PIMLICO

832

'A SENSELESS, SQUALID WAR'

Norman Rose is a graduate of the LSE and now holds the Chair of International Relations at the Hebrew University, Jerusalem. A distinguished historian and Fellow of the Royal Historical Society, he is also the author of much-acclaimed biographies of Churchill, Chaim Weizmann, Harold Nicolson, Sir Lewis Namier, and studies of 'The Cliveden Set' and 'The Gentile Zionists'.

'The most complete and detailed account of the British and Zionists during the era of the mandate . . . All in all, a masterpiece.' Wm Roger Louis, Editor in Chief of *The Oxford History of the British Empire*

'Norman Rose's eloquent, comprehensive, and even-handed book says it all, from Palestine in the late 19th century to Gaza right now . . . (his) typically vivid phrases resound in his truly excellent book.'
Jonathan Mirsky, *Spectator*

'Norman Rose pulls together witnesses, official and unofficial, to the battering relations between Jews who were looking for Zion and the British who were trying to keep order in Palestine . . . Rose has written something close to a definitive version of how the British and Jews engaged in their dialogue of the deaf . . . if you want to know all the facts and their nuances and complications, Norman Rose has supplied them. And any new context for thinking about Palestine, that murderous stalemate, is a kind of intellectual miracle nowadays.'
Michael Pye, *Scotland on Sunday*

'Norman Rose, of the Hebrew University, charts in meticulous detail the last bloody years of the Palestine Mandate. He neither conceals nor excuses the the excesses of the Irgun and the Stern Gang, but carefully places them in the wider contexts in which they must be seen . . . Professor Rose's book is a work of scholarship.'
Geoffrey Alderman, *Jewish Chronicle*

'Norman Rose, in his lively recounting of that period of history . . . with telling comments from the major players of the day - Jewish, Arab, British, American - extracts from hitherto unpublished correspondence and archival material . . . Norman Rose, who holds the chair in international relations at the Hebrew University of Jerusalem has written a scholarly book . . . But it is no dry academic account.'
Hyam Corney, *Jerusalem Post*

'Norman Rose . . . makes excellent use of contemporary sources to give a generally dispassionate account, which is sometimes all the more hair-raising for that, whether he is describing the blatant anti-semitism of some British officials . . . or the behaviour of Zionist ultras who sent letter bombs to British politicians and planned to infect the London water supply with cholera.'
Geoffrey Wheatcroft, *London Review of Books*

'Rose, a distinguished Israeli historian, writes objective, hard-hitting history . . . He gives a powerful, detailed and meticulously documented account of that violence, shaming to both the contending parties.'
Sir Martin Gilbert, *Standpoint*

'Rose's book is, to a considerable degree, a tripartite indictment, highlighting the cruelties and the ineptitude displayed not only by the Arabs, but also by the Jewish Zionist movement and the British mandatory authorities in Palestine . . . Rose's account of those three or four tortured years in the momentous history of the Middle East is both accessible and authoritative. It is not entirely sombre – among its smaller gems are the revelations of minor but significant roles in support of the Zionist cause played by Marlon Brando and Frank Sinatra.'
Gerald Jacobs, *Tablet*

'Norman Rose's excellent new history of the Mandate of Palestine offers a detailed account of the final years of British rule . . . Rose's history should be read by anyone interested in the history of Palestine, as well as anyone who wishes to understand how not to wage a successful counter-insurgency.'
Calder Walton, *Times Literary Supplement*

'A SENSELESS, SQUALID WAR'

Voices from Palestine 1890s to 1948

NORMAN ROSE

PIMLICO

Published by Pimlico 2010

2 4 6 8 10 9 7 5 3 1

Copyright © Norman Rose 2009

Norman Rose has asserted his right under the Copyright, Designs
and Patents Act 1988 to be identified as the author of this work

First published in Great Britain by The Bodley Head in 2009

Pimlico
Random House, 20 Vauxhall Bridge Road,
London SW1V 2SA

www.vintage-books.co.uk

Addresses for companies within The Random House Group Limited can be found at:
www.randomhouse.co.uk/offices.htm

The Random House Group Limited Reg. No. 954009

A CIP catalogue record for this book
is available from the British Library

ISBN 9781845950798

The Random House Group Limited supports The Forest Stewardship Council (FSC),
the leading international forest certification organisation. All our titles that are printed on
Greenpeace approved FSC certified paper carry the FSC logo. Our paper procurement policy
can be found at www.rbooks.co.uk/environment

Printed and bound in Great Britain by
Clays Ltd, St Ives PLC

Every human benefit, every virtue and every prudent act, is founded on compromise.

Edmund Burke, *On Conciliation with America*

From abroad we are accustomed to believing that the Arabs are all desert savages, like donkeys, who neither see nor understand what goes on around them. But this is a big mistake . . . The Arabs, and especially those in the cities, understand our deeds and our desires in *Eretz-Israel*, but they keep quiet and pretend not to understand, since they do not see our present activities as a threat to their future . . . yet they mock us in their hearts . . . If the time comes when the life of our people in *Eretz-Israel* develops to the point of encroaching upon the native population, they will not yield easily their place . . .

Asher Zvi Ginsberg (Ahad Ha'am, 'One of the People') from *Emet me-Eretz-Israel* (*Truth from Eretz-Israel*, 1891), text in Alan Dowty, 'Much Ado About Little: Ahad Ha'am's "Truth From *Eretz-Israel*", Zionism and the Arabs', *Israel Studies*, vol. 5, no. 2 (Fall, 2000)

Two important phenomena, of identical character but nevertheless opposed, which till now have not attracted attention, are now making their appearance in Asian Turkey: these are the awakening of the Arab nation and the latent efforts of the Jews to re-establish, on an extremely large scale, the ancient Kingdom of Israel. These two movements are destined to struggle continuously with one another, until one prevails over the other. The fate of the entire world depends on the result of this struggle between the two peoples, which represent two contradictory principles.

Najib Azouri, *Le Réveil de la Nation Arabe dans l'Asie Turque* (Paris, 1905) p.5, quoted in Yehoshua Porath, *The Emergence of the Palestinian-Arab National Movement, 1918–1929* (London, Frank Cass, 1974), p.26

'£80 million since the Socialist Government came into power squandered in Palestine, and 100,000 Englishmen now kept from their homes and works, for the sake of a senseless, squalid war with the Jews in order to give Palestine to the Arabs, or God knows who.'

Winston Churchill, House of Commons,
12 March 1947

Contents

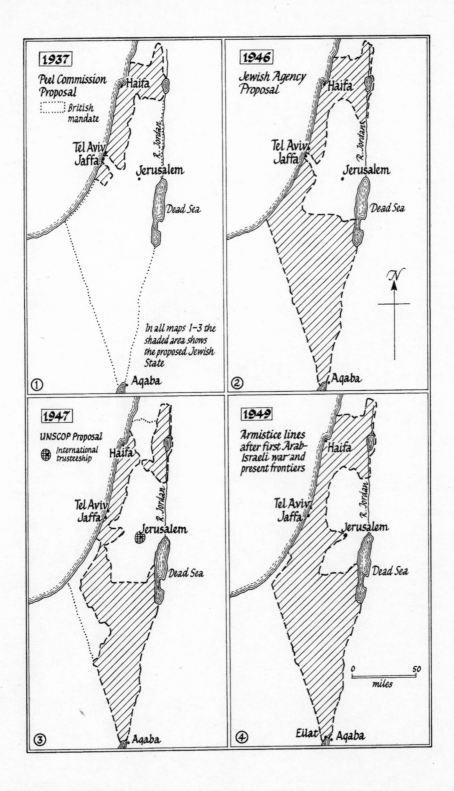

1937
Peel Commission Proposal
········· *British mandate*

Haifa

Tel Aviv Jaffa

Jerusalem

R. Jordan

Dead Sea

In all maps 1–3 the shaded area shows the proposed Jewish State

① Aqaba

1946
Jewish Agency Proposal

Haifa

Tel Aviv Jaffa

Jerusalem

R. Jordan

Dead Sea

N

② Aqaba

1947
UNSCOP Proposal
⊕ *International trusteeship*

Haifa

Tel Aviv Jaffa

⊕ Jerusalem

R. Jordan

Dead Sea

③ Aqaba

1949
Armistice lines after first Arab-Israeli war and present frontiers

Haifa

Tel Aviv Jaffa

Jerusalem

R. Jordan

Dead Sea

0 ———— 50
miles

④ Eilat Aqaba

I

The Promised Land

On 3 September 1897, a Jewish intellectual living in Vienna, an acquaintance of Freud, Gustav Mahler, Arthur Schnitzler and Hugo von Hofmannsthal wrote in his diary: 'If I were to sum up the Congress in a word – which I shall take care not to publish – it would be this: "At Basel I founded the Jewish State. If I said this out loud today I would be greeted by universal laughter. In five years perhaps, and certainly in fifty years, everyone will perceive it. The essence of a State lies in the will of the people for a State, yes, even in the will of one powerful individual – *l'état, c'est moi*: Louis XIV." '[1]

The diarist was Theodor Herzl. A month earlier, at the Basel Municipal Casino, feeding off the emotions his pamphlet *Der Judenstaat* (February, 1896) had stirred up – for its 'daring, clarity and energy', as the future first President of Israel, Chaim Weizmann, recalled[2] – he had, almost single-handedly, organised and convened the first Zionist Congress, moulding a disparate group of societies and associations into a spirited political movement.

Yet in 1897 the vision of an independent Jewish state was no more than the most fragile of hopes. The two hundred and eight delegates, representing sixteen countries, who had gathered at the Casino spoke for only the tiniest of minorities among the dispersed Jewish people: their ultimate goal, a Jewish state, fiercely opposed both by orthodox Jewry and the assimilationists. As for the Jewish masses, they regarded this outlandish venture with studied indifference. From the 1880s to 1914, in the wake of a series of pogroms in Russia, there had occurred a mass exodus of Jews from eastern Europe – it being estimated that of the approximately four and a half million Jews who resided in the Pale of Settlement, well over two million had fled the organised anti-Semitism of the Czarist regime. But these persecuted Jews, voting with their feet, preferred the far-off, speculative attractions of western Europe, and in particular of the United States, to the hardships and uncertainties of life in Palestine under Ottoman rule. Even so, some fifty years later, on 29 November 1947, the United Nations General Assembly voted in favour of establishing a Jewish (and Palestinian) state. By any reckoning, this must be counted as one of the most remarkable diplomatic-political success stories of the twentieth century: one which half a century before had been but a figment of the wildest of imaginations, the aspiration of a zealous minority among the Jewish people. Although these visionaries – or romanticists – barely grasped it at the time, the road leading to a Jewish state would be strewn with unpredictable diplomat upheavals, considerable political skulduggery and much bloodshed.

Herzl was a most improbable candidate to lead the Zionist movement. Born in Budapest in 1860 to a well-to-do middle-class family, he moved, at the age of eighteen, to the bewildering and contradictory world of *fin-de-siècle* Vienna: elegant, sophisticated, cosmopolitan, intellectually stimulating, yet at the same time intolerant and violently anti-Semitic, a centre of Austrian chauvinism jealously bent on preserving its prerogatives. Viennese society reflected in an exaggerated and hysterical manner the internal stresses of a multinational empire coming apart at the seams. Herzl made his way in this milieu, and by the 1890s he had acquired a reputation as an established journalist, a minor playwright, and a widely read and popular *feuilletoniste*. Possessed of an extraordinarily complicated character, subject to fits of depression, fascinated by the sense of physical danger – he was involved in at least three duelling incidents – Herzl was given to a vivid sense of high drama and mapped out for himself the role of martyr, tragically to be realised, as 'the Parnell of the Jews'.

Myth has it that the Dreyfus affair awakened him from his torpor as an assimilated Jew. The story, alas, as dramatic as Herzl's commanding presence, is merely legend. It was impossible to grow up in Vienna and remain immune from its anti-Semitism. At the age of twenty-three he had resigned from his student fraternity, handicapped, as he wrote, 'by the impediment of Semitism'. The Jews, he reflected, were 'living perpetually in enemy territory'. He concocted the most grandiose of schemes: the mass conversion of Jews to Christianity. He toyed with the notion of investigating the Jewish condition, analysing the state of

Jewish communities throughout the world, including the new Jewish colonies being established in Palestine. These thoughts, never absent from his mind, surfaced when he witnessed the terrifying scene at the *École Militaire* in December 1894 when Dreyfus was publicly humiliated and degraded to the accompaniment of the menacing bays of the Paris crowd threatening '*À mort! À mort les juifs*'. For Herzl this was 'merely the last straw'.[3]

Whether Herzl – an assimilated German-speaking Hungarian Jew, with only a sketchy knowledge of Jewish ritual, tradition, literature or history – knew it or not, he was building on a rich heritage. The Judaeo-Roman wars, symbolised by their most dramatic act, Titus's destruction of the Second Temple in 70 CE, gave rise to the most enduring of the Jewish Dispersions. Defeated and scattered, the Jews continued to pine for their lost patrimony.

> There is no other example in history [wrote Arthur Koestler], of a community which has been chased round the globe quite as much, which has survived its death as a nation by two thousand years, and which, in between *autos-da-fé* and gas chambers, kept praying at the proper season for rain to fall in a country on which they have never set eyes, and drinking toasts to 'Next year in Jerusalem!' during the same astronomical stretch of time, with the same untiring trust in the supernatural.[4]

Where the majority of the Jewish people was located, in Europe, in particular in the Pale of Settlement in Russia, the promoters of the *Haskala* (Enlightenment) had introduced a new dimension into Jewish life, generating a climate for the introduction of freethinking, radical ideas. By the mid-nineteenth century, revolutionary nationalist sentiments, that stirred nationalist movements in parts of Europe, filtered down to excite the minds of Jewish intellectuals. In 1862 Moses Hess, a German socialist, drawing his inspiration from the Italian *Risorgimento*, published *Rome and Jerusalem*. Now a Zionist classic, it called for the rebirth of a Jewish state. Twenty years later Yehuda Leib (Leon) Pinsker, a semi-assimilated Russian Jew born in Odessa, who had abandoned the legal profession for medicine, published his pamphlet, *Autoemancipation! Mahnruf an seine Stammesgenossen von einem russischen Juden* (Auto-emancipation! a warning to his kinsfolk by a Russian Jew).

Reeling under the impact of the pogroms of 1881, Pinsker perceived a pathological hatred of Jews everywhere, concluding that only by restoring a viable Jewish nationhood can full equality for the Jewish people be realised. 'A people without a territory is like a man without a shadow,' he wrote. And this would be achieved, not by the charitable efforts of others, but by self-help. Pinsker did not point specifically to *Eretz Israel* (the Land of Israel) as the future Jewish homeland, but neither did he exclude it.[5]

Herzl was pushing at an open door in another sense. In the latter decades of the nineteenth century groups of Jews – known as *Hovevei Zion* (Lovers of Zion) – drawing on the ideas of Hess and Pinsker, began to meet, often independently of each other, to discuss ways and means to promote immigration to Palestine. Located mainly in Russia and Romania, these associations, some secular, some religious, inevitably disparate in views and approach, often petered out into little more than talking shops. The most radical of these societies was formed in 1881 in Kharkov by a group of high-school and university students. These young idealists comprised the nucleus of the *Biluim.** One of its founders, Ze'ev Dubnow, laid out an ambitious nationalist programme.

> The aim of our journey is rich in plans. We want to conquer Palestine and return to the Jews the political independence stolen from them two thousand years ago. And if it is willed, it is no dream. We must establish agricultural settlements, factories and industry . . . And above all we must give young people military training and provide them with weapons. Then will the glorious day come, as prophesied by Isaiah in his promise of the restoration of Israel. With their weapons in their hands, the Jews will declare that they are the masters of their ancient homeland.[6]

The *Biluim* formed the core of what became known as the first wave of immigration, or *Aliyah* (literally 'to ascend', 'to go up'). However, their youthful exuberance was matched only by the paucity of their skills in establishing 'agricultural settlements, factories and industry'.

---

*An acronym from the Hebrew *Bilu* – *Beit Ya'akov Lechu ve-Nelecha* – 'House of Jacob, come ye and let us go', Isaiah 2:5.

Largely sustained by the largesse of Jewish philanthropists – chiefly Baron Edmond de Rothschild – the colonies they founded – Rishon le Zion, Rosh Pina, Zichron Ya'akov among others – survived, but only just, with bankruptcy a constant threat.

In Palestine they encountered a small Jewish community that viewed these intruders with foreboding. For two thousand years there had always been a Jewish presence in Palestine, sometimes in the thousands, at other times in the tens of thousands. Accurate figures for the number of Jews residing in Palestine circa 1880 are hard to come by: one source puts the figure at almost 15,000, another at 25,000, yet another at about 34,000.* These were mostly ultra-orthodox Jewish communities centered on Jerusalem, Safad, Tiberius and Hebron, praying and waiting patiently for the Messiah to arise and lead the dispersed Jewish people back to the Promised Land, His, and only His, prerogative. To many of these Jews the *Biluim* were an anathema, little more than heretics meddling in God's master plan to redeem the Jewish people.

A second *Aliyah* followed at the turn of the twentieth century. Stunned by a fresh wave of pogroms,† galvanised by Herzl's initiative, imbued with Tolstoyan ideas, inspired by the concept of a return to the land, of the sanctity of Jewish self-labour, these pioneers – who included among their number David Ben Gurion, Israel's first Prime

---

*For the more modest figure see Justin McCarthy, *The Population of Palestine* (New York, Columbia University Press, 1990), p. 10; for the intermediate figure, Yehoshua Porath, *The Emergence of the Palestinian-Arab National Movement, 1918–1929* (London, Frank Cass, 1974), p. 16; and for the greater number, ESCO Foundation for Palestine, *Palestine. A Study of Jewish, Arab, and British Policies* (Yale University Press, 1949), i, p. 53.

These discrepancies, also relevant for the Arab population, are understandable: there were no reliable censuses for that period. It should also be noted that under Ottoman rule 'Palestine' was little more than 'a geographical expression'. What we now regard as Israel/ Palestine included a number of Ottoman administrative areas: the Independent Sanjak (District) of Jerusalem, together with the Sanjaks of Beirut, Acre, and Balqa, all part of the Vilayet (Province) of Beirut.

†At Kishinev, between 19 and 20 April 1903, an incited mob savagely attacked its Jewish community: forty-nine Jews were killed, men, women and children, more than five hundred were injured, property was looted and destroyed. Carefully timed to coincide with the Easter holidays, it was followed by fifty other pogroms throughout Czarist Russia. By today's distorted standards the blood-letting at Kishinev was small beer indeed, but it sent shockwaves throughout the civilised world. Strong protests

Minister – were, in the main, committed socialists. They founded
Labour parties, established the first kibbutzim, laid the foundations for
the renaissance of Hebrew as a living language. Plans were made to
establish a Hebrew University on Mount Scopus, Jerusalem. By the
outbreak of the First World War fifty-five settlements – including the
new town of Tel Aviv – had been established. From the early 1880s to
1914 an average of 2,000–3,000 Jews entered Palestine each year – many
of whom eventually left. By the latter date most authorities put the
total Jewish population of Palestine at about eighty-five thousand.[7]

These were considerable achievements of which Herzl, who had
set these breakthroughs in motion, could be justly proud. But in one
crucial particular he had failed: all his efforts to attain a Charter, a
covenant that would grant international legitimacy for a Zionist
entity in Palestine, came to nought. It was not from want of trying.
He had stalked the chancelleries of Europe. Frederick, Grand Duke
of Baden and uncle to the Kaiser, William II, received him, and
through his good offices the Kaiser agreed to grant him an audience
in Palestine in a scene recorded famously outside Mikveh Israel, an
agricultural school on the road to Jerusalem, where a mounted
William, clad in military uniform, complete with pickelhaube, gazes
down on a bare-headed, seemingly humble Herzl.* In London he
saw Joseph Chamberlain, the energetic Secretary of State for the
Colonies, who expressed some sympathy for Herzl's ideas. In Italy he
attended the King, Victor Emmanuel III, and secured an audience
with the so-called 'peasant' Pope, Pius X: barren of concrete results,
the parties simply exchanged pleasantries. Most provocative of all, he
met Vyacheslav von Phleve, the Russian Minister of the Interior. Von

---

were voiced in London, Paris and New York. Theodore Roosevelt, President of the
United States, issued a statement expressing 'the deep sympathy felt not only by
the administration but by all the American people for the unfortunate Jews who have
been the victims in the recent appalling massacres and outrages'.

Chaim Bialik, the poet of the Hebrew national revival, composed his best-known
work, *City of Slaughter*, with Kishinev in mind. These appalling events radicalised
Jewish opinion, a terrible reminder that the Jews remained powerless and vulnerable
to the whims of anti-Semites.

*As the original photograph was bungled, the picture that has gone down in history is
in fact a photomontage of the Kaiser, the horse, belonging to a member of his
entourage, and a photograph of Herzl for which he had posed separately on a later day.

Phleve, a notorious anti-Semite who had encouraged the pogroms of 1903, promised to intervene with the Sultan, Abdul Hamid II: his aim merely a more sophisticated means of ridding Russia of its Jews. But whatever von Phleve's purpose, his petition fell on deaf ears at Constantinople.

Obviously, the attitude of Constantinople, the hub of the Ottoman Empire, from where Palestine was administered, was the key factor. Herzl was an intermittent visitor at the Golden Horn, dangling before the Grand Vizier promises of economic aid and the visions of international support – which, in fact, were far beyond his reach – only to see his offers disappear in the quicksands of the byzantine politics of the Ottoman administration. Exhausted by this relentless, and ultimately fruitless, grind, frustrated by internal wrangling within the movement he had created and already subject to a heart condition, he collapsed and died in July 1904. No leader of the same stature emerged to replace him until the appearance of Chaim Weizmann at the end of the First World War. Zionist diplomacy temporarily entered the doldrums.

Israel Zangwill's picturesque conceit, 'A land without a people for a people without a land', was entirely without foundation.* Estimates vary, but on the eve of the First World War the Arab population of Palestine, still overwhelmingly rural, was put at around 640,000–650,000.[8] In the late 1890s and early 1900s Arab nationalism began to take shape: first among intellectual and student circles centred in Damascus and Beirut, then in groups meeting in Constantinople, Cairo and Paris. Initially, few Palestinians participated in these debating societies. Over time, interest grew. At the first Arab Congress, held in Paris in 1913, out of 387 signatories, 130 Palestinians registered their support for its aims.[9] One factor that deeply affected their position was the policies of the 'Committee of Union and Progress', now in power in Constantinople following the 'Young Turk' revolution of 1908. The committee, pressing for reform, forced the despotic Sultan, Abdul Hamid II, to summon a

---

*It was not an original saying. Zangwill had cribbed it from the nineteenth-century philanthropist and gentile Zionist, Lord Shaftesbury. In its original form, it read: 'A country without a nation for a nation without a country'.

parliament and restore the liberal constitution of 1876.* The high
hopes invested in the 'Young Turks' were soon dashed: they proved
to be very much like the 'Old Turks', their regime characterised by an
aggressive pan-Ottomanism (that eventually shaded off into pan-
Turkism and pan-Turanianism) and an inability, or unwillingness, to
establish effective constitutional rule.

Ruthless in its methods, the new regime's repressive measures
generated a duel response: some Palestinians advocated decentralisation, greater local autonomy, to soften the process of
Ottomanisation; others, perhaps apprehensive of outright confrontation with the 'Young Turks', rejected decentralisation – a stand
adopted by *Filastin*, a leading Palestinian newspaper in Jaffa, which
wished to remain loyal to the Ottoman Empire.[10] This ambivalence
was reflected in the equivocal comments of one prominent
Palestinian intellectual. At first, Khalil al-Sakakini, an Orthodox
Christian by religion and an educator by profession, greeted the
'Young Turk' revolution with joy, seeing it as a liberating force,
freeing him from the parochialism that had frustrated him in the
backwaters of Palestine: 'Now I can serve my country. Now I can
found a school, a newspaper, and societies for Youth. Now we can
lift up our voices without impediment.' Three months later he
joined the local committee of 'Union and Progress', swearing
allegiance in a melodramatic ceremony shielded by masked men,
guns, and blood-curdling oaths. But which country al-Sakakini was
alluding to is not entirely clear. Less than three weeks after these
theatricals, he was inducted into the Arab Brotherhood, a secret
society that opposed the Union. Much later, in the immediate
aftermath of the First World War, he became a leading advocate of
pan-Arabism, drawing inspiration from the Sharifian regime in
Damascus.[11] One theme, however, remained constant in his world
outlook. As early as February 1914, when addressing a Zionist
official, Benjamin Ivri, he robustly defended his position as an
obdurate Arab nationalist:

*The constitution was wide-ranging. It called for the indivisibility of the Ottoman
Empire; liberty, equality and justice for all Ottomans, Muslims, Christians and Jews
alike; freedom of conscience, the press and education; equality of taxation; irremov-
ability of judges; and parliamentary government based on general representation.

If I hate Zionism, it isn't because I object to the revival of the Jewish nation, thereby allowing it to escape from the twin abyss of weakness and misery. Rather, it's because I despise its, Zionism's, underlying principle: its attempt to reconstruct its nationalism upon the ruins of others. For by seizing Palestine, it is as though it has conquered the heart of the Arab nation.[12]

Al-Sakakini was merely expressing what many of his compatriots felt. In 1891, a group of Jerusalem notables sent a petition to the central government in Constantinople calling for the cessation of Jewish immigration and land sales to Jews.[13] It was the first recorded political opposition to Zionism by Palestinians and its two central demands – to curtail immigration and land sales – remained at the heart of Palestinian grievances until the end of the British mandate. These early displays of open anti-Zionist hostility were sporadic and did not manifest themselves systematically until after the Young Turk revolution. Its standard bearers were the Arab press – *al-Karmil* in Haifa and *Filastin* in Jaffa, both owned by Greek Orthodox Palestinians, a position ardently adopted by the urban educated elite.[14] Over time the agitation spread to Syria and other centres of the nascent Arab national movement outside Palestine, including the Ottoman parliament, where Palestinians too were represented. Not that it did them much good as the Ottoman administration, hostile to any challenge to its pan-Ottoman programme, had no need of yet another national problem.

As early as the 1900s protests were being heard that the Zionists were busy laying the foundations of 'a state within a state'. Together with the symbols of an ambitious nationalist movement – the Zionist anthem, *HaTikvah* (The Hope), and the Zionist flag (two blue stripes on a white background – representing a Jewish prayer shawl – with the shield of David in the centre) – the protesters could point to the dispossession of Arab lands, an expanding network of Jewish settlements, a financial institution – the Anglo-Palestinian Bank – and a separate educational system. Consistently exaggerating the extent of Jewish immigration, putting it at anything between 100,000 and 300,000, some Arabs suspected that the Zionists intended to create a Jewish state extending as far as Iraq.

Other matters intruded. Zionist mores were often at odds with Arab convention, threatening the customs and moral assumptions that lent cohesion to a socially conservative, traditional Palestinian society. The status of women, their active political role in the *Yishuv* (the Jewish community in Palestine), were judged particularly offensive. Although calls for more forceful measures to combat the encroachment of Zionism were voiced, it was still far too early to speak of a consolidated Palestinian national movement. The preferred options – neither, admittedly, sympathetic to Zionism – remained: either a pan-Arab movement or loyalty to Ottoman unity.[15]

While extremely nervous about wide-ranging Zionist goals, there was some talk of cooperation between the two communities, even expressions of admiration, perhaps envy. *Filastin,* for example, wrote admiringly of the revival of Hebrew as a living language and hailed the agricultural accomplishments of the Jewish settlements. Occasionally, friendships were formed, but purely on a personal basis. No support of Zionism took root among the Arabs. Quite the contrary, inflamed even further by what they viewed as unfair economic competition, there were calls for violent action against these overbearing colonists. Clashes over water rights or land boundary disputes were frequent; crops were often set on fire. Sporadic, uncoordinated acts of Arab violence broke out, leading every so often to killings. The Jews responded. Instead of relying on non-Jewish guards, often Bedouin or Circassian, they founded in 1909 *Hashomer* (the Watchman). Mounted on horseback and clad in Arab dress, these self-styled guards of the Jewish settlements had, for the most part, been active in Jewish self-defence in Russia in earlier times. At this stage, any talk of an inevitable conflict between the developing *Yishuv* and the Palestinian Arabs would have been premature; but the pattern for future discord can already be discerned.

The British government had long indicated an interest in Palestine, well before it ordered the occupation of Egypt in 1882. While noting Napoleon's incursion into Egypt, it was the Syrian crises of the 1830s, precipitated by Muhammad Ali's advance from Egypt into Syria, that first drew the attention of the British government to its strategic interests in Syria and Palestine. Compelled to intervene militarily at Acre and Beirut to safeguard its interests, Britain's role was crucial in bringing the crisis to an end. Averting the threat of war between Britain and France, the Straits Convention of July 1841 regulated relations between the Ottoman Empire and the Great Powers – Britain, Russia, France, Austria and Prussia. One unexpected by-product of the crisis was the setting up of a British consulate in Jerusalem in 1838 with instructions to British representatives in the Levant to protect local Jewish communities,[17] perhaps the first instance of British imperial policy merging with a benevolent interest in the fate of the Jewish community in Palestine. In the late 1870s British concern took another turn. Collaborating with the Palestine Exploration Fund, the War Office seconded officers – including one Horatio Herbert Kitchener – to conduct a detailed survey of Palestine, west of the River Jordan, an exercise with a clear military purpose. It resulted in a twenty-six-sheet map, on a scale of one inch to the mile, of western Palestine from Dan to Be'ersheva.[18]

With the British occupation of Egypt and control of the Canal, those areas to the north-east of Egypt, the Sinai peninsula and Palestine, assumed crucial significance. Indeed, most British observers would not have taken exception to the definition of Palestine as 'the Clapham Junction of the Commonwealth'. To protect the quickest and cheapest route to India and British interests in the Far East it was vital to preserve these regions as a buffer zone, free of any rival imperialist predators – France taking pride of place in British suspicions. The possibility of an autonomous Jewish settlement in El-Arish – an area strategically located in northern Sinai astride the coastal route to Syria and the Lebanon – was raised by British ministers, Joseph Chamberlain and Lord Lansdowne, the Foreign Secretary, with Herzl in 1902. Nothing came of it. Asserting a lack of sufficient water supplies to sustain the project, the Egyptian government, presided over by Lord Cromer, Egypt's Proconsul, who also happened to be 'the most disagreeable Englishman' Herzl had ever met, effectively stymied the scheme.[19]

Fortunately Joseph Chamberlain proved far more amenable, though not in quite the way Herzl had envisaged. In August 1903 Herzl reported to Congress Chamberlain's latest proposition: a self-governing Jewish community in East Africa, 'everything of course under the sovereign jurisdiction of Great Britain'. Herzl emphasised to a hot-tempered Congress that the new territory could never dislodge the ultimate goal of Palestine, but this radical, unconventional, and temporary, solution would help alleviate the desperate situation of eastern European Jewry, still reeling from the effects of the Kishinev pogroms. Hoping to disarm his critics, he underlined his allegiance to Palestine. In a gesture of high theatre, Herzl raised his right hand and recited in Hebrew: 'If I forget thee, oh Jerusalem, may my right hand forget its cunning.'[20] But despite Herzl's vigorous advocacy, opposition was widespread – first and foremost among the Russian delegates, who viewed Herzl's strategy as little more than apostasy. Conveniently for the *nein-sagers* the government, under pressure from British expatriates in East Africa, began to back-pedal. Following a negative report by a Commission of Inquiry, the scheme was finally buried in 1905, but only after stirring up the gravest crisis yet experienced by the Zionist movement. For the Zionists the controversy over the so-called 'Uganda crisis'* had one positive outcome: it confirmed for them the centrality of Palestine in the Zionist programme. Palestine remained very much on the agenda – and this filtered through to some British policy-makers.[21]

Factored into these political-strategic arguments were more scriptural considerations. Ever since Oliver Cromwell had decided to allow the Jews to return to England in December 1655, the concept of the Return of the Jews to Palestine had been a topic for public debate, much of it highly polemical. The restoration of the Jews to Palestine, it was held, was a necessary precursor of the 'Latter Days', when 'the Messiah would come once again to inaugurate the reign of righteousness and justice, brotherhood, freedom and peace'. Nurtured on the Scriptures and strengthened by a deeply held bond with the Old Testament, there emerged an influential school of British politicians and publicists who acted and felt as though they were fulfilling an historic mission when furthering the cause of the Return. A colourful assortment of Victorian personages took up this challenge: Lord Shaftesbury, George Eliot, Laurence Oliphant, Colonel Henry Churchill among others. Some prominent British policy-makers of the early twentieth century – Lloyd George and Balfour, Smuts and Milner among them – were the natural heirs to this rich inheritance. 'Towards

---

*This offer is popularly and inevitably referred to as the 'Uganda crisis' and no amount of nitpicking by professional historians has managed to shake this label. In fact, the original territories discussed with representatives of the British government were some 40,000 square miles between Nairobi and the Mau escarpment, an area finally whittled down to 5,500 square miles compromising the Gwas plateau to the north-east of the first-mentioned zone. These lands lie clearly in Kenya.

such a people one has a feeling of awe,' recorded one gentile Zionist, 'they are so well known, and yet so old and eternal.'[22]

It was the First World War that afforded Britain the opportunity to define in earnest her intentions towards the Middle East in general and Palestine in particular. Only days after Constantinople had joined the Central Powers the Prime Minister, Henry Herbert Asquith, in a speech at the Guildhall, spelled out the 'death-knell' of the Ottoman Empire. 'The Turkish Empire', he proclaimed, 'has committed suicide and dug its grave with its own hand.'[23] With the western front frozen in a bloody stalemate, the drive began to unravel the Ottoman Empire. Britain's purpose was defined early on, set out in the de Bunsen Committee report, an interdepartmental assessment of British interests, or 'desiderata', in their preferred term. Later, Britain's allies – France and Russia – were brought in by the Sykes-Picot agreement, a much maligned and misconstrued accord. And to round off the picture, the British also drew in the nascent Arab and Zionist nationalist movements, dispensing pledges distinguished only by a studied vagueness.

The future of Palestine was considered in all of these documents. Owing to the sensitivity of the Holy Places and the interests of the Great Powers, de Bunsen called for 'Palestine [to] be recognised as a country whose destiny must be the subject of special negotiations, in which both belligerents and neutrals are alike interested'. In the event of partition, de Bunsen went on, Britain's strategic position in the eastern Mediterranean would be maintained by controlling the area from the line 'Tadmor (Palmyra)-Acre' in the north and, following 'the coast as far as the boundary of Egypt, include the whole Sinai peninsula, and then run from Akaba to the Persian Gulf'. In effect, this would include all of western and eastern Palestine in the British sphere of interest. Sir Mark Sykes* – a prime mover also in the de Bunsen Committee – was

---

*Sykes may genuinely be portrayed as a classic illustration of that truly authentic figure of British public life, 'the amateur'. Heir to an estate at Sledmere, Yorkshire, he had travelled extensively in the Near East in his youth. He was not conversant with its languages – Arabic, Turkish, or Persian – he had no formal training in oriental studies nor as a professional diplomat. None of this tarnished his reputation. A prolific author and skilful cartoonist, and moving in the right circles as a baronet and Conservative MP, he came to be credited by his masters as an expert on the region.

more circumspect in his talks with the French diplomat François Georges-Picot and, while echoing de Bunsen's insistence on the international significance of Palestine, he made it abundantly clear that Britain required a foothold in Palestine. Accordingly, in the final draft of the document they drew up, Britain was awarded the ports of Haifa and Acre – naval bases in the making – together with the right to own and administer a railway link from an enclave around Haifa bay to 'Area B', which itself extended to Akaba in the South and to the Euphrates in the east, a zone designated as the British zone.[24]

British negotiations with the Arabs were conducted on an entirely different plane. Since February 1914, intermittent contacts between the parties had taken place, broaching ways of political, even military, cooperation against the Turks. Nothing came of these early gambits. Now, anxious to involve the Arabs in their war against the Ottomans, the British, through Sir Henry McMahon, High Commissioner in Egypt, pursued a labyrinthine correspondence with the Sherif Husayn of Mecca, the titular head of the Arab nationalist movement, who, together with his sons, Abdullah and Faysal, was intent on attaining the greatest measure possible of Arab statehood. The exchange ended in a stand-off. The original Arab demands, although recorded under Husayn's name, had in fact been formulated by Abdullah. He set out an audacious programme: a greater Arab state bounded by Persia and the Indian Ocean in the east, the Red Sea in the south, the eastern Mediterranean littoral up to Mersina (lying on the Turkish coastline) in the west, and in the north, on a line from Mersina and Adana to the Persian border.

The British agreed in principle, but with several reservations. They excluded 'portions of Syria lying to the west of the districts of Damascus, Homs, Hama, and Aleppo', and emphasised time and again that they were not free to enter into any obligations detrimental to the regional interests of their allies, the French. As these clearly included significant areas of the hinterland of the eastern Mediterranean coastline, Palestine, almost by definition – but never referred to by name in the correspondence – was also excluded. Husayn reluctantly accepted these caveats, but promised to return to his initial claims 'at the first opportunity after this war is finished'. Despite this proviso, Husayn launched his revolt against the Ottomans some months later, in June 1916.[25]

The Zionists barely entered into this dialogue at this stage. In England, Chaim Weizmann – not yet the dominant figure in Zionism – was engaged in what he called 'reconnoitring', hobnobbing with influential socialites, politicians and journalists, his wartime work as an organic chemist on behalf of the British government smoothing his path into these exclusive circles.

Weizmann was an imposing figure. In almost every particular he differed from Herzl. Born in Motol, a shtetl near Pinsk, he was an authentic child of the Pale of Settlement. Steeped in Jewish ritual and tradition, his mother tongue was Yiddish. A convinced Anglophile in later life, he wrote as a child of eleven: 'All have decided: THE JEWS MUST DIE, but England will nevertheless have mercy upon us.' An active Zionist from his earliest days, he concluded in the same letter: 'In conclusion to Zion! – Jews – to Zion! let us go.'[26] A truly charismatic figure, he possessed superb diplomatic qualities. Pragmatic in approach, he was ready for compromise without ever losing sight of the main aim. Unhappy at Herzl's strictly political strategy, he set out his own formula: 'synthetic Zionism', combining practical work in Palestine with political canvassing among the nations.

But in these early days, neither the force of his personality nor the cogency of his arguments produced concrete results. Yet the notable contacts he made – Balfour, Lloyd George, Churchill among them – were to prove crucial in the future; and none more so than at one such reconnoitring session in December 1914 when he met Herbert Samuel, President of the Local Government Board and the first practising Jew to sit in a British Cabinet. Samuel astonished Weizmann. Although not a paid-up member of the Zionist move-ment, he spoke like a true Zionist, arguing on traditional Zionist lines for a Jewish state in Palestine, while, as a responsible cabinet minister eager to secure British imperial interests, he also maintained that it should fall under British protection. Samuel translated these ideas into an official memorandum that he placed before Cabinet at the end of January 1915. Its reception was mixed: Sir Edward Grey, the Foreign Secretary, and Lloyd George, then Minister for Munitions, registered varying degrees of approval. Asquith pooh-poohed the idea: 'Dithyrambic', the Prime Minister called it, concluding that 'it is a curious illustration of Dizzy's favourite maxim that "race is every-thing"'. With this rebuff the government's attention turned to other, more pressing, wartime emergencies. The realisation of Zionist aims was put on the back burner until Lloyd George came to power in December 1916.[27]

A month after he assumed the premiership, Lloyd George was asked about the future of Palestine. 'Oh! We must grab that,' he replied with a smile, 'we have made a beginning.'[28] His remark was more than apposite. For Sinai-Palestine was the one theatre of operations where British forces were actually advancing, cautiously but steadily. In December 1916 El Arish, a large town commanding the coastal road to Palestine, was occupied; the following month Rafah, some twenty-five miles further north, was captured. The British were poised to conquer Palestine. Against this background, Anglo-Zionist negotiations were begun in earnest, the ubiquitous Sir Mark Sykes leading for the government, Weizmann for the Zionists. The bargaining, prolonged and involved, culminated in the contentious Balfour Declaration of 2 November 1917, a note sent by Arthur James Balfour, the Foreign Secretary, to Lord Rothschild.* Weizmann recognised immediately that it signified a milestone in Jewish history. For the first time since the destruction of the Jewish state in 70 CE, a major power had recognised the national identity of the Jewish people. It promised great things. And, on a personal note, it also confirmed Weizmann's ascendancy over the Zionist movement. The Charter, that had eluded Herzl, was bestowed upon him, allowing him to inherit Herzl's mantle as the greatest figure in world Jewry.

Yet Weizmann was not entirely satisfied with his triumph. The misty phraseology of the Declaration left him on edge: it was not 'the boy' he had expected. The Balfour Declaration left all options open – and this is what disturbed Weizmann. It contained no firm British commitment to administer the National Home, a shortcoming that

---

* The Declaration was subjected to five drafts before the final text was agreed upon. The most pertinent passage read:

> His Majesty's Government view with favour the establishment in Palestine of a national home for the Jewish people and will use their best endeavours to facilitate the achievement of this object, it being clearly understood that nothing shall be done which may prejudice the civil and religious rights of existing non-Jewish communities in Palestine or the rights and political status enjoyed by Jews in any other country.

All five drafts can be seen in Stein, *Balfour . . .*, p. 664.

raised the grim prospect of an international regime for Palestine.*
Again, it hinted at partition: from the first draft that spoke of Palestine
as the National Home, it evolved into establishing 'in Palestine' the
National Home. Both these outcomes were as unacceptable to Lloyd
George as they were to Weizmann. But in the current wartime context
there was probably no other recourse for the British but to cover their
declarations in a cloak of vagueness. For in November 1917 it was by no
means certain that Britain was going to win the war, whatever
happened in Palestine – a campaign that Lloyd George, under no
illusions, passed off as a mere 'sideshow'. It was, however, to prove a
'sideshow' of great moment. By December 1917 Allenby's forces took
Jerusalem, Lloyd George's 'Christmas present' to the British people.
Ten months later, allied – mainly British – armies had completed the
conquest of Palestine, Syria and the Lebanon.

In Europe, on 11 November 1918, the First World War finally came
to an end. The great German March offensive, a last fling, had
collapsed: the Kaiser fled to Holland; an untested German republican
government, its armies in full retreat, its economy shattered, had no
option but to sue for an armistice.

At the beginning of December the same year Georges Clemenceau,
the French Prime Minister, visited London for talks with Lloyd
George, a preliminary meeting of minds before the forthcoming Paris
peace conference. No official record of this conversation was kept, but
Maurice Hankey, Secretary to the Cabinet, noted its contents in his
diary. ' "Tell me what you want," asked Clemenceau. "I want Mosul,"
said Lloyd George. "You shall have it," said Clemenceau. "Anything
else?" "Yes I want Jerusalem too," continued Lloyd George. "You shall
have it," said Clemenceau . . . Thus and thus is history made!'[29] The
original Sykes-Picot agreement was crumbling; a more fashionable one
was taking its place, based on the new realities of the aftermath of the
war: the British conquest of Palestine, Syria and Iraq; French
ambitions; above all, the need to preserve the Anglo-French alliance in
both Europe and the Middle East. This would ultimately hurt both the

*As noted previously, in the de Bunsen report Palestine was reserved for special
treatment, a commitment that was expressed in a more subtle form in the McMahon-
Husayn correspondence, but was later reiterated plainly in the Sykes-Picot
agreement. Now, it was hinted at again in the Balfour Declaration. Overall, one can
trace a thread of flexible continuity in British policy in the Near East.

Arabs and the Zionists. In the tremendous conflict of interests between the Great Powers and the aspiring nationalist movements, whether Arab or Zionist, the balance moved inexorably in favour of the former.

There can be no doubt about what was in the minds of the chief architects of the Balfour Declaration.[30] The evidence is incontrovertible. All envisaged, in the fullness of time, the emergence of a Jewish state. For the Zionists, accordingly, it was the first step that would lead to Jewish statehood. Yet for Weizmann – a confirmed Anglophile – and the Zionist leadership there proved to be adverse repercussions. As the British attempted to reconcile their diverse obligations, there began for the Zionists a period full of promise but also of intense frustration. One cynic noted that the process of whittling down the Balfour Declaration began on 3 November 1917. In his darker moments Weizmann would have concurred.

For the Arabs the Declaration was not so much the starting point of the conflict as a turning point, aggravating an already resolute antiZionist trend that can be traced back well before 1914. Although the substance of the Declaration was well known, it was not, astonishingly, published officially in Palestine until February 1920. Arab hostility towards it remained implacable, a position readily fostered by the Palestinian Arab leadership. A contemporary report testified very much in this sense. The King-Crane Commission, after spending six weeks in 1919 evaluating opinion, concluded that 'antiZionist feeling in Palestine and Syria is intense and not lightly to be flouted. No British officer, consulted by the Commissioners, believed that the Zionist programme could be carried out except by force of arms.'[31] In essence, little changed until the establishment of the state of Israel in 1948 – and for many years thereafter.

Not surprisingly then, for the British the Balfour Declaration inaugurated one of the most controversial episodes in their imperial history. Undone by the complexities of wartime diplomacy, unable to bridge the gap with either of the interested parties, the Declaration impaired their relations with both Palestinian Arabs and Zionists. And no less, it stained Britain's reputation throughout the Arab Middle East for generations to come. Yet all this was in the future. It would be quite wrong to ascribe to the British conquest of Palestine Machiavellian intentions. Imperialism was not yet the dirty word it has since become:

hindsight is a poor servant for historians. At the time, Britain's squabble was more with the French than with the Arabs or Jews, who were, in truth, bit players in the unfolding Middle East drama. As T. E. Lawrence colourfully put it: 'we can rush right up to Damascus, & biff the French out of all hope of Syria'.[32] Britain came to Palestine with clean, albeit 'imperial', hands. Relying on its vast empire-building experience and solid democratic heritage at home, Britain genuinely believed it to be possible to guide the Middle Eastern peoples under its tutelage to reconciliation and eventual self-government. Sadly, reality ultimately intruded, swamping Britain's original intentions in the mire of inter-communal strife.

As the war ended, Britain emerged from it weakened and virtually bankrupt, a debtor nation. Yet its Empire was more extensive than ever before. In the Middle East it had acquired new acquisitions, extending from Egypt to the Persian Gulf, comprising client states and the mandated territories. In this roundabout manner, the 'desiderata' of the de Bunsen Committee had been realised, and refined. Lloyd George – and Sir Mark Sykes – had long come to the conclusion that the Sykes-Picot agreement was a dispensable encumbrance, that it was necessary to keep the French at arm's length from the Canal zone and so consolidate Britain's position in the region. Despite the widespread accusations of double-speak, befitting the image of Perfidious Albion, Britain's Middle East diplomacy, given the fluctuations of wartime priorities, followed a generally coherent line.

2

'Beginnings are always troublesome'*

Until July 1920 Palestine was governed by the military authorities under a regime clumsily named 'Occupied Enemy Territory Administration (South)'. Sucked into a vortex of conflicting nationalist emotions at variance with their soldierly expertise, the military administrators, frustrated by the ungrateful natives they had liberated from oppressive Ottoman rule, instinctively thought in terms of 'a plague o' both your houses'. 'I dislike them all equally,' fumed Lieutenant-General Walter Norris 'Old Concrete' Congreve, Commander-in-Chief British armies in Egypt and Palestine. Ronald Storrs, first military (later civilian) Governor of Jerusalem, a highbrow who aired his erudition at the drop of a hat, put it more artfully: 'I am not wholly for either, but for both. Two hours of Arab grievances drive me to the Synagogue, while after an intensive course of Zionist propaganda I am prepared to embrace Islam.'[1]

OETA (South) rapidly acquired a reputation for embracing a distinctly anti-Zionist bias.[2] Congreve again, in a circular issued to his officers in October 1921:

> Whilst the army officially is supposed to have no politics, it is recognised that there are certain problems such as those of Ireland and Palestine, in which the sympathies of the Army are on one side or the other. In the case of Palestine these sympathies are rather obviously with the Arabs, who have hitherto appeared to the disinterested observer to have been the victims of the unjust policy forced upon them by the British Government.[3]

*George Eliot.

As Brigadier-General Sir Gilbert Clayton, chief political officer of the Egyptian Expeditionary Force, had already stressed: 'The Palestinians desire their country for themselves and will resist any general immigration of Jews, however gradual, by every means in their power including active hostilities . . . Fear and distrust of Zionist aims grow daily and no amount of persuasion or propaganda will dispel it.'[4]

The generals were not necessarily opposed to Zionism as such, but supremely conscious of the rising, often violent, wave of Arab hostility, they pressed for a Zionist policy that would not arouse the anger of the Arabs and so interfere with British control of Palestine. Clearly, a contradiction in terms. Nor were matters helped by the quality of the first batch of civilians brought in to help govern the country. Storrs, in typical style, made light of the calibre of his colleagues, among whom he spotted 'a cashier from a bank . . . an actor-manager . . . a clown, a land valuer . . . an Alexandria cotton broker, an architect . . . a taxi driver from Egypt, two school masters and a missionary'.[5] This particular circumstance, however, improved over time.

Events in Palestine were, inevitably, influenced by outside forces, at times without reference to the two interested parties, Arab or Zionist, and often beyond their control. At San Remo, in April 1920, Britain and France emerged as the mandatory powers for the Arab Middle East – Lebanon and Syria being awarded to France; Palestine (which by inference included Transjordan) and Iraq taken by Britain. Although both Arabs and Jews were present at San Remo, they were there as bystanders only, their fate determined by the imperial powers. The settlement well suited the Zionists: Weizmann had never disguised his predilection for a British mandate; and Lloyd George had never hidden his desire to impose one.

For the Arabs the outcome at San Remo foretold painful consequences. A month earlier, on 11 March 1920, the Syrian Congress, in an attempt to intimidate the powers at San Remo, had convened and proclaimed Faysal King of a United Syria, resulting in a wave of nationalist fervour, which swept through Palestine. But if this provocative step was an attempt to strong-arm the Great Powers, it clearly backfired. Britain and France would not be deflected from their purpose. On 1 July the British inaugurated its civil administration in Palestine, with Sir Herbert Samuel installed as its first High Commissioner. Three weeks later French armies – with the

British conveniently signalling a green light – advanced on Damascus, expelled Faysal (eventually compensated by the British with the kingdom of Iraq), and so brought to an end the dream of a great Arab state.

Faysal's banishment to Baghdad finally put paid to attempts, fragile at best, to square the circle by way of an Arab-Zionist agreement. In June 1918, encouraged by the British, Weizmann and Faysal had met at Wadi Waheida, an oasis just north of Akaba, the meeting formalised in an agreement signed a few months later. In general terms it set out the grounds for political and economic cooperation between the parties, promising to put into effect the Balfour Declaration. Faysal appended a 'Reservation' in his own hand. Written in Arabic (and translated by T. E. Lawrence) it read: 'If the Arabs are established as I have asked . . . I will carry out what is written in this agreement. If changes are made, I cannot be answerable for failing to carry out this agreement.'[6] But changes were made, as Faysal – whose capacity for leadership was vastly overrated – proved incapable of controlling his own extremists. Worse, by appeasing them he played into the grasping hands of the imperial powers. The Weizmann–Faysal accord proved to be a brief, transient moment of optimism in Jewish-Arab relations.

'We considered ourselves as Arabs, not a separate Palestinian identity,' said Dr Khalil al-Budayri, a self-styled Marxist and member of the Al-Nadi faction that advocated unification of Palestine with Syria.[7] The actions of the Great Powers dashed these hopes. The greater Arab national movement fragmented into its component parts. Palestinians now acted as an independent entity. Gradually the term 'Southern Syria' was erased from the lexicon of Palestinian nationalists; instead they spoke in the name of the 'Arab people of Palestine'. Anti-Zionist manifestos at Palestinian conventions now took on a distinct local character, insisting on representative government.[8] In April 1920, and again in May 1921, anti-Zionist riots flared up, mainly in Jerusalem and Jaffa, but also in a number of more remote Jewish settlements such as Hadera and Petach Tikva. Many were killed and wounded, Jews and Arabs alike. In the wake of the May blood-letting a Commission of Inquiry was set up. The Haycroft investigation found the Arabs culpable of fomenting the riots, but concluded that Arab enmity stemmed from fear of endless Jewish immigration and by the Jews' conception of the ultimate goal of Zionist policy. The whole tone of the document was highly critical of Zionist aims and methods.[9] It was the first in a long series of similar government statements.

Matters were not improved when, in May 1921, Haj Amin al-Husayni was appointed Mufti of Jerusalem by Sir Herbert Samuel, a post that carried not only spiritual authority but also commanded great financial and political clout. Haj Amin, a rabid anti-Zionist, had been tried *in absentia* for his role in the 1920 riots and sentenced to fifteen years' imprisonment. He had fled Palestine. Now he returned covered with glory. Eight months later a Supreme Muslim Council was set up with Haj Amin as its President, a position that confirmed his status as 'Head of the Muslim Community in Palestine'. He came to embody a deadly combination: overweening ambition, ruthlessness, fanaticism – all buttressed by dipping into the considerable funds at his disposal. Never shrinking from instituting a reign of terror against his rivals, Haj Amin dominated Palestinian politics until the *Nakba* (Catastrophe) of 1948–9 engulfed the people he professed to lead.

In Zionist politics too there were those who adopted a more pugnacious approach, the most prominent among them being Vladimir (Ze'ev) Jabotinsky. Born in Odessa to a middle-class family, his early experiences in Italy as a student and journalist left him in thrall to the myths of the *Risorgimento*, in particular to those of its mercurial military chieftain, Garibaldi, and its ideologue, Mazzini. An outstanding publicist and a firebrand orator, Jabotinsky was a loyal, if unpredictable, member of the Zionist leadership. As a member of the Jewish Agency Executive he had acquiesced in the final draft of the mandate in 1921 – that effectively excluded Transjordan from the provisions of the Jewish National Home; and the Churchill White Paper – that redefined the Balfour Declaration in more restrictive terms the following year.[10]

Then, in 1923, at odds with Weizmann and frustrated by the Fabian-like tactics of mainstream Zionism, he flounced out of the Executive. After two years he set up a new party, the World Union of Zionist Revisionists; a decade later he seceded from the movement and founded the New Zionist Organisation. His aims were maximalist: to establish a Jewish state along both banks of the River Jordan, and to proclaim immediately Jewish sovereignty over these areas. This may well have been a case of the wish being father to the thought, for the extent of Britain's international and regional commitments rendered Jabotinsky's creative thinking well beyond the realm of practical politics.

Like Weizmann, Jabotinsky was a convinced Anglophile. At one time he advanced the notion of incorporating Palestine as the 'Seventh Dominion' of the British Empire, a quite fanciful proposition. His British orientation also led him in other directions. In the First World War Jabotinsky was the driving force behind the formation of the Jewish Legion, five battalions of Jewish volunteers that served with the Royal Fusiliers. Commissioned as a lieutenant, he was decorated for bravery, but a setback followed. Involved in Jewish defence in the wake of the riots of 1920, he was imprisoned: later, his sentence was quashed, but in 1930 the authorities refused to grant him residency, effectively exiling him from Palestine.

Although the British had disappointed him, he did not lose faith. In a roundabout way, he returned to the British connection in his well-known 'Iron Wall' article. It postulated that, owing to visceral Arab hostility,

> Zionist colonisation must either stop, or else proceed regardless of the native population. Which means that it can proceed and develop only under the protection of a power that is independent of the native population – behind an iron wall, which the native population cannot breach . . . And we are all of us, without any exception, demanding day after day that this outside Power, should carry out this task vigorously and with determination.[11]

Yet Jabotinsky's iron wall stood on shaky foundations, for it assumed that Britain – 'this outside Power', for there was no other – would either actively or passively be a party to its construction, extravagant conjectures to an extreme.*

Mainstream Zionism had no quarrel with Jabotinsky's demand for adequate defence forces to protect the National Home. But its leaders

---

*Throughout his career Jabotinsky aimed at the Zionist leadership, to inherit Weizmann's mantle. He never succeeded, despite his many talents. Until his untimely death in August 1940, Jabotinsky remained the stereotype of the eternal oppositionist. But he was elevated to the rank of spiritual godfather by the more fanatical elements that followed him and that claimed, often on the flimsiest of evidence, his legacy. For Jabotinsky, despite his intransigent image and hardline rhetoric, deplored gratuitous violence.

were under no illusion that the British would act decisively in their cause. Ben Gurion detected immediately the defects in Jabotinsky's reasoning. 'I believe that it is impossible for a Jewish brigade under the command of a British General – and not the *Va'ad Leumi* [the *Yishuv's* National Committee] – to offer us adequate defence . . . His psychology would prevent him – the British General – from employing such a brigade within a Jewish environment. Jewish self-defence is the only means of securing and protecting our settlements!'[12] *Hashomer* was an early indication of the *Yishuv's* fighting ability. Later, the *Haganah*, the official defence body of the *Yishuv*, served the same purpose, though it acted over a wider canvas. Although the British, 'this outside Power', classified it as an 'illegal' organisation, there would be brief periods of cooperation between the *Haganah* and the British military, but only in the most extreme circumstances of the approach of the Second World War.

The inauguration of a civil administration did little to ease relations between the three interested parties. Samuel's appointment as High Commissioner only aroused Arab suspicions. Although no longer a practising orthodox Jew, his self-evident Jewish background left ample room for speculation that he was in fact a closet Zionist and would act accordingly. The Zionists thought this absurd – and could point to facts on the ground to prove it. For not only had Samuel (temporarily) halted immigration in the wake of the May 1921 riots, he had appointed that notorious agitator, Haj Amin, a mischievous and malign force in Zionist eyes, Mufti of Jerusalem. Was this not appeasement to Arab extremism? The Zionists certainly thought so. But Samuel, an experienced politician – having held high Cabinet office in Asquith's administrations – took the British way: compromise, conciliation, building bridges to parties in dispute. Damned if he did, and damned if he didn't, Samuel was caught in a cleft stick, as were to be so many of his successors.

Although Britain and France had crowned themselves as the mandatory powers, their resourcefulness had still to be confirmed in a lasting peace treaty with Turkey and ratified by the League of Nations. In July 1923, at Lausanne, the treaty with Turkey was at last formalised, a foregone conclusion, retroactively affirming the San Remo decisions. The jockeying over the terms of the mandate was more involved. Arab and Zionist lobbies now focused on London. The Arabs pressed strongly for the abrogation of the Balfour Declaration, but the British would have none of it.* This was a commitment the government would not renege on, as Churchill made abundantly clear. Largely held responsible for creating a new order in the Middle East, Churchill, at a conference in Cairo in March 1921, dispatched Faysal to Iraq as King, and later in Jerusalem mollified Abdullah, encamped in Transjordan, breathing revenge for his brother's expulsion from Damascus, by granting him 'one Sunday afternoon' the emirate of Transjordan. Some months later the final draft of the mandate was agreed upon: Transjordan remained subject to the British mandate, but the provisions relating to the Jewish National Home were excluded from it.[13] It was the first partition of the San Remo-style Palestine.

The Zionists swallowed this setback mainly because the actual terms of the mandate ran very much in their favour. Incorporating the Balfour Declaration, it can easily be read as a Zionist document. In some ways this was a triumph for the Zionist camp no less than the Balfour Declaration, perhaps even more so, for it flew in the face of a fresh wave of anti-Semitism – that slipped effortlessly into an anti-Zionist mode – throughout Europe. The Bolshevik revolution, inspired, or so it was widely believed, by villainous Jewish agitators, saw the re-emergence of a fantastical conspiracy theory. 'The Protocols of the Elders of Zion', which first saw the light of day in 1903, inevitably made an appearance in Palestine, as reading material for many serving British officers. Although soon established as a forgery by *The Times*, its message of an international Jewish conspiracy to achieve world domination resonated strongly among the gullible. (To this day it remains a popular read in most Arab countries.) These prejudices found an echo in the Arab–Zionist debate in Britain. The Northcliffe press was openly anti-Zionist, while Beaverbrook was conducting a public campaign for Britain 'to evacuate Mesopotamia

---

*They gained a pyrrhic victory in the House of Lords. In June 1922 the Lords voted in favour of a motion that questioned the validity of the mandate 'in its present form', despite a brave maiden speech by Balfour, newly created an earl. The vote was not binding on the government, but it came as a rude shock to the Zionists, highlighting as it did the depth of anti-Zionist feeling in England. A few days later the Commons endorsed the final text of the mandate. See *PD*, Lords, Fifth Series, vol. 50, c.994–1034, 21 June 1922; and *PD*, Commons, Fifth Series, vol. 156, c.263–340, 4 July 1922.

and Palestine bag and baggage *and at once*'. At times, this paper war was scarcely distinguishable from anti-Semitism. Who is this ' "Mysterious Chaim" [Weizmann]', asked the *Daily Express*, who has inveigled the innocent and unsuspecting British into the mire of the Middle East?[14]

By the summer of 1922 the struggle over the ratification of the mandate was moving to its climax. In June, the government published a summary of its discussions with the Arab and Zionist delegations together with a statement of policy: this was the famous Churchill White Paper – in fact drafted by Samuel.[15] It reaffirmed that the Balfour Declaration 'is not susceptible to change'. But it then redefined the Declaration, not in the enthusiastic, positive terms previously expressed by Lloyd George and Balfour, but in more limiting phrases. Immigration was now to be determined by 'economic absorptive capacity', a flexible yardstick given to much ill-natured haggling. Although the British review recognised that the Jews were in Palestine 'as of right and not on sufferance', it viewed as 'impracticable' the proposition, expressed by Weizmann at the Paris Peace Conference, that Palestine would become 'as Jewish as England is English'. A month later the League of Nations, taking note of these caveats, ratified the mandate: a year later it was endorsed by the United States in a special Convention. These commitments received an added boost when Andrew Bonar Law, famously labelled 'the Unknown Prime Minister', took office in October 1922. Bent on retrenchment, his administration initiated a reappraisal of Britain's Palestine policy. After extensive investigations, in July 1923, the Cabinet agreed to continue with the policy of the Balfour Declaration, mainly, but not only, for reasons that stressed Palestine's strategic importance to the Empire.[16]

The Zionist Executive subscribed, albeit reluctantly, to the qualifications of the Churchill White Paper – not that it had much choice – for despite its provisos, there was much cause for satisfaction. The British government had stood firm in its obligations, or at least, as the cynics would have it, had not surrendered entirely to anti-Zionist pressure. The mandate remained, slightly soiled, but substantially intact. However, overshadowing all else was the fact that the concept of a Jewish National Home in Palestine had won international recognition. For the Arab delegates the story ran differently. They had gamely tried to force public opinion in their direction, but with limited success. Although the British had wavered on occasion, the government would not yield to their ultimatory demands. Thwarted and resentful, they returned home empty-handed from London. Unwilling, or unable, to soften their all-or-nothing demands, perhaps perfectly reasonable from their point of view, they had hit upon a bankrupt formula to conduct a negotiation to a successful conclusion, staking all on a zero-sum game. Having set such a gloomy precedent, similar disappointments would follow. For the British, this whole espisode signified the beginning of a protracted learning curve. It slowly dawned on them that the mandate for Palestine, which they had fought so strenuously to obtain, was *sui generis*, unlike any of their other imperial acquisitions. Bitter experience would not shake this assumption, only reinforce it.

The Ottoman Turks had imposed a savage wartime regime on Palestine. Disease and incidents of famine compounded the misery. The economy slumped. Many fled the country to seek sanctuary elsewhere; others were expelled by the Turks as security risks. Both communities, Jewish and Arab, suffered. With the end of hostilities, a degree of stability was restored. Slowly the exiles began to return. Immigration was resumed, mainly Jewish, but Arabs too. By 1922, according to a British-conducted census, the population of mandatory Palestine stood at 744,431: 660,641 Arabs, 83,790 Jews. Once things had settled down after the 1920–1 riots, Samuel's more forward-looking administration promoted steps appropriate to Britain's ideal of a well-run dependency, measures that also accorded with Britain's mandate to prepare the country for self-government. Palestine's transport system was overhauled; communications with the outside world improved; more social services were made available; a non-partisan civil service began to function, that included a restricted number of Jews and Arabs; and of paramount importance, an independent judicial system was put in place, rescued from the baksheesh culture of Ottoman times.

Highly commendable as all this was, it did not penetrate to the root of the problem of mandatory Palestine. One notion, professed by some Zionists, held that economic growth that benefited Arabs and Jews alike would somehow unravel the political stalemate. This was idle speculation. The stumbling block was political: it overshadowed everything. As a mark of compromise towards the Arabs, Samuel proposed establishing representative bodies, including an Arab Agency similar to the status of the Jewish Agency as laid out in the mandate.[17]

These offers were unceremoniously shot down by the Arab leadership, holding that any surrender to such gestures would imply recognising the legitimacy of the mandate. Other attempts in the future suffered the same fate, and for the same reason.

Samuel's period in office ended in 1925, without any further violent disturbances. His replacement was a soldier, Field Marshal Viscount Herbert Charles Onslow Plumer. With his squat figure, ruddy countenance and white walrus moustache, Plumer cut a somewhat comical figure. In fact, he was one of the few British generals to emerge from the First World War with his reputation intact – no mean feat! His Colonel Blimp image masked a tough, no-nonsense personality. When an Arab dignitary – reportedly Haj Amin – made clear to Plumer that *he* could not be held accountable for any breakdown in law and order, Plumer retorted: 'You don't have to be responsible, I'm responsible'; and again, on being asked to comment on the 'political situation', he snapped back, dropping his monocle from his eye, 'there is no political situation, and don't you create one' – *bons mots* that rebounded to haunt other High Commissioners.[18]

The mid-1920s was a period of relative tranquillity, so much so that the British authorities felt it appropriate to reduce the security forces. One reason for this untimely measure was the state of the Jewish National Home: the *Yishuv* appeared to be in bad shape, a key factor in the lessening of tension. World Jewry had not responded in kind to Weizmann's dramatic challenge 'to rebuild and re-establish the Jewish nation in the Jewish land'.[19] By 1928 the Jewish population had crept up to 151,656 (compared to 775,092 Arabs), a far cry from Zionist aspirations. In 1927 more Jews emigrated than made *Aliyah* to the Promised Land.[20] Moreover, the Zionist Organisation was virtually bankrupt. One solution was to tap the resources of American Jewry. 'Eating [his] way from coast to coast', Weizmann claimed for himself the accolade of the greatest tax collector in the history of the Jewish people: reception committees and speeches, breakfasts, lunches, teas and dinners followed each other with soul-destroying regularity, all strikingly similar in appearance, content and taste.[21] These heroic chores produced only limited, though life-saving, results. As foreign capital trickled into the country, mainly from Jewish sources, the standard of living rose, slowly but perceptibly, benefiting the population as a whole, though not to an equal degree.

But this was only half the story. In other ways the *Yishuv* was developing along lines that later led the Peel Commission to define it as 'a state within a state'.[22] The Jewish Agency spawned departments that mirrored government ministries. The *Histadruth* (General Federation of Jewish Labour), founded in 1920, was much more than a multi-trades union; it was also a provider of social services and an employer on a large scale. And together with advanced forms of large-scale collective agriculture and diverse light industries – all based on the high-minded principle of the 'conquest of Jewish labour' – it nurtured an economic infrastructure that foretold a lively growth rate in the years to come. Progressive educational and health systems were also set up, independent of the central Palestine administration. Furthermore, political life thrived – including much infighting – offset by a flourishing cultural life, its crowning accomplishment, the Palestine (later Israel) Philharmonic Orchestra, premiering in December 1936. The British found nothing untoward in all this extra-curricular activity, probably assuming, rightly, that it saved the British taxpayer money.

There was no such radical transformation of Palestinian society. It remained much as it had been, mainly rural in character, its political and intellectual life dominated by the wealthy and influential great families – the notables, all too often at (frequently violent) odds with each other. In particular, the al-Husayni family network, led by the Mufti, Haj Amin, manipulating his pre-eminent position on the Palestinian Arab Executive Committee and later the Supreme Muslim Council, gained an ascendancy over Palestinian Arab politics. His no-compromise mentality reinforced widespread tendencies from before the First World War. Zionism was perceived as a movement that planned to mutate the religious and national character of the country, depriving its indigenous (Palestinian) inhabitants of their legitimate natural birthright. Suspicion slowly turned to enmity. Perceiving Zionism in such absolute terms only ensured further inter-communal conflict.[23]

If there was one thing that concentrated Zionist minds wonderfully, it was the conviction that British officials were hopelessly biased against them, not all of them, of course, but the overwhelming majority. There was some evidence to support this belief. Samuel told Weizmann in August 1921:

It is quite true that a great many, I might almost say all, of the British officials in Palestine are not sympathetic to a Zionist policy which would be detrimental to the Arabs, and are not prepared to carry out with any good will a policy which is likely to result in a regime of coercion. But if the whole of the present staff were changed and replaced by others chosen by yourself, in six months the newcomers would hold precisely the same views.[24]

The diaries of Owen Tweedy, a British journalist who covered the Middle East and later acted as press officer to the Palestine government from 1936 to 1941, tell much the same story, naming high-ranking officials for their anti-Jewish bias, singling out for special mention Archer Cust, Stewart Perowne, Ernest Richmond and, finally, the new High Commissioner himself, Sir John Chancellor, appointed in 1928, who admitted to Tweedy that he did not like Jews, 'an ungrateful race'.* Theodore White, the American writer, passing through Palestine on his way to China, unfortunately fell out with a pugnacious British officer. 'You Jews are simply a bloody nuisance', he was told. Whatever racist prejudices these, and other, officials may or may not have held, politically the problem could be traced back to 'that fateful mental aberration known to history as the Balfour Declaration', as one functionary delicately put it.[25] Another official, in the best traditions of colonial administration, put this inflammatory issue on a different footing. The Jews might be 'a bloody nuisance', they might be uppity and argumentative, refusing ever to take 'NO!' for an answer, yet: 'It does not seem to have occurred to the Zionists that it is possible for an English official to have a personal dislike for a type yet to do his duty conscientiously in spite of it.'[26]

The British viewed the Arabs from another perspective. At the most select level there was some social intercourse. Katy Antonius's salon,

*Cust served as private secretary to Sir John Chancellor, the High Commissioner; Perowne in the Education Department; Richmond, Assistant Civil Secretary in the Palestine administration, resigned in 1924 in protest at Samuel's alleged pro-Zionist policy, but returned in 1927 as Director of the Department of Antiquities. See, in general, Evyatar Friesel, 'Through a Peculiar Lens: Zionism and Palestine in British Diaries, 1927–31', *Middle Eastern Studies* (1993), vol. 29, no. 3, pp. 419–44.

William Mathieson, a Colonial Office official dealing with Palestine, denied that the Office was tainted with anti-Semitism, but admitted that it was 'definitely' anti-Zionist in outlook. See MSS Brit. Emp., s.527/10, vol. 3, RH.

held in Jerusalem, where the great and the good would regularly convene to discuss the 'who and the why', evolved into a much sought-after venue throughout the Middle East. The Antoniuses resided in the Sheikh Jarrah quarter in Jerusalem at a junction that led to the Mount of Olives. The house, known as 'Karm al-Mufti' (the Mufti's Vineyard), originally belonged to Haj Amin, though he never actually lived in it. Forced into exile, he first rented and subsequently sold the Mufti's Vineyard to his confidants, George and Katy Antonius. Set in a spacious garden, and replete with books, beautiful carpets and musical recordings, it provided the perfect backdrop for the gregarious Katy Antonius to emerge as the pre-eminent hostess of the social and cultural life of Jerusalem in the 1930s and 1940s.* 'Katy gave a very nice little dance for about 60 people, and supper at her house,' recorded a satiated British officer. Richard Crossman, another guest, was more perceptive.

> Mrs Antonius seems to have a political salon in true French style. It was a magnificent party – evening dress, Syrian food and drink, and dancing on the marble floor. As far as I could see the party was fifty-fifty Arab and British. It is easy to see why the British prefer the Arab upper class to the Jews. This Arab intelligentsia has a French culture, amusing, civilised, tragic and gay. Compared with them the Jews seem tense, *bourgeois*, central European.

As Crossman left the *soirée*, a British official said to him, 'There are two societies in Jerusalem, not three. One is Anglo-Arab and the other is Jewish. The two just can't mix.'[27]

But whatever passed for conversational niceties in Katy's parlour could not disguise the air of condescension that betrayed her British guests' innermost feelings. 'One must remember that we British can always feel superior to the Arab,' a high-ranking British police officer told Richard Crossman. Untrustworthy and amoral, Arabs could not be counted on. 'I am not prepared to trust them as a body and I doubt if we shall be able to do so,' said Sir William Denis Battershill, Chief

---

*Later, she became the subject of widespread rumours, never denied, that she was romantically involved with General Sir Evelyn Barker, British Military Commander in Palestine 1946–8. A scandalous episode, it accorded her celebrity status.

Secretary to the Palestine Administration from 1937 to 1939 (later Deputy Under-Secretary of State at the Colonial Office), and went on: 'I doubt whether any Arab has any ethical feeling against murder . . . [they] look upon murder as a justifiable and satisfactory weapon . . . we shall never get them to change their fundamental beliefs on this point.' Were they also backward? 'The Arabs never bother about the clock – the sun is good enough for them', derided Mary Burgess, a high-school teacher in Jaffa, to her mother. Sir Henry Lovell Goldsworthy Gurney, the last Chief Secretary to the Palestine government, added his own variation on the same theme: Arabs were subject to

> intrigue and chicanery . . . [they were] completely intransigent and wooden in the face of any argument or persuasion to recognise the hard facts . . . easy-going to the point of indolence, disposed to cruelty and capable of only about one idea at a time. The idea is formed on emotion rather from any rational thought; it is nursed and chewed over on innumerable occasions in coffee-houses and in the press, until it is firmly stuck and nothing on earth will shift it.[28]

Despite these preconceived and oversimplified impressions, the Palestine administration functioned efficiently enough. Both Arabs and Jews served in it. Teamwork was vital. Cooperation, at times even fraternisation, existed between all parties. One Jewish District Officer recalled being invited to his superior's home and 'sipping beer and chatting about trivia' with his chief, the hospitable Mr Musgrave. On another occasion he was persuaded by an Arab colleague, Jamal Bey, into founding (during Ramadan!) a two-man coffee clutch to meet every day at 10 a.m. sharp.[29] Obviously some relationships worked. But this was only scratching the surface. The stereotypes noted above stuck firmly in the British imagination and were not to be easily dislodged. The Arabs, for their part, assumed that the Jewish National Home was prospering on the points of British bayonets, while the Jews viewed the British as being hopelessly prejudiced, wilfully sabotaging the development of the National Home. Moreover, both Jews and Arabs continued to regard each other with barely concealed suspicion and resentment, while reserving much of their animosity for the hapless British. A vicious circle indeed, and a sure recipe for outbreaks of violence.

3

Rebellion

From 23 until 29 August 1929 bloody communal disorders flared up throughout Palestine. In all, some 472 Jews and 268 Arabs were either killed or wounded. These events came as a climax to eleven months of mounting inter-communal tension, the culmination of one of those (seemingly) petty religious squabbles that have periodically disgraced the Holy Land. At the Wailing Wall on 24 September 1928, the Jewish Day of Atonement, a screen used to divide Jewish male and female worshippers was forcibly removed by the police, acting on a complaint by the Arabs that the screen constituted an infringement of the status quo. Baseless allegations and needlessly provocative demonstrations, with extremists from both sides on the march, fanned an already incendiary situation, culminating in the outbreaks of August 1929[1]*

These rabble-rousing incidents were, of course, merely symptoms of a much more pernicious malaise. Only days earlier, on 11 August, Weizmann had opened the Constituent Assembly of the enlarged Jewish Agency, described as 'coextensive with the Jewish people everywhere'. Many Jewish luminaries – including Albert Einstein, Leon Blum, Sir Herbert Samuel, Lord Melchett and Felix Warburg – were associated with this reincarnation of the Jewish Agency. Baron Edmond de Rothschild was elected its Honorary President. Was this

---

*Actually seeing the Wailing Wall in action gave rise to some quirky reactions. 'What did you think of the Wailing Wall?' asked Mrs Bentwich, wife of Norman, the first Attorney General of the mandatory government. 'A horrible, stinking, little alley with a pack of dirty, greasy Jews howling against this Wall,' replied Rear-Admiral Sir William Milbourne James, Chief of Staff of the Mediterranean Fleet, 'If I'd had a revolver on me I would have shot the lot of them. I'd have given 'em something to howl for.' Mrs Bentwich's response was not recorded. See Sidney Moody (a ranking official of the Palestine administration) to Jane ?, 22 September 1930, Brit. Emp., s.382, Box 8/2, RH.

not, suspicious Arabs might ask, an ominous reminder of the power of world Jewry, of its grandees, with untold wealth and influence at their fingertips, now conscripted to advance the cause of the Jewish National Home? While the timing of this occasion might have been coincidental, its significance could not have escaped the Arab leadership in the run-up to the August riots.

'All night firing went on around us,' recorded Miss Irvine, an English schoolteacher in Jerusalem. 'Hebron, of course, was the worst,' she continued, 'an entirely unprovoked attack on these quite inoffensive Jews . . . between 50 and 80 Jews were murdered in cold blood, I believe, women and children as well.' These were ultra-orthodox, non-Zionist Jews, intent only on praying in their City of the Patriarchs. The more fortunate among them were rescued by their Arab neighbours. 'Dr Abd-al-Al was splendid, and personally saved a large number of Jews. He conducted them to a café where the Muslim notables were gathered, put them in their care, saying he knew every one of the Jews and of the notables there.' Others were rescued by British officers – Raymond Cafferata, 'who killed as many of the murderers as he could, taking to his fists even', being singled out for special mention. Killings were also recorded in Jerusalem, Tel Aviv, Safad and some outlying settlements. As a matter of course the Jews retaliated; but the overwhelming majority of Arab casualties fell to British bullets. Sir John Chancellor, in defence of his security forces, spoke of 'acts of unspeakable savagery upon Jewish people'.[2]

What followed soon became a familiar routine: commissions of inquiry, investigations, reports, political manoeuvring, partisan lobbying, backtracking, stitching together temporary solutions: few were assuaged, most continued disaffected, the country remained what it had always been, a tinderbox.

The overriding tone of these official papers was exceedingly critical of Zionist methods in Palestine, particularly regarding immigration policy and land purchases. Only in one particular could the Zionists draw some satisfaction: the violence, it was affirmed, had resulted from attacks by Arabs upon Jews for which there was no excuse. Otherwise, the overall conclusion was equally explicit: that the fundamental cause of the riots lay in Arab frustration at their failure to satisfy their political and national aspirations, as well as concern for their economic future. Fearing that it would provoke 'a shriek of anguish from all Jewry', Lord Passfield, the Colonial Secretary, encapsulated these findings in his statement of policy: it envisaged drastic restrictions in the scale of Jewish immigration and land purchases, and far-reaching constitutional proposals inimical to the National Home. Even Beatrice Webb, Passfield's wife, herself no friend of Zionism, thought it 'Badly drafted [and] tactless'. It resulted in a major crisis in Anglo-Zionist relations.

Weizmann and other leaders of the Jewish Agency resigned in protest at the government's overtly hostile attitude, designed, they argued, to throttle the Jewish National Home. Exploiting a vulnerable minority Labour government, the Zionists responded by launching an efficacious exercise in worldwide political lobbying that rectified much of the damage inflicted by Passfield, at least from their point of view. In a letter to Weizmann that was laid before the Council of the League of Nations as an official government document, dispatched to the High Commissioner as a Cabinet instruction and tabled and recorded in the proceedings of Parliament, Ramsey MacDonald, the Prime Minister, partially made amends. It did not abrogate the Passfield White Paper, but its style and substance modified it to a degree that rendered it virtually meaningless. Bolstered by outside factors, the MacDonald letter heralded a period of unprecedented growth and expansion of the *Yishuv*. The Arabs, naturally, viewed it differently, as yet another example of the sinister power wielded by the international Jewish-Zionist lobby, capable of beating down any opposition. Disparagingly, they dubbed it 'the Black Letter'.[3]

The appointment of General Sir Arthur Grenfell Wauchope as High Commissioner anticipated the turn in policy signified by MacDonald's recent guidelines. A Boer War veteran, he arrived in Jerusalem in November 1931, taking up residence at Government House, a newly designed edifice situated on a knoll – popularly (and perspicaciously?) referred to as the 'Hill of Evil Counsel' or the 'Mount of Offence' – to the south of the city. For the Zionists, Wauchope was 'perhaps the best High Commissioner Palestine has had',[4] a verdict challenged forcefully by the Arabs. Although rich in military experience, he came as a novice in the arts of colonial administration. He could be 'pretty horrid and rough' when dealing with people, remembered his secretary, Ralph Postan, badgering his petitioners with 'questions, questions, questions'.

At the same time, Wauchope fostered a more easy-going style. A confirmed bachelor, he persuaded 'an elderly widowed lady' to act as his
hostess at the dinner parties he regularly held for fifty to sixty people,
taking great pains over the *placement*, agonising over the right 'pecking
order'. Jews were entertained more often than Arabs, as they spoke 'our
language intellectually' and shared with Wauchope a passion for music.
He kept a 'luxurious summer camp' at Athlit, a small coastal town south
of Haifa, where he would unwind from the demands of his day-to-day
administrative chores, preferring to fly there rather than suffer a bumpy
car journey. I'm giving you 'a good man, a fellow Scot', Ramsey
MacDonald had assured Ben Gurion. Wauchope tried to live up to his
down-to-earth image, not only in matters of high policy, but also in
more day-to-day routine, surprising his servants by eating his porridge
or yoghurt at breakfast in the traditional Scottish way, 'standing up!'[5]

Unlike Wauchope, some officials and soldiers thought 'the English
way of life' in Palestine 'plain boring'. Others, like their chief, made the
best of it, sparing no effort to amuse themselves, keeping up appearances until the last days of the mandate. There was 'a small Red Light
district' in Haifa, worthy of an occasional visit, recollected one patron.
Afterwards, 'wonderful meals' were to be relished, 'perfectly cooked
schnitzels' at the Slavia restaurant, or 'super mixed grills' at the
Olympia, washed down by a Tom Collins or a bottle of Carmel Hock.
When not enjoying the delights of Haifa, there were more traditional
pastimes to engage the sporting types: football, cricket and boxing.
Teams drawn from the Palestine Police, the Army and the administration competed regularly against each other. 'Smashing swimming
excursions' provided another outlet: 'Caesaria has a wizo beach, bang
on!' wrote one enthusiast to another. More upmarket sports also
beckoned. 'The Jack Hunters', a makeshift polo team based at Sarafand,
rode 'pretty old horses, between 16 and 20 years!' – but they persisted.
Or alternatively one could hunt with the Ramle Vale, tracking down
jackals – the Commander-in-Chief at the time, General Archibald
Percival Wavell, excelling as 'a strong rider'. A more junior officer
remembered the experience as 'good fun, but not much jumping – just
a few cactus hedges and we drew orange groves'.[6]

Wauchope's more benign administration witnessed a sharp rise in
Jewish immigration. The years 1933–5 saw 134,540 authorised immigrants

enter Palestine, a truly dramatic increase from the overall figure of 247,404 for the period 1921–35. Hitler's accession to power in January 1933 provided the impetus for this surge in Jewish immigration, that if allowed to continue threatened to change the demographic structure of the country. The 'Aryanisation' of Nazi Germany, with the Jews marked out for special treatment, ensured that there would be no let-up of Jewish refugees seeking shelter elsewhere, including Palestine, particularly as other countries in central and eastern Europe were engaged in similar racist policies.[7]

Resentful at MacDonald's 'Black Letter', bitter at continued Jewish land purchases, and now inflamed by the current upsurge in immigration, the Arabs saw no option but to adopt a more radical line. In October 1933 riots broke out in Jaffa, Nablus, Haifa and Jerusalem, directed mainly, but not exclusively, against the British, whom the Arabs regarded as the sponsors and protectors of the Zionist experiment: in all 26 Arabs were killed, 178 injured, with the police also incurring a number of casualties.[8] Soon afterwards the Arabs found a potent symbol in the figure of Sheikh Izz-a-din al-Qassam. Syrian born, he took up residence in Haifa after studying in Cairo, first teaching at an Islamic school, later haranguing the faithful at the Istaqlal mosque. Preaching fundamentalist Islamic precepts, he nourished the concept of armed struggle against the mandatory power and the National Home. 'You are a people of rabbits who are afraid of death,' he upbraided his devotees. 'You must know that nothing will save us but our arms.' Attacks on British installations and Jewish settlements followed, with Kibbutz Yagur and Nahalal, symbols of Zionist enterprise, singled out for special treatment. Finally, in November 1935, cornered in a cave in the hills around Jenin, al-Qassam was killed in a clash with the security forces. His funeral, attended by thousands, became the occasion for a massive demonstration against the authorities and the *Yishuv*. Elevated to iconic status, al-Qassam came to personify militant Palestinian nationalism. (The Izz-a-din al-Qassam Brigades, the armed wing of Hamas, boast his name.)

The same month that al-Qassam met his death, a united Arab delegation presented a memorandum to Wauchope. It repeated long-standing Arab demands: the establishment of a democratic government; the prohibition of land sales to Jews; and the immediate cessation of Jewish immigration. In an attempt to quell this surge of

Arab nationalism, countered by an increasingly combative mood in the *Yishuv*, the British re-introduced proposals for a Legislative Council. Already rejected by both sides in 1923, the later negotiations for a Council, hotly rejected by the Zionists, with the Arabs still vacillating, petered out in early 1936, overtaken by the outbreak of the Arab rebellion of 1936–9.[9]

On 19 April 1936 Arab riots broke out in Jaffa: after two days nine Jews were dead and many more wounded, a curfew had been imposed and emergency regulations brought into force.* An Arab Higher Committee (AHC), led by Haj Amin, thereupon proclaimed an Arab general strike to end only when its demands had been met. Infringements of the strike were common and, as is usual in such cases, the poorer sections of the Arab community suffered most. By contrast, the strike stimulated the Jewish economy – its proudest, most publicised achievement, the construction of 'the first Jewish port in two thousand years': in fact a modest wooden wharf off Tel Aviv to offset the loss of Jaffa. By October the strike was called off, the dictates of the AHC hanging fire. Tiredness, the approach of the citrus season and the intervention of outside Arab states – a precedent that some thought dangerous as it widened the scope of the Palestinian dispute – were all factors in ending the strike. One Arab source emphasised how the violent events in Palestine forged a bond between the Palestinians and the rest of the Arab world, and concluded, somewhat rashly, that the strike, and later 'the Revolt', were directed from Damascus, Beirut and Baghdad.[10]

Even during the strike there was no let-up to the violence, directed also against British personnel. A bankrupt British government, putty in the hands of the Jews, had to be taught a terrible lesson, decided Khalil al-Sakakini, listing some of the punishments to be meted out: bomb and shoot the British and Jewish invaders, torch Jewish fields and orange groves, ambush routine traffic, block roads, derail trains, cut power lines. 'The battle in Palestine is in full force,' cried al-Sakakini, in a burst of nationalist fervour. 'Victory is in the hands of God . . . If we

---

*The riots were preceded by a series of tit-for-tat killings that began when Arab highwaymen held up a bus, dragged two Jews from it and shot them. Retaliation swiftly followed. For the background and general course of these events, see *Cmd.5479* (the Peel report), chapter IV and *Col.* No. 129, *Report by HMG. to the League of Nations on the Administration of Palestine* (1936), pp. 5–20, 22–36.

live – we shall live with honour. If we die – we shall die with honour.'
The achievements of the rebellion were 'too many to list', he thought:
'suffice it to say that Palestine which had been as good as dead has
revived, returned to life. God be praised.'

In August the Syrian-born Fawzi al-Kaukji, a notorious professional
rebel – sentenced to death *in absentia* by the French – infiltrated
Palestine at the head of 200 Iraqi, Syrian and Transjordan volunteers.
As the self-styled 'Commander-in-Chief of the Revolt in Southern
Syria', al-Kaukji brought some order to the Palestinian bands operating
in Samaria, though he failed to eliminate the inevitable friction
between the Palestinians and his foreign mercenaries. After two
months, with the strike called off, he retreated back across the Jordan.[12]
However, al-Kaukji's presence in Palestine, though short-lived, caused
Palestinian resistance, directed against the Jews and, as they saw it,
their British watchdogs, to move up a gear.

For their part, the British took steps to combat the breakdown in law
and order, both on the military and political fronts. The British armed
presence was beefed up. At times, when the rebellion peaked – in the
summer and autumn of 1937, or September 1938, for example –
approximately 20,000 soldiers (two divisions), were actively engaged in
suppressing the insurgency. The balance of power between the civil and
military authorities swung towards the fighting services. The insurgency
also led to the oddest of occurrences in the history of the mandate:
cooperation between the *Haganah* and the British army. The initiative
came from Captain (later Major-General) Orde Charles Wingate, an
eccentric, unorthodox – some would add, unbalanced – officer, but who
would prove himself to be a master of guerrilla-style tactics. Raised
among the Plymouth Brethren, he saw the creation of a Jewish state as a
religious duty, the literal fulfilment of Christian prophecies. His declared
ambition was to command the Jewish army. 'Lucky for us', observed
'Baffy' Dugdale, 'that Wingate's fanatical Zionism gets the better of his
sense of duty as an Intelligence Officer. He is clearly one of the
instruments in God's hand.' Now serving in Palestine, his 'ferocious
eloquence' was sufficient to convince Generals Wavell and Haining to
set up 'Special Night Squads', armed groups of *Haganah* volunteers
(among whom was Moshe Dayan) led by British officers and NCOs.[13]

Wingate aimed at 'a system of general and undetected movement of
troops by night, across country and into villages, surprising gangs,

restoring confidence to peasants, and gaining government control of rural areas'. After only a month's work he reported that eleven engagements had been fought and that 'between sixty and seventy rebels have been killed . . . [and] double this number must have been wounded'.[14] Despite the conspicuous success of his innovative military tactics, Wingate's commitment to Zionism was so absolute, so uncompromising, that he became an embarrassment to his superiors and was subsequently transferred out of Palestine in 1939, though this did not bring to an end his pro-Zionist activity.*

While cooperation between the *Haganah* and the military in Palestine was in full flow, the Jewish Agency and the British government were squaring up for a showdown. As the international situation deteriorated, Britain's position became more vulnerable. Italy, having swallowed Libya by 1930 and Ethiopia by May 1936, threatened Britain's control of the Mediterranean and its lines of communication with the Far East. From Bari, its radio station blared out an incessant, and highly provocative, barrage of propaganda, openly encouraging the Arabs to liberate themselves from British imperialism. In Damascus, at the Italian consulate, 'chauffeurs and mechanics' occupied themselves in their ample spare time in fund-raising, gun-running, and gang-raising enterprises on behalf of the Palestinian rebels.[15]

With the Italians aspiring to inherit Britain's position in the Near East and the Japanese menacing British possessions in the Far East, the government had also to contend with Nazi Germany's mission to

---

*Wingate continued to press for a Jewish army to contain the Middle East on behalf of Britain. Whenever in London, he would participate in top-level meetings at the Zionist headquarters in Great Russell Street. Posted to Ethiopia, Wingate fought a successful campaign against the Italians, leading his 'Gideon Force', a guerrilla troop of British, Sudenese, and Ethiopian soldiers, with a sprinkling of SNS veterens. Hospitalised after a bout of malaria, he made an unsuccessful suicide attempt by stabbing himself in the neck. Benefiting from Wavell's patronage, he was transferred to India and Burma in 1942, where he founded his Long Range Penetration Units, the 'Chindits'. In March 1944, now holding the rank of Major-General, Wingate was killed in an air crash over Burma. He never lost his passion for Zionism and a Jewish army. 'Baffy' Dugdale made this reserved comment on hearing of his death: 'He was evidently a guerrilla leader of genius, whatever he might have been in handling larger bodies of men. I never liked him, and have always wondered whether his influence on the *Yishuv* would have been as splendid as his friends think, if he had returned to Jewish work after the war. Now we shall never know. *Dugdale Diaries*, 30 March 1944, pp. 211–12.

dominate Europe. Nor were the Germans bashful about making their presence felt in Palestine. About 2,000 'Aryan' *Reichdeutsche*, the majority of whom were members of the Templar sect, resided in the Holy Land. By 1937 this community was 'completely under the influence' of the local branches of the Nazi Party, 'which treated the German settlements as advance posts of the Third Reich'.[16] Time and again the Chiefs of Staff warned that Britain could ill afford, and was totally unprepared, to fight a war on three fronts. When, after the *Anschluss*, the French asked what force the British could contribute in the event of a European war, His Majesty's ministers replied, 'two divisions . . . inadequately equipped for any offensive operations'.[17] Clearly, there was a pressing need to conserve Britain's limited resources. And Palestine figured large in these calculations, for two divisions, 'inadequately equipped', was more or less the size of the force being used to crush the Arab rebellion. In fact, it appears that about forty per cent of Britain's total field force, the equivalent of what was tentatively being offered to France in the event of a European war, was tied down in Palestine.

You are instructed 'to ascertain the underlying causes of the disturbances . . . [and] to make recommendations for their removal and for the prevention of their recurrence'. So read the terms of reference to the 'Royal (Peel) Commission on Palestine' that began its inquiries in November 1936. The appellation 'Royal' lent the Commission not only greater dignity but also, at least in theory, greater political clout. It carried out the most wide-ranging and thorough investigation yet conducted into the history of the mandate. Its main recommendation, published in July 1937, was revolutionary in concept: the partition of mandatory Palestine. The reactions to this far-reaching proposition were mixed. The Zionists accepted it in principle; the Arabs rejected it, also in principle.* Wauchope, the High Commissioner, thought it 'to be the best of a bad job'; Battershill, his Chief Secretary, thought it 'an historical crime'; the British government at first concurred, but then backtracked.

*Among the more conciliatory-minded Arabs there were those who were prepared to consider the partition proposal; but there were none who were prepared to defy Haj Amin's ascendancy, backed as it was by the rule of the gun. See J. C. Hurewitz, *The Struggle for Palestine* (New York, 1950), pp. 78–9, 90.

In Britain, a most formidable combination emerged to bury the idea (at least for the time being): the Chiefs of Staff, the Foreign Office and its representatives throughout the Middle East, and Parliament, which responded coolly to the report, including the usually reliable pro-Zionist lobby. Their arguments were persuasive. Apart from the obvious point, belaboured by Foreign Office mandarins and military chiefs, that partition would inflame the Arab-Muslim world – India was for ever at the back of their minds – against the British Empire, an argument that slotted in neatly with that of a majority of gentile Zionists who asserted that partition would signal an abdication of responsibility, a spineless capitulation to violence that would set a calamitous precedent for an imperial power. All the Jews could do was 'persevere, persevere, persevere' with the mandate, as Churchill pithily put it. Nor could one ignore the technical difficulties of partition. Herbert Samuel, in 'a brilliant piece of destructive criticism', remarked: 'The commission seems to have gone to the Versailles treaty and picked out all the most awkward provisions it contained. They have put a Saar, a Polish corridor, and half a dozen Danzigs and Memels into a country the size of Wales.' These voices, among the most influential in the land, proved to be too powerful for the Royal Commissioners. By the late autumn of 1938 Peel's partition proposal was effectively buried. The debate over partition, however, remained – and remains – as an ongoing option.[18]

Apparently incapable of coping with 'the troubles' – as those with recent memories of Ireland would often refer to the Rebellion – an air of desperation blanketed the British civil administration. At times it seemed as though the situation verged on anarchy. Matters came to a head in the autumn of 1937. At Bludan, Syria, a pan-Arab Congress referred to Zionism as 'a cancer in the bodies of Arab countries which must be removed', a duty it imposed on 'every Arab'. The delegates then took an oath 'to continue the struggle for Palestine until she had been liberated and Arab sovereignty over the land had been attained'. Two weeks later, on 27 September, Mr Lewis Andrews, Acting District Commissioner for Galilee, and his police escort, Constable McEwan, were shot and killed as they left the Anglican church in Nazareth. Provoked by this outrage, the administration acted vigorously. It declared the AHC illegal, disbanded it, exiled some of its leaders to the Seychelles Islands, and detained others. Some fled the country, including Haj Amin, who, after seeking sanctuary in the Dome of Rock compound, fled (reputedly disguised as a woman) to Beirut from where he continued to direct the Rebellion by his traditional methods of terror and assassination, intimidating those Palestinians who opposed his tactics. One of his more prominent targets, Hasan Bey Shukri, Mayor of Haifa from 1927 to 1940, decamped to the Lebanon after two assassination attempts on his life. Others were not so fortunate, falling victim to Haj Amin's gunmen.[19]

'The Yids became so cock-a-hoop' at the news of Haj Amin's flight, commented one high-ranking officer, 'that they had to be told severely to keep quiet'. Yet for the British, as for the Jews, Haj Amin was plainly the unscrupulous mastermind overseeing the chaos. The generals spoke with one voice. Sir Richard Nugent O'Connor, Commander of 7th Division and Military Commander of Jerusalem: 'The Husseinis have openly declared war on the British regime; they instigate assassination, arson and every sort of disloyalty; whilst I find on all sides the inclination to act at their dictation and to find excuses for their conduct'; or the Commander-in-Chief, General Sir Robert Hadden Haining: 'The Mufti will never be a party to calling anything off until there is an Arab Kingdom and he is at its head. That is his objective based on overwhelming conceit.'[20]

The administration's robust response proved effective, but only in the short run. 'The gangs rule this country,' concluded Sir William Battershill, returning to his post after a short holiday, 'in fact if ever there was a complete breakdown of a civil administration we have it here.' Relations with the military were strained – at times almost to breaking point. General Haining vented his anger at the Chief Secretary in no uncertain manner, 'cursing' Battershill for the mess the civilians had caused and that he was now called upon to clean up.[21] If the civilians were unable to cope, the military were determined to come up with an answer.

Houses in Arab villages suspected of being involved in terror activities were routinely blown up. On occasion the soldiers interpreted their orders in a flexible manner. 'I saw to it that the R [oyal] E[ngineers] put in enough explosives to not only demolish the culprits' houses but also those adjoining it,' reported Lieutenant-General Carr to his wife. 'In all I had eight houses obliterated.' In Haifa, the streets were cleared by taking potshots at the rioters: 120 casualties were sustained. 'But they managed to keep that hushed up!' recorded Major-General Vivian Wakefield Street, breathing a sigh of relief. Another common practice was to drive 'a bus loaded up with villagers' backwards and forwards over mined roads, ostensibly to teach them a lesson. From Damascus the *Bureau Nationale Arabe* emphasised the brutality of British actions that included, according to their informants, assassinations, burning villages, torturing and killing their inhabitants – at Jenin, it alleged, 8,000 were left homeless. Other reports spoke of the violation of Arab homes, looting, destroying contents, the use of foul language.[22]

There were also flourishes of a dying tradition as General Sir John Winthrop Hackett led 'the last cavalry charge . . . with all the appropriate trumpet calls' in the Beisan valley, only to see the insurgents melt away before his fearsome 'Arab ponies'. Bernard Law Montgomery, then commanding an infantry brigade in Haifa, summed up his role in characteristic fashion: 'I do not care whether you are Jews or Gentiles [sic] – I care nothing for your political opinions. I am a soldier. My duty is to maintain law and order. I intend to do so.' And so he did, as did his fellow soldiers. Precise figures are difficult to come by, but military sources estimated that between 1936 and 1938, 2,150 rebels were killed (no figures were available for the number of wounded), 108 executed, and 2,000 houses demolished. Estimates of those imprisoned, lashed, or exiled, or of collective fines imposed were not given. Over a similar period the British incurred 265 fatalities, the Jews 495.

While these tactics might have appeased the military hardliners, the methods employed invited criticism. Were these actions effective? And more particularly, were they legal? 'The soldiers are always going out on great and unproductive operations,' Judge Lamon Evan Evans disclosed to his wife. 'Some of them seem to be behaving in a way that will not be forgotten.'[23]

The official Jewish Agency response to the terror launched against the *Yishuv* was encapsulated in the expression *Havlaga* (self-restraint) – Wingate's 'Special Night Squads' excepted, of course. This, for the time being, was politically expedient. As the international situation deteriorated and the prospect of war threatened, an eventual showdown with the British authorities was very much on the cards. The key issue was immigration. Figures had dropped dramatically after the peak years of 1933–6. Yet the need was never greater as Central and East European Jewry found itself trapped in an anti-Semitic hell on earth, with few avenues of escape. But for the moment there was no need to exacerbate matters. British actions against the insurgents, heavy-handed as they often were, also benefited the Jews. So all in all, limited, but justifiable, military cooperation with the British was preferable to all-out confrontation with them: an impending political flare-up, as circumstances would inevitably dictate, was kept on the back burner.

Havlaga held, though not without some difficulty. Even in more moderate circles the concept began to wear thin and there occurred some measured responses. For others the concept had broken down irrevocably. The temptation to respond in kind to Arab violence was too strong for some to resist. Conscience-struck, a few held back, only to succumb finally to a logic of their own invention. This inner conflict is dramatically portrayed in Arthur Koestler's novel, *Thieves in the Night*.

Bauman, a one-time *Haganah* leader, now commander of the 'Black Squad' (the hit team of the *Irgun Zvai Leumi*, the military arm of the Revisionist movement) and whose 'spiritual leader' is Avraham ('Yair') Stern (later head of the notorious 'Stern Gang') is talking to Joseph, a member of the kibbutz Ezra's Tower:

> I have no quarrel with Ezra's Tower. But those lovable idiots think they have a quarrel with me . . . their roots are still in the twenties and their heads in the clouds. They are pacifists and legalists like all honest-to-God Social Democrats, and if it were left to them we should share the fate which befell their comrades in Austria, Germany, Italy and so on – all who lived in their own Ezra's Tower. I love them but I hate their muddled thinking.
>
> You once said to me that we are nationalists *faute de mieux*. That's true enough of you and me, but you can't expect my boys to work up much enthusiasm for it. Nobody will choose to die *faute de mieux* . . . We have to use violence and deception, to save others from violence and deception.

After a long silence, Joseph capitulates: 'You win Bauman – as usual. I have to agree with you, *faute de mieux*. So what's the next step?' Joseph, a passive recruit, pursues his double-life in Ezra's Tower. But, revealingly, as he sets off to found a new *kibbutz* he quotes from Isaiah: 'And they shall build houses and inhabit them; and they shall plant vineyards, and eat the fruit of them . . .'*

The real-life Baumans, prisoners of their own twisted reasoning, perpetrated indiscriminate acts of counter-terrorism of the most horrendous nature, their actions reaching a ghastly climax in July 1938 when bombs set off by the *Irgun* exploded in a market in Haifa killing fifty-six Arabs and three Jews.[29] At least one British officer protested that the authorities were not dealing severely enough with Jewish atrocities. Lieutenant Aubrey Trevor Owen Lees was suspended from service for his pains. (A committed anti-Semite and recognised as a maverick figure, Lees was subsequently active in the British Union of Fascists, and on the outbreak of war was arrested and imprisoned under the Emergency 18B Regulations.[25]) These indiscriminate reprisal killings, defying the authority of the elected representatives of the *Yishuv* and threatening its future, poisoned relations between the Jewish Agency–*Haganah* and the Revisionists–*Irgun*. It split the movement, and left both camps teetering on the brink of all-out civil war. An appalled Weizmann would write: 'And now at this terrible critical moment the Revisionists are our cruellest enemies.'[26]

---

*See *Thieves in the Night* (London, Macmillan, 1946), pp. 297–8, 300, 353.

Koestler admitted that his novel was part autobiography. In the 1920s he had made his way to Palestine, joined kibbutz Heftseba, but left after a short period. Since his student days he had been active in Revisionist circles, in touch with Vladimir Jabotinsky, the Revisionist leader, a relationship that he pursued in Palestine, even collaborating with Jabotinsky on a Hebrew newspaper, *Doar Hayom*, Koestler claiming credit for composing the first Hebrew crossword. The archetype European cosmopolitan, Koestler finally left Palestine in 1929 absolutely certain that the revival of Hebrew as a living language (for some, Zionism's most meaningful achievement) was too limited and parochial for him, sensing that if he stayed he would surrender himself to 'provincial chauvinism', thereby cutting himself off from the European cultures that had fostered and enriched him. See his *Arrow in the Blue* (London, Collins, 1952), pp. 106-10, 121, 146, 184, 246.

Later, Koestler distanced himself from Zionism – though the Holocaust temporarily revived his interest – holding that Jews should either assimilate totally into their local cultures or else emigrate to Israel; there could be no third way. He later wrote a bizarre book, *The Thirteenth Tribe* (Picador, 1976), that argued, not at all convincingly, that East European Jewry were descended, not from Abraham, but from the Khazars of the Caucasus region, who had converted to Judaism in the eighth century.

By April 1939 General Haining could report: 'It can now be fairly claimed that the rebellion is rapidly being stamped out. The main rebel leaders have been killed, have surrendered or fled. The villagers are no longer prepared to submit to the depredations of the "warriors", and information improves daily.'[27] Worn down by three years of struggle, subject to unrelenting military pressure, its ranks crippled by inter-factional killings, the Revolt gradually wound down.

The temper of the Palestine administration had also changed. 'A remote figure', Sir Harold MacMichael had replaced the more amiable Wauchope as High Commissioner. Fondly characterised by one of his colleagues as 'a lovable bit of inhumanity', MacMichael was highly critical of the Jewish Agency, 'an alternative government' in his view. The Jews damned him as their preferred bête noire – until a better candidate would appear. In August 1944 MacMichael survived an assassination attempt by members of the Stern Gang.[28]

The last attempt to reach a negotiated three-way agreement at St James's Palace – involving the Jewish Agency, a Palestinian delegation and representatives of the Arab states – collapsed on 15 March 1939, the same day the Germans marched into Prague, destroying the Munich settlement. The symbolism linking these two events was not lost on the participants of the conference. On 21 March the Germans annexed Memel. Two weeks later the Italians conquered Albania. In the face of mounting German and Italian aggression in Europe – coupled with a renewed Japanese offensive in China – it was clear that the British government would seek to rid itself of its embarrassing obligations elsewhere. Safeguarding vital British interests in the Middle East, the gateway to the British Empire in India and the Far East, was of paramount concern. Should the Arab states adopt an anti-British position in the coming war, these could well be jeopardised, and with it the fate of the Empire and the mother country.

Having abandoned partition (temporarily, at least), the British government was forced to improvise an immediate solution, made increasingly urgent by the approach of war. Once again, it fell back on the Peel report, ratcheting up its (often overlooked) 'palliatives' that spoke of 'a political high level of immigration' and land sales for Jews that were to include 'zonal restrictions', and applied them in draconian fashion in the May 1939 White Paper.* These measures came as no surprise to the Zionists. Ever since September 1938, a month that witnessed the digging of trenches in Hyde Park, preparations for a war that was averted only at the last moment, but the danger of which remained a distinct reality, the British had made plain that they intended to take a tougher line – what Weizmann sardonically dubbed 'the doctrine of temporary expediency'.[†]

In Palestine, rumours were rife of an imminent government statement. Feelings ran high. Susanna 'Espie' Emery, teaching in Haifa, heard bombs going off everywhere. *Irgun* bombs, she assumed, as the Arabs 'were very excited & happy because they had heard rumours of a favourable settlement'.[29] It was not favourable enough to satisfy Haj Amin, however, who held out for an immediate Palestinian state and whose obduracy overcame those among the Palestinian leaders who would have acquiesced, *faute de mieux*, in the May White Paper, regarding it as a hesitant step forward. Rather than adopt an all-or-nothing tactic, four members of the AHC sought to cooperate with the government in implementing the White Paper.[30] They were joined by Musa Alami, a Palestinian Arab grandee. A Cambridge graduate in law, he served the administration in various capacities as a legal adviser. Hoping to profit from his family connection to Haj Amin, Jewish Agency leaders had sought him out as a conduit to the Palestinian leadership. Ben Gurion cast about for 'an Arab nationalist who cannot be bought with money or favours, but is not a hater of Israel'. He found Musa Alami 'sincere, straightforward and sensible': perhaps too

---

*See *Cmd.5497*, 366–67, for 'palliatives'. And *Cmd.6019*, 'Palestine. A Statement of Policy' (May 1939). The May White Paper limited immigration to a maximum of 75,000 over five years; after that period it could be resumed only with Arab consent. Land sales included prohibited, regulated and free zones: only five per cent of the country's area – Zone C – would remain open to unrestricted Jewish land purchases. Finally, a Palestinian state, in treaty relations with Britain, was envisaged after a transition period of ten years. There were additional flourishes: the possibility of a federal solution, or that independence would be withheld until the British government was entirely satisfied that Arabs and Jews could and would work together.

[†]'The doctrine of temporary expediency' held even after *Kristallnacht*, the organised pogrom against German and Austrian Jewries on the night of 9–10 November 1938, an ominous harbinger of more terrible things to come. It brought no change in Britain's immigration policy to Palestine, as the May White Paper indicated (see also Cabinet minutes of 5 December 1938, CAB.23/96, NA), although as a humanitarian gesture the government allowed 9,000–10,000 Jewish children from Germany, Austria, Poland, Czechoslovakia and the Free City of Danzig to enter Britain.

'straightforward', for despite a number of encounters there was to be no meeting of minds.*

The Zionists rejected the White Paper out of hand – although some preferred to believe that it was a 'sort of mental and moral aberration', and that once the current international crisis had faded away, so too would the May statement: it never did.[32] The *Yishuv* demonstrated against the new policy and planned a campaign of civil disobedience. Crowds in Tel Aviv and Jerusalem chanted 'If I forget thee O Jerusalem'. Ben Gurion proclaimed the beginning of a new era, the era of 'fighting Zionism'. So-called 'illegal' immigration was stepped up; and in a conspicuous, defiant challenge to the government, twelve new Jewish 'tower and stockade' settlements were established in the month of May.

Nor did the May White Paper generate great joy for the government. It survived the parliamentary debates, but with a greatly reduced majority of only eighty-nine, a result that could – and was – interpreted as a vote of no-confidence, as its usual majority was around 250.[†] The chief target of these widespread recriminations was Malcolm MacDonald, the Colonial Secretary. Once a friend of the Zionists, he

*Eventually Musa Alami fell out with the AHC, not over the principle of founding a Palestinian state but over the tactics to be employed in realising it. For Musa Alami, Haj Amin had now become a dangerous and disruptive figure. During the war, Haj Amin, overcome by his blind hatred of Zionism in particular and Jews in general, fled to Nazi Germany, was officially received by Hitler, and actively and eagerly collaborated with the Nazi regime in its crimes against humanity, conduct that led to his being charged as a war criminal. Aware that Haj Amin's notorious reputation rendered him damaged goods, appalled by his brutal methods of 'persuasion', conscious that his long-term game plan was both unrealistic and counter-productive, and was only leading the Palestinians into a blind alley, Musa Alami advised General Sir Alan Gordon Cunningham, the last High Commissioner, that Haj Amin (now under house arrest in France) should be 'exiled' to Switzerland, where 'he would lose much of his power': at present, he explained, 'he is doing a great deal of harm' (Cunningham Papers, GB165:0072, Box 5/1, MEC). Though by now he was very much a fringe figure, Musa Alami remained active in Palestinian politics. A fervent nationalist to the last, he advocated an independent Palestinian state within the framework of a 'United States of Arab countries'. See Musa Alami, 'The Lessons of Palestine', *Middle Eastern Journal* (October, 1949), vol. 3, no. 4.

†It is worthwhile noting that the government majority in this debate was only eight more than in the debate over the Norwegian debacle in May 1940, a vote that led to the fall of the Chamberlain government.

For the debate, see *PD*, Commons, vol. 347, c.1937–2056, and c.2129–90, 22 and 23 May 1939.

was now blackballed by them as an apostate. Was he tormented by guilty feelings? With good grace, he admitted that British policy 'had a touch of cynicism in it' in that the Jews were bound to support the British war effort – but what, he wondered, of the Arabs? MacDonald told Sir John MacPherson that 'the balance' of his policy 'may be a little too much to the Arab side', so, he added, 'if you can be kind to the Jews, will you please do it'. It was left to Ivan Lloyd Phillips, a high official of the Palestine administration, who confessed to being 'no longer a lover of Zion', to flesh out the practicalities of the new policy. 'The Jews are determined to resist this new regime with all means in their power,' he told his father. 'Actually,' he went on, 'very considerable concessions were made to the Arabs . . . In point of fact we have let the Jews down rather badly; the National Home is practically "liquidated"; and the Jews are condemned to be a permanent minority in an Arab country which loathes them . . .'[33]

It was, however, far too late to talk of the National Home as 'liquidated'. The MacDonald Letter had ensured that the National Home would prosper, even if at a slower rate than the Zionists desired. Clearly, the White Paper was a blow that no Zionist could accept: but it was not a knock-out blow. 'Illegal' (and legal) immigration continued; settlements were established; sharp-minded lawyers sought and found loopholes to circumvent the clauses regarding land sales restrictions;[39] and the armed strength of the *Yishuv* took on a new, more menacing dimension with the founding of the *Palmach* in May 1941, the elite strike force of the *Haganah*.

Three months after the promulgation of the May White Paper, while all the parties concerned were grappling with its ramifications, Britain found itself at war with Germany. Palestine's strategic, imperial importance to Britain now assumed an added significance.

4

War

On Sunday, 3 September 1939, at 11.15 in the morning, a bitterly disillusioned Neville Chamberlain broadcast to the nation that Britain was at war with Germany. Five days earlier he had received a letter from Chaim Weizmann:

> I wish to confirm, in the most explicit manner, that the Jews stand by Great Britain and will fight on the side of the democracies . . . and therefore would place ourselves, in matters big and small, under the co-ordinating direction of His Majesty's Government. The Jewish Agency is ready to enter into immediate arrangements for utilising Jewish man-power, technical ability, resources, etc.
>
> The Jewish Agency has recently had differences in the political field with the Mandatory Power. We would like these differences to give way before the greater and more pressing necessities of the time.

Weizmann was calling for temporary truce, hoping, in one observer's phrase, to put 'the White Paper into refrigeration and create conditions in which it would appear after the victory as a grotesque and unseemly anachronism'.*

Things, however, were not quite as straightforward as that. The Zionists assumed that the White Paper was 'in abeyance'. They were to

---

*For Weizmann's letter, see *WL*, XIX, no. 123, p. 145. Copies of this letter were sent to other leading British politicians. Chamberlain replied, acknowledging 'with pleasure' Weizmann's offer, adding, 'You will not expect me to say more at this stage than that your public spirited assurances and welcome aid will be kept in mind.'

For 'into refrigeration', see Abba Eban's essay in *Chaim Weizmann. A Biography by Several Hands*, eds. Meyer Weisgal and Joel Carmichael (New York, Atheneum, 1963), p. 253.

be rudely brought down to earth. In an abrupt, uncompromising note, Lord Halifax, the Foreign Secretary, ruled: 'It is not possible to modify or postpone the application of the White Paper policy.' Proving his point, the Cabinet approved the Land Regulations in February 1940, despite a last-minute appeal for a reprieve by Churchill. The Regulations roused the *Yishuv* to new heights of indignation. Mass demonstrations, that often spilled over into violence, swept the country for six consecutive days.[1] For the Jewish Agency, the implementation of the land regulations signalled an ominous portent of things to come.

As the war progressed, and the White Paper held, particularly regarding its brutal immigration quotas, the Jewish Agency Executive in Jerusalem sought to square the circle by indulging in semantic acrobatics. Its chairman, Ben Gurion, adaptive as ever, declared, 'We shall fight the White Paper as if there were no war, and the war as if there were no White Paper' – without doubt a catchy, populist slogan. But despite its thrilling rhetoric, it also revealed a fundamental weakness in the Zionist position. It would prove to be easier 'to fight the war as if there were no White Paper', than 'to fight the White Paper as if there were no war'.

The standing of the Palestinian Arabs was far more problematical – indeed, in the eyes of the British, highly ambivalent. They entered the war 'a house divided against itself', the most striking example being the ongoing internecine feud between the Nashashibi and Husayni clans. Battered by their 'Rebellion' against the *Yishuv* and the mandatory power, their leader, Haj Amin al-Husayni, discredited and in exile, they were more than ever dependent on the active assistance of the neighbouring Arab states – and of no less consequence, highly vulnerable to the conflicting national interests of these states. As the war expanded these trends intensified. And in one particular instance took an ugly turn, at least from the Allies' point of view.

Haj Amin's first contact with Nazi Germany occurred as early as July 1936. Hoping to recruit support for his cause, he approached its Consul-General in Jerusalem, expressing sympathy with the aims of the 'new Germany'. In late 1937, with the Rebellion in full flow, he was declared *persona non grata* by the authorities. Turfed out of Jerusalem, Haj Amin found his way to Beirut and from there to Baghdad, where he arrived in October 1939. Already in receipt of Italian money and *matériel*, by the autumn of 1940 the Germans were also replenishing his coffers. A few months later he was heavily involved in Rashid Ali's abortive coup to link Iraq with the Axis powers, an insurrection crushed ruthlessly by Britain's military forces. Later, as Rommel advanced through the western desert towards Alexandria, threatening the British position in the Middle East, he was active in egging on those anti-British elements in Egypt bent on purging their country of the imperialists. Once again, Britain acted vigorously, quashing these conspiracies with an iron fist. When Soviet–British forces marched into Iran in August 1941, Haj Amin was compelled to cut and run from Teheran where he had sought sanctuary after the Rashid Ali debacle. He ended up in Rome, conferring with Mussolini and Count Ciano, from where he eventually made his way to Berlin.

On 28 November 1941 Haj Amin was received by Hitler and Ribbentrop. Here, there occurred a meeting of minds. After expressing firm confidence 'that Germany would win the war', Haj Amin assured Hitler that 'The Arabs were Germany's natural friends because they had the same enemies . . . namely the English, the Jews, and the Communists'. Paying tribute to the Reich's 'military leaders of genius', he emphasised that 'the Arabs were striving for the independence and unity of Palestine, Syria, and Iraq' and requested that Hitler make a public declaration to this effect 'so that the Arabs would not lose hope'. In return, Haj Amin was ready and willing to aid Germany's war effort, not only by 'acts of sabotage and the instigation of revolutions, but also . . . by the formation of an Arab Legion'. The Führer explained that, for the moment, he was unable to comply with Haj Amin's request, but he stressed his resolve to wage an 'uncompromising war against the Jews', reiterating his 'active opposition to the Jewish national home in Palestine'. He elaborated, pledging his commitment 'to the total destruction of the Judaeo-Communist empire in Europe', as well as 'the destruction of the Jewish element residing in the Arab sphere'. Haj Amin felt 'fully reassured and satisfied' by these remarks.

After their meeting, Hitler recalled his impressions of the Palestinian leader. A 'principal actor' in Middle East affairs, Hitler said, 'a realist rather than a dreamer' and 'pre-eminently a sly old fox'. And, conferring on Haj Amin the ultimate compliment, Hitler noted that with 'his blond hair and blue eyes, he gives one the impression that he is, in spite of his sharp and mouselike countenance, a man with more than one Aryan among his ancestors and one who may well be descended from the best Roman stock . . . When he does speak, he weighs each word very carefully. His quite exceptional wisdom puts him almost on equal terms with the Japanese.' Clearly a chemistry of sorts existed between them. Later in the war, Haj Amin was instrumental in recruiting Moslems from the Balkans and the Soviet Union into units of the Waffen SS.[2]

The British had reacted vigorously to protect their regional interests. They had ensured that the ruling political party in Egypt, the *Wafd*, and the ruling dynasties in Iraq and Transjordan, the Hashemites, together with the House of Sa'ud's Wahhabist regime in Saudi Arabia remained secure. While not wildly friendly towards the Allies, they nevertheless maintained a benevolent, if frosty, neutrality, which held throughout the war. But under Haj Amin the Palestinian leadership opted for a different course. Having committed itself to the Axis powers, it left itself with little room for manoeuvre. After the war, with the same leaders pulling the strings, it found itself an orphaned political entity. Virtually devoid of political clout, the Palestinians became almost totally reliant on the Arab states if they were to attain any concrete political gains, a factor that paradoxically worked against them in the crucial period of 1947–9 as the conflicting national interests of these states prevailed over their support of the Palestinian interest. One may, or may not, make out a case regarding the conceptual poverty of the Palestinian leadership, of its inability to read correctly the political map, all depending on one's point of view. Of one thing, however, there can be no doubt. Haj Amin, sullied by his wartime record – a case history that also stained his cohorts – emerged fatally compromised into a post-war world grappling with the unspeakable horrors of the Holocaust, a key outcome of the war that would help determine the fate of Palestine.

For the first three years of the war, until the autumn of 1942, the catalogue of British military disasters on all fronts makes grim reading. The ill-conceived Norwegian campaign misfired calamitously; and, despite the heroic rhetoric, the evacuation at Dunkirk signalled the fall of western Europe. In the Far East, Singapore, its garrison yielding to a Japanese force less than half its number, surrendered: 'a disgrace' Churchill called it. By March 1942, with Japanese units approaching India, the British Empire in the Far East had in effect collapsed. The situation in the Mediterranean–Middle East was no better. Franco menaced Gibralter; Crete, Greece and Yugoslavia were occupied by German armies. The Italian peninsula cut across the Mediterranean, disrupting the lines of communication to the Arab East and India, while the Italian conquest of Ethiopia pressurised Egypt from the south. And, most alarmingly of all, Rommel, his Afrika Korps reinforced, struck eastwards through Cyrenaica towards the Egyptian border, after having inflicted upon Britain's Army of the Nile a humiliating defeat at Tobruk.*

For Britain, her resources overextended, it was imperative to mobilise all possible allies to sustain her war effort. How did the rival communities in Palestine measure up to British expectations? Invoking the spirit of Weizmann's letter, the *Yishuv* responded immediately and impressively. The right of the Jews to arm themselves against their most savage persecutor was, in their judgement, defensible on every imaginable ground – a moral and political right, reinforced by military necessity. By the end of September, out of a community of less than half a million, 136,000 Palestinian Jews – 90,000 men and 46,000 women – had registered, through the Jewish Agency, for some kind of essential national service, the overwhelming majority of men specifically mentioning their readiness to serve with the British army.[3] The British response was muddled. Considering it politically ill-advised to openly favour one group over the other, the authorities initially proposed raising mixed Jewish–Arab 'Pioneer' units to serve on the western front, an idea spurned by some Jewish Agency leaders. Despite their disapproval, the 'Pioneers' eventually saw action in northern France before Dunkirk. Even after the fall of France and Italy's entry in the war, strategic blows that necessitated strengthening pro-British forces in the region, the principle of even-handedness prevailed. Palestinian companies were now to be raised on the basis of strict numerical parity

---

*In stark contrast to this dreadful litany of military disasters, Britain's high strategic fortunes had improved out of all recognition. In June 1941 Hitler launched 'Operation Barbarossa', the code name for his onslaught on the Soviet Union, an act of aggression that made Britain and the Soviet Union full partners in the war against Nazi Germany. The Japanese attack on Pearl Harbor followed in December of the same year. Hitler, succumbing to his monstrous hubris, then declared war on the United States. In this unforeseen way the Grand Alliance was formed and victory ensured. Now it was only a question of how long it would take, and at what cost.

between Jews and Arabs, and were to be incorporated in the 'Buffs' (the Royal East Kent Regiment). As the Arab response was less than enthusiastic, this limited the Jewish contribution to a bare minimum, inspiring one wit to assess the niggardly British proposal as the 'Buffs and ReBuffs'.

Efforts to boost the Jewish contribution to the war effort continued. One enterprise that stirred the imagination concerned thirty-four Jewish volunteers, trained by the British, who were parachuted into Nazi-occupied Europe. Their mission: to spy for the Allies and to rescue Jews. Some escaped capture and saw action with Tito in Yugoslavia and in the Balkans. But twelve were captured by the Germans, seven of whom were executed, including the diarist, poetess and playwright Hannah Senesh, who later attained iconic standing in the collective memory of the *Yishuv* (and Israel). Not one Jew was saved by their efforts. But their mission – largely symbolic, as one survivor, Peretz Rosenberg, freely admitted – was not without value. 'The very fact that Jews were coming to jump out of planes in the name of the Jewish people of Palestine', he recollected, 'gave those still alive a spark of hope to continue, to live, and to persevere. These were the decisive factors – and not necessarily how many Jews were rescued or how many succeeded in escaping because of guidance received from the parachutists.'[4]

In the summer of 1942, prompted by Rommel's renewed advance into Egypt, the British government decided to abandon its principle of strict numerical parity. This offered some encouragement. But for the *Yishuv* the formation of an independent Jewish Fighting Force (JFF), that would fight under its own insignia, took priority. First petitioned early in the war, the negotiations to establish the JFF deteriorated into a dreary squabble. Not even the presence of a sympathetic Churchill as Prime Minister substantially improved the situation as the wrangling dragged on until September 1944 when the Jewish Brigade was finally approved. By the end of the war approximately 27,000 Palestinian Jews were enlisted in all services of the British forces, including 1,100 in the Royal Navy, and 4,000 women serving in the ATS (Auxiliary Territorial Service) and WAAF (Women's Auxiliary Air Force).[5]

The Palestinian response was more modest. Figures vary, but one source has 9,000 Palestinian Arabs enlisting for service in the British forces (though many were later discharged or deserted with their arms).[6] Sir John MacPherson, the Chief Secretary, explains: 'Well, the Arabs – I don't want to be unfair as I've got a lot of good friends amongst them – but I think they would have touched their hats to any new conqueror. When Rommel was very near Cairo I think a lot of the locals were getting ready with the appropriate coloured flag to say hello . . .'[7]

The scale of the Jewish response, although it indicated a massive show of support for the war effort, was also a source of disquiet for the British. As General Sir Alan Brooke, Chief of the Imperial Staff, warned the Commander-in-Chief, Middle East, General Sir Henry Maitland Wilson: sooner or later these 'well-trained men' would be turned against us as *Haganah* fighters. Reports were already circulating in Whitehall forecasting a Jewish revolt either before or immediately after the war.[8]

Initially, the British had cracked down on the *Haganah*, detaining forty-three of its members – including one Moshe Dayan – in October 1939, sentencing them to ten years' imprisonment. Reproving the sentence as 'savage and stupid', the then CIGS, Field Marshal Edmund Ironside, swiftly revoked it. Cooperation between the *Haganah* and the military authorities resumed, mainly in intelligence gathering and sabotage operations.* None of this assuaged the growing suspicion of *Haganah*'s long-term intentions. What, the authorities could well ask, was the precise nature, the ultimate intentions of its elite force, the *Palmach*, raised in May 1941. According to Sir John MacPherson, the Jews mainly 'wanted to fight the Germans'. One *Haganah* contingency plan, the 'Northern Plan', called for a last-ditch stand, concentrating resistance around the Haifa–Carmel area, should Rommel succeed in breaking through the British lines and penetrating into Palestine. Yet Sir John, no less prescient, noted that none of this 'really makes them much more friendly with the British administration'. Ben Gurion elaborated: 'We have two armies, the Australian and the British. With the Australians we get on very well indeed.'

---

*In June–July 1941 *Haganah* forces participated in the campaign to free the Lebanon and Syria from Vichy rule. One Palestinian casualty from the fighting, Moshe Dayan, lost his left eye when he was hit by a sniper's rifle bullet while scanning enemy positions with his binoculars. After making a partial recovery, Dayan began wearing the black eye patch that became his symbolic trademark. On the recommendation of an Australian officer, Dayan received the Distinguished Service Order, one of the British Empire's highest military honours.

That the *Haganah* was engaged in 'a great deal of secret military training with thoughts about the post-war period', as Sir John put it, was not in doubt. The British were particularly irked by the sophisticated methods employed by the *Haganah* in gun-running. Again, Sir John MacPherson explains: 'The exploits they did were brilliantly conducted. They would pinch Army trucks, send them through all the check points with forged papers down into Cairo, go and get from Army stores machine guns and ammunition and things on false chits and bring them back. They were brilliant.'[9]

Arms-smuggling led to government-coordinated arms searches. In November 1943 a particularly violent one occurred in Ramat HaKovesh, a kibbutz in the Sharon coastal plain a few miles north of Tel Aviv. A combined force of 800–1,000 British police, Indian troops and Polish military police, backed up by tanks, descended on the kibbutz looking for arms caches and a secret *Haganah* training camp. The kibbutznikim, men and women, were rounded up and thirty-five arrested, some of whom were beaten. Shots were fired. One settler was hit and died later from injuries. Angry demonstrations broke out in Tel Aviv, where a government office was torched. Hot-tempered protests spread throughout the country, civilians and police taking casualties. No arms or ammunition were found,[10] though that did not mean that none existed. Ingenious steps were devised to conceal arms caches, or 'slicks' as they were commonly called. George Lowe, a sergeant in the Intelligence Corps, after innocently pulling the chain in an 'outside loo', was startled to see that it sprang a trapdoor concealing a tunnel that led to a 'slick', where he retrieved 500 rifles and 3,000 grenades.[11]

A few British soldiers, either low on cash or principle, or both, procured trivial quantities of rudimentary arms for both sides. Clearly insufficient, the Arabs supplemented their stockpile by also engaging in weapons trafficking, a practice first begun in the early days of the mandate. Some arms were filched from Arab Legion stores, but in the main arms were smuggled in from the surrounding Arab countries – Syria, Transjordan, Egypt, or Iraq – including 'leftovers' abandoned by the armies that fought in the First World War.[12] These were not (usually) for immediate use. The level of inter-communal violence had dropped significantly since the outbreak of war. The dominant force in Palestinian politics, the hard-line Husayni party, led by Haj Amin, was in disarray: its leaders were in Germany consorting with Nazi bigwigs or imprisoned by the British in the Seychelles Islands. Resentment had not diminished. Indeed, the gap between the mutually antagonistic nationalist movements remained as wide as ever. When 768 Jewish survivors from the killing fields of Europe, making their way to Palestine, were drowned at sea, the tragedy touched Khalil al-Sakakini's conscience, but he still regarded them as invaders, not as refugees. Already the view was taking hold among the Arabs of Palestine that they should not be required to pay the price for Europe's barbaric persecution of the Jews.[13] But saving the 'invaders' or 'refugees' very much preoccupied the mind of the *Yishuv*.

News of the mass killings of Jews (and Gypsies, Slavs and homosexuals) in eastern Europe and the Soviet Union reached the West and Palestine in late 1941, early 1942. Initially, these reports were received with scepticism, reminding many of the atrocity rumours from the First World War. Many in the *Yishuv* regarded them as inconceivable, too monstrous for the human mind to grasp. In August 1942, Gerhart Riegner, secretary of the World Jewish Congress in Geneva, sent a telegram to London and Washington that outlined the plan and implementation of the 'Final Solution'. Although detailed in its findings, both the Foreign Office and the State Department were reluctant to take the 'Riegner telegram' at its face value.

By December of the same year further doubt was impossible. Authenticated reports reaching the West made abundantly clear the gratuitous butchery, the mass murder being perpetrated by German forces in the East. The scale of the killings was too great, too extensive to be kept secret for long. Hundreds of thousands – including women and children – were simply shot and dumped into pits, often that they themselves had dug. The most notorious executions – thought to constitute the largest single massacre in the history of the Holocaust – were carried out in September 1941 at Babi Yar, a ravine near Kiev, where 33,771 people, mainly Jews but also Gypsies, were massacred in two days. From 1942 the death camps where millions perished – Auschwitz-Birkenau, Belzec, Treblinka, Sobibor, Chelmno – were fully operative. The accounts of the carnage were too graphic to be ignored. A day of fasting and mourning and prayer was declared in the *Yishuv*. In London, on 17 December, the House of Commons heard Anthony

Eden, the Foreign Secretary, tell of the ongoing tragedy in Nazi-occupied Europe. When he finished the Members rose and stood in silence. This was an unprecedented act. Lloyd George said, 'I cannot recall a scene like that in all my years.' On the same day the Allied governments (and the 'Free French National Committee') sombrely announced that the Jews of Europe were being exterminated, vowing that 'those responsible for these crimes would not escape retribution'.[14]

The impact of the Holocaust on the *Yishuv* (and later on the state of Israel) cannot be exaggerated. To a large extent it defined its character, its inner being, its *raison d'être*. At no time was this more acute than in these years, when a trickle of survivors from the Holocaust were painfully making their way to Palestine.

For the Jewish Agency, extricating German Jews from the torments of Nazi terror began as early as August 1933 with the signing of the *Ha'avara* (Transfer) agreement. Called 'unsavoury but necessary', it allowed emigrants to transfer their assets out of Germany, though only after submitting to a tortuous bureaucratic procedure.[15] Early in the war, by one of those quirks of history, an arrangement was devised between *Mossad L'Aliyah Beth* (the Jewish Agency body that facilitated 'illegal' immigration) and leading Nazis – namely the Jewish 'experts', Reinhard Heydrich and Adolf Eichmann – to effect the emigration of German Jews to Palestine via Romania, the Black Sea and the Bosphorus. Fewer than 13,000 Jews left the Reich and the Protectorate under this deal; even fewer reached Palestine. Although it provided an escape route of a sort, it was an extremely hazardous one, and often the prelude to heart-rending tragedies. The agreement held between June 1939 and March 1941.[16] Even after it had officially come to an end, these asylum-seekers were prepared to risk their all by embarking upon this perilous journey. The 768 fatalities that so touched al-Sakakini's heart provides a pertinent example.

The SS *Struma*, an unseaworthy hulk of 240 tons, carrying mostly Romanian Jews fleeing from Ion Antonescu's rabidly anti-Semitic regime, left Constanza on 12 December 1941. It limped into Istanbul where it was holed up for two months, the refugees having to endure the most appalling sanitary conditions; inevitably cases of dysentery were recorded. These unfortunates aimed to reach Palestine, though they held no permits to do so legally. Negotiations regarding their fate dragged on. The British ambassador to Turkey, Sir Hughe Knatchbull-

Hegesson, tentatively suggested that rather than send an ancient and defective vessel back into the Black Sea, where it was likely to founder and sink, it would be more charitable to allow the refugees to reach Palestine where, despite their illegality, they might receive 'humane treatment'. His suggestion was shot down by the Colonial Office, judging it to be 'absurdly misjudged on humanitarian grounds', restating the by now discredited canard that Nazi agents, somehow hoodwinking the Jewish Agency, were masquerading as Jewish refugees. Lord Moyne, the Colonial Secretary, argued that allowing the refugees to reach Palestine was 'in flat contradiction to govern-ment policy' as inscribed in the May White Paper, a view reinforced by Sir Harold MacMichael, the High Commissioner. 'Palestine was under no obligation to them . . . enemy nationals from enemy or enemy-controlled territory should not be admitted to this country during the war,' he rationalised. A case was made for admitting the children, but eventually they too were excluded.

In late February 1942, the SS *Struma*, faulty engines and all, was towed back into the Black Sea and cast adrift. It had not gone more than twelve kilometers before an explosion occurred, almost certainly caused by a torpedo (though whether of German or Soviet origin remains unclear). Of the 769 passengers, only one survived.*

The Zionists held Moyne and MacMichael largely to blame for the *Struma* disaster. But they were backed to the hilt by their officials, seemingly bent on implementing the White Paper whatever the cost. Even taking into account the tenacity, single-mindedness and

---

*Full details of the *Struma* incident in Bernard Wasserstein, *Britain and the Jews of Europe, 1939–1945* (Oxford, Clarendon Press, 1979) pp. 143–56; and Ronald Zweig, *Britain and Palestine During the Second World War* (London, Royal Historical Society, 1986), pp. 118–24.

There were other chilling incidents involving 'illegals'. In November 1940 two ships, the *Milos* and the *Pacific*, were escorted into Haifa, carrying 1770 'illegals'. It was decided that they were to be transferred to the SS *Patria*, their ultimate destination Mauritius. Meanwhile, another death ship, the *Atlantic*, arrived. On 25 November, as its cargo of 'illegals' was being transferred to the *Patria*, a gigantic explosion rocked the boat, ripping open its hull. It later transpired that an attempt had been made by the *Haganah* to immobilise the ship's engines with the intention of keeping the refugees in Haifa, thereby exerting pressure on the authorities to allow them entry into Palestine: the plan had gone horribly wrong with the most tragic consequences. The death toll numbered 267; the survivors were later incarcerated at an internment camp at Athlit.

intemperate language of Zionist demands for greater flexibility in dealing with the contentious immigration issue, the statements issued from the pens of Colonial and Foreign Office officials, given the circumstances of the time, make for incredible reading – some, it might reasonably be assumed, were slipping in and out of fits of paranoia. 'Sob stuff and misrepresentations' said one. 'These wailing Jews' noted another. Sir John Shuckburgh, Deputy Under-Secretary of State at the Colonial Office, wrote, 'I am convinced that in their hearts they [the Jews] hate us and have always hated us; they hate all Gentiles . . .' Harold Frederick Downie, the most significant figure in the Colonial Office regarding Middle East policy, was thought to be 'anti-Semitic to a degree which prevents his conducting reasonable discussions with Jews'. 'This sort of thing [a pro-Zionist publication]', he remarked, 'makes one regret that the Jews are not on the other side in this war.' A Foreign Office mandarin pointed to Downie's 'inward and spiritual conviction' which led him to believe that 'illegal immigration is only the outward and visible sign of a world-wide scheme to overthrow the British Empire'; but we should not 'tar [ourselves] with the brush of Mr Downie's curious and unprofitable beliefs', penned the official.[17]

The *Struma* tragedy has been described as 'a psychological watershed for the *Yishuv*', a landmark that confirmed for Jews that they could no longer rely on Britain for their salvation. It released, and strengthened, forces in the *Yishuv* that could now only envisage armed resistance to counter the callousness of British immigration policy. The Stern Gang – a fanatical offshoot of its parent movement, the *Irgun Zvai Leumi* (National Military Organisation) – stepped up its campaign of terror, its leader Avraham ('Yair') Stern overcome by messianic dreams of a revived Jewish kingdom to be brought into existence in alliance with the Axis powers. His contacts with Germany and Italy came to nothing. In February 1942, led by Superintendent Geoffrey Morton, the British police raided Stern's hideaway flat in Tel Aviv. Marked down by the authorities as a 'megalomaniac, fifth column gangster', he was gunned down in what amounted to a summary execution.[18]

Two years later Menachem Begin, who had arrived in Palestine with Anders Polish army, was appointed Commander-in-Chief of the *Irgun*. His unprepossessing physical appearance belied his self-styled role as a gung-ho military commander. From the outset he was determined to implement his 'military-style Zionism', a concept he had first put to a

Betar (the Revisionist paramilitary youth movement) world convention in Warsaw in the autumn of 1938. Later, after Jabotinsky's death in August 1940, he claimed for himself the mantle of Jabotinsky's ideological and political heir. In fact, Jabotinsky had taken issue with Begin's 'Death or Victory' speech at Warsaw, deriding his tub-thumping as 'the creaking of a door', insisting that 'it is vital to repress ruthlessly all such creaking', arguing that the 'way proposed by Mr Begin' is the way to 'commit suicide'. Jabotinsky aimed at 'curbing the spirit of extremism he had discovered in *Betar*'. As one prescient observer has recorded, 'His outlook was diametrically counter to the idea of military Zionism, which prepared itself for a show of arms.'[19] Some old-style Revisionists, 'broad-minded, secular, Odessan Jabotinskyites', viewed Begin, the young pretender, with studied disdain. His Polish origins, his excessive emotionalism, rendered him somewhat 'plebeian or provincial'. Not sufficiently 'a man of the world, not quite *charmant* enough', he lacked 'poetry . . . the ability to radiate the charisma, the grandeur of spirit, that touch of tragic loneliness, which they felt became a leader possessed of the qualities of a lion or an eagle'. 'Begin', they thought, 'did not look much like a lion.'[20]

Nevertheless, Begin won the day at Warsaw; the convention appointed him *Natziv* (literally Commissioner) of *Betar* in Poland. Times had changed. Jabotinsky, a child of *fin de siècle* Europe, at once more tolerant, more liberal, more cosmopolitan, had been eclipsed by a more rough-and-ready generation, conditioned by the violent strong-arm politics of Continental Europe in the 1920s and 1930s.

Begin's first act in Palestine was to proclaim a 'Revolt' against British rule,[21] a synonym for the resumption of terror-style tactics. It marked a new and controversial phase in the inter-party politics of the *Yishuv* and the history of the mandate (and later of the state of Israel). The *Haganah*, not given to gesture politics, stuck to its policy of *Havlaga* (self-restraint), concentrating, not on headline-catching operations, but on the more substantial policies of bringing in more 'illegal' immigrants and founding new settlements. During the war approximately 52,000 Jewish immigrants entered Palestine, of whom 12,000 were 'illegals'; over the same period sixty-one new settlements were founded.[22]

While immigration remained a festering sore, poisoning Jewish Agency–British relations, politically things were beginning to look brighter. Churchill never recognised the validity of the May White

Paper. Seeing it as a monstrous betrayal of previous government pledges – including his own – he had voted against it. It was, he reminded the House, a shameful act of appeasement, 'another Munich'. He scolded his critics: 'The slaughter of European Jews can only be redeemed by establishing Palestine as a Jewish country.' At the end of the war, he promised, 'The creation of a great Jewish state inhabited by millions of Jews will be one of the leading features of the Peace Conference'. A Cabinet committee on Palestine was convened. And in January 1944 the Cabinet accepted in principle its recommendation in favour of partition.[23] All this very much squared with mainstream Zionist policy since 1937. Most recently it chimed with a resolution adopted at an 'Extraordinary Zionist Conference', attended by 600 delegates, held at the Biltmore Hotel, New York on 9–11 May 1942. Urging 'that the gates of Palestine be opened; that the Jewish Agency be vested with control of immigration into Palestine and with the necessary authority for upbuilding the country . . . and that Palestine be established as a Jewish Commonwealth integrated in the structure of the new democratic world', it was approved by general consent.[24] Although the resolution spoke of Palestine 'as a Jewish Commonwealth', on the face of it a maximalist programme, Zionist leaders had shown before that they were ready for a reasonable compromise, if offered.

Eleven months later this honeymoon period came to a violent end. In the early afternoon of 6 November 1944, Eliyahu Bet-Zuri and Eliyahu Hakim, two members of the Stern Gang, ambushed Lord Moyne, now Minister Resident in the Middle East, near his home in Cairo. Shot three times, Moyne was rushed to hospital but died of his wounds that evening. The two assassins were apprehended by the police, sentenced to death and hanged on 11 January 1945. Natan Yellin-Mor, a top commander of the Stern Gang who was deeply implicated in contacts with the Axis powers, justified the brutal slaying: Moyne was 'guilty of many crimes', he charged, citing in particular the *Struma* incident, but he was also 'a symbol of the British Empire'. Our mission, Yellin-Mor spelled out, was to strike at the British government, not the Palestine administration, which receives its orders from London. Our aim: to blackmail the British people through terrorist acts in Palestine and elsewhere so that they should exert pressure on the government, forcing it to evacuate Palestine. After Moyne, MacMichael, the High

Commissioner, was singled out as the prime quarry. Barely escaping from an attempt to kidnap him, he later survived a botched assassination plot.[25] Ironically, unknown to the zealots – would it have made any difference? – both Moyne and MacMichael were now born-again partitionists, having reluctantly reversed their previous position.

Moyne (Walter Guiness) was a long-standing and intimate friend of Churchill, and his senseless murder affected the Prime Minister profoundly. One of Churchill's secretaries, John Martin, remarked that it was impossible to talk to him of Palestine for months after Moyne's death. Typically, Churchill's revulsion first found expression in the flavour of his rhetoric – though it would also result in dire political consequences. Bracketing 'Zionism' and this 'new set of gangsters worthy of Nazi Germany', he threatened to reconsider his position. Leo Amery, Secretary of State for India and a staunch, lifelong Zionist supporter, noted in his diary that Moyne's murder, perpetrated by 'insane fanatics', had 'inflicted a possibly fatal injury to their [the Zionists'] own cause'. But Churchill was not panicked into taking punitive measures against the *Yishuv*, as he was being pressed to do. Weizmann, who compared Moyne's murder with that of the loss of his son Michael (reported missing in action with the RAF in 1942), assured Churchill that the Jewish Agency would cooperate with the British authorities to stamp out the terrorist organisations, 'to cut out root and branch, this evil from its [Palestine Jewry's] midst'.[26]

Weizmann kept his pledge. The Jewish Agency Executive instructed the *Haganah* to launch an 'open season', the so-called '*saison*', against the extremist groups, a controversial decision challenged by some *Haganah* commanders. But a majority of the elected bodies of the *Yishuv* favoured it, a 'national decision' in the words of one reluctant *Haganah* commander.[27] The *saison* was directed mainly against the *Irgun*. Exact figures are difficult to come by, but it has been calculated that dozens of *Irgun* members were kidnapped by the *Haganah* and handed over to the British authorities, together with a list of 700 names.[28] For all that, the Moyne assassination was a real turning point. Something snapped in Churchill's relations with the Zionists. Their most powerful political ally in British government now temporised, reluctant to press ahead with his Cabinet's partition proposal. While not officially discarded, it was set aside and put into cold storage.

★ ★ ★

Armed Arab resistance to British rule and the Zionist presence in Palestine had all but died out during the war, eclipsed by the operations undertaken by the *Haganah* and the dissident groups, the *Irgun* and the Stern Gang. Were other political solutions at hand, amenable to Arab aspirations? There was some talk of promoting Arab unity, broached initially by the British. 'It seems to be both natural and right', declared Anthony Eden at the Mansion House, 'that the cultural and economic ties between the Arab countries . . . and the political ties, too, should be strengthened. His Majesty's Government for their part will give their full support to any scheme that commands general approval.' But differences of outlook, of ambitions, of agenda among the Arab leaders soon surfaced: Transjordan, Syria, Egypt, Iraq and Saudi Arabia adopting independent, at times contradictory, approaches. Resurrecting a traditional goal, the Nationalist Bloc in Syria aimed at a Greater Syria, to incorporate Lebanon, Transjordan and Palestine, where the Jewish colonies would be allowed 'a certain autonomy'.

In September–October 1944 Arab leaders met at Alexandria where these differences were ostensibly ironed out in the so-called Alexandria Protocol. Apart from agreeing to form an Arab League, the Protocol dealt in some detail with the Palestine problem. It was a brave declaration: 'Palestine constitutes an important part of the Arab world and the rights of the Arabs [in Palestine] cannot be touched upon without prejudice to peace and stability in the Arab world.' The Protocol went on to declare 'its support of the cause of the Palestinian Arabs and its willingness to work for the achievement of their legitimate aims and the protection of their just rights'. Stoppage of Jewish immigration, safeguarding Arab land, and independence for an Arab Palestine were registered, yet again, as 'their just rights'.[29] These fine-sounding proclamations, however, could not paper over the divergent policies of the Arab states concerning the future of Palestine, nor hide the internecine rivalries within the Palestinian national leadership.

Musa Alami represented the Palestinian Arabs at the Alexandria Conference. Although increasingly disillusioned with Haj Amin's character and policies, he still persevered with the Husayni clan: perhaps his family connection (his sister was married to Jamal al-Husayni) kept him in the fold – at least for the time being. He put the Palestinian case skilfully. As a result, he was charged with conducting a worldwide propaganda campaign on behalf of his people and to raise funds to prevent further land sales to the Zionists. After two frustrating years, marked by self-destructive Arab squabbling and a blunt refusal to fund his projects, he had little to show for his efforts.[30] This outward display of unity of purpose had imploded into disorder and division.

Towards the end of the war, acting through its proxy, the Palestine Arab Party, the Husayni faction was undergoing something of a revival. Despite his notorious reputation, his proven record as a Nazi collaborator, Haj Amin had lost none of his appeal to many of his constituents. His arrival in Damascus after the war, having escaped the surveillance of the Allies, became the occasion for great rejoicing. Many Palestinians made the pilgrimage to congratulate him. 'Britain seems to allow it to happen,' complained Mary Burgess, a government official, to her family in Dumbartonshire: 'All the Arab world is celebrating his return. Every inch of every bus, horse, camel, donkey, shop and street is decorated with flags and flowers. Pictures of the 5 kings of the Arab world are hanging everywhere.' The Palestinians are 'very excited', noted Susanna Emery, an English teacher from Haifa, 'flying flags and decorating their cars with green-stuff, and holding processions. The Christians, I am sure, wish that the Mufti had stayed in France, but I doubt if anyone will say so. He is an old rascal, but he has been exalted by public clamour into a hero and a national leader.'[31]

With hostilities drawing to a close, the Jewish Agency was geared for confrontation, either militarily or politically, or both, with either the Arabs or the British, or both. All scenarios were feasible, all options open. As Weizmann once said, 'it's hard to be a prophet in Palestine. There's too much competition.' The strong arm of the Yishuv, the Haganah, was prepared for any eventuality. By 1944 various intelligence sources put its strength at around 35,000 men, of whom fifty to seventy per cent were armed – its elite striking unit, the Palmach, numbering some 1,500 fighters.* To these forces, local but considerable, responsible to the elected leadership of the Yishuv, must be added the dissidents, the

*Both of these forces could be – and were – expanded considerably should a national emergency emerge. With the outbreak of war in May 1948 the Haganah rapidly escalated to 65,000 personnel by July, mounting to 95,000 by December, while the Palmach had grown to three fighting brigades and auxiliary aerial, naval and intelligence units. See Zweig, Britain and Palestine . . ., p. 165, notes 68 and 69; and Slutsky, History of the Haganah.

Irgun and Stern Gang (some 2,000 to 3,000 in number), responsible to no one but themselves and all too often prepared to embarrass the *Yishuv* with their reckless terrorist tactics.

The last months of war had shown ominous signs of an erosion in the Zionist position. Rumours were afoot that at Yalta the Big Three had promised Palestine to the Jews. 'Pure moonshine,' ridiculed one British official, so much hearsay. Stalin remained adamantly anti-Zionist. Weizmann, in an attempt to blunt Soviet hostility, proposed a meeting with Stalin after Yalta, an idea quashed by the British on the grounds that it was 'impracticable'.[32] The Arab League, first broached at Alexandria, was formed in March 1945. Fundamental differences still separated its seven member states, but the very existence of such a League remained as a threat to Zionist aims. Lastly, the myth that Ibn Saud would one day underwrite an Arab–Zionist understanding was finally punctured.* Roosevelt, who had met the Saudi ruler on an American warship on his return from Yalta, proclaimed that he had learned more about 'the whole problem, the Moslem problem, the Jewish problem by talking with Ibn Saud for five minutes than I could have learned in an exchange of two or three dozen letters'. The President told Rabbi Stephen Wise, who repeated the message to Weizmann, 'that the one failure of his mission was with Ibn Saud . . . Every time I mentioned the Jews he would shrink.' Had not the Jews reclaimed Palestine? persisted Roosevelt. 'My people don't like trees,' Ibn Saud retorted. 'We are desert dwellers.' Even Churchill's persuasive tongue, Roosevelt added, had failed to dent the desert king's hostility.[33]

Nor was there much to be gained from Churchill himself. On 22 May Weizmann appealed to him in the name of the Jewish Agency: 'The White Paper still stands. It is prolonging the agony of the Jewish survivors. Will you not say the word which is to right wrongs and set

---

*Harry St John ('Jack') Bridger Philby – Arabist, explorer, writer; confidant to Ibn Saud; converted to Islam; known as Sheikh Abdullah – chanced to meet Lewis Namier at the Athenaeum Club in London early in the war. He laid out before a sceptical Namier a grandiose vision of future Arab–Jewish cooperation, which turned chiefly on granting Ibn Saud a dominant role in a future Arab federation and massive Jewish economic aid to Saudi Arabia. Namier never fully trusted Philby, but he passed on the details of this scheme to Zionist leaders. Nothing materialised from these contacts. See Rose, *Lewis Namier*, pp. 94–5.

the people free? . . . This is the hour to eliminate the White Paper, to open the doors of Palestine, and to proclaim the Jewish State.' Churchill's concise and unambiguous reply shattered Weizmann. The Palestine question would not be 'effectively considered until the victorious allies are definitely seated at the Peace table', he was told. Weizmann, the moderate Anglophile, the movement's premier diplo-matist, whose credit stood high in the international arena, felt his world collapsing around him. 'I stand before young Jews today,' Weizmann reflected later, 'as a leader who failed to achieve anything by peaceful means.'[34] More strident voices than his would soon be heard.

As the war came to an end, the triangular conflict of interests in Palestine dividing the British, the Arabs and the Jews had not sub-stantially changed; if anything, the gaps separating the parties had significantly widened. For the Jewish Agency, there was little alter-native: should the government persist in its callous immigration policy, a showdown was inevitable. The May White Paper, in operation throughout the war, blocked any chance of a compromise. The struggle to nullify it consumed the Jewish Agency leadership. If its immigration restrictions were intolerable in 1939, they were even more odious in the grim reality of the war and post-war years. In Zionist eyes there was a moral, no less than a political, obligation to save the remnants of European Jewry, a calculation that was paramount in their reasoning. For the *Yishuv* – for all Zionists (and most Jews) – this was a make-or-break issue in its relations with the British government.

5

The 100,000

On 25 July 1945, the eve of election day in Britain, Graham Charles Tylee, a flight mechanic serving at Ramat David, noted that all his mates would vote Labour. It had little to do with fine points of party politics, he insisted, it was simply that 'we had seen too much of the class system and were sick to death of it. We had all observed that posh accents without ability outweighed working class accents with ability.' They had seen the Aussies, the New Zealanders, and the Canadians, Tylee went on, who treated everybody as their equals, 'while accepting that not all men had the same abilities'.[1] The election results bore out Tylee's forecast. Churchill, the victorious war leader, was sent packing. 'Yes, I won the race,' he remarked bitterly, 'and now they have warned me off the turf.' Attlee, his wartime deputy, took over, his position securely anchored in Labour's overall majority of 146.

On the face of it the Jewish Agency had nothing to fear from the Labour Party. Only a few months earlier it had adopted an extreme pro-Zionist resolution. Drafted by Hugh Dalton, a London School of Economics don, it read:

> There is neither hope nor meaning in a 'Jewish National Home' unless we are prepared to let Jews, if they wish, enter this tiny land in such numbers as to become a majority. There was a strong case for this before the war. There is an irresistible case now, after the unspeakable atrocities of the cold and calculated German Nazi plan to kill all Jews in Europe. Here, too, in Palestine surely is a case, on human grounds and to promote a stable settlement, for transfer of population. Let the Arabs be encouraged to move out as the Jews move in.

The Arabs, Dalton went on, should be 'compensated handsomely' for their land and their resettlement 'generously financed' in the 'many wide territories' ruled by the Arabs. Perhaps, he speculated, we should even explore the possibility of 'extending the present Palestinian boundaries by agreement with Egypt, Syria, or Transjordan'.[2]

For the Zionists, the new, untried Labour government had still to prove itself. Initially, there was room for optimism. As in so much else, Clement Attlee, the Prime Minister, was an unknown quantity. But Ernest Bevin, a burly, no-nonsense trade union boss, the newly appointed Foreign Secretary (having dashed Dalton's chances for the post) had served the Zionists well in the past. Dalton, the author of the controversial pro-Zionist resolution, now held the office of Chancellor of the Exchequer, while Arthur Creech Jones, soon to become Colonial Secretary, was on familiar terms with many of the *Yishuv*'s Labour leaders.* Would the Labour Party, its principals now occupying high government office, remain bound by its earlier extravagant pledges, or not? This question must have troubled the minds of Zionist leaders. The answer was not long in coming.

On 18 June the Jewish Agency asked the British to release 100,000 certificates to allow Jewish survivors in Europe to enter Palestine for immediate relief. Why 100,000? So far, no accurate assessment of the number of Jewish survivors in Europe had been made, nor of those among them who wished to emigrate to Palestine.[†] But in an interview with Churchill in November 1944, Weizmann spoke of bringing 'something like one-and-a half million Jews' into Palestine in fifteen years. Calculated at 100,000 a year, the figures matched. This hypnotic

---

*On his previous visits to Palestine, Creech Jones had been most impressed with Jewish achievements, particularly in the fields of health and education. He was especially friendly with Dov Hos, a Labour leader, from whom he received a box of oranges every year. See Creech Jones Papers, MSS. Brit. Emp., s.332, Box 3/1,4, RH.
†The figures varied. In immediate post-war Europe approximately 170,000 Jews were under UNRRA protection; the Anglo-American Commission of Inquiry reported (1946) that of 138,320 Jewish DPs, 118,570 opted for Palestine – see Michael Marrus, *Unwanted. European Refugees in the Twentieth Century* (New York, OUP, 1985), pp. 323, 334. Another source put the number of DPs by the late summer of 1946 at 'probably over 250,000' – see Amikam Nachmani, *Great Power Discord in Palestine. The Anglo-American Commission into the Problems of European Jewry and Palestine* (London, Frank Cass, 1987), p. 236.

number filtered down to President Truman, by way of the 'Harrison Report'. Drafted by Earl G. Harrison, his special emissary to Europe, the report of 1 August 1945 stated that the Jewish Agency's demand for 100,000 'makes a persuasive showing', with Palestine as 'definitely and pre-eminently the first choice', a conclusion Harrison reached after having taken stock of the appalling conditions prevailing in the displaced persons camps.

Truman's concern was not conceived overnight. According to Clark Clifford, his special counsel, the President, a 'fine Bible student', conscious of the age-long injustice done to the Jews and shocked beyond belief by the obscene revelations of the Holocaust, felt that the Jews had no other place to go but Palestine. (As befits a discreet lawyer, Clifford tactfully refrained from mentioning electoral considerations.)[3] At Potsdam Truman had appealed to Churchill 'to lift the restrictions of the White Paper on Jewish immigration into Palestine'. Attlee, who had replaced Churchill at the conference, put off a definite answer. On his return to Washington Truman told the press 'that we want to let as many of the Jews into Palestine as it is possible to let into that country'. He hoped that something could be worked out diplomatically with the British and the Arabs, not least because 'I have no desire to send 500,000 American soldiers there to make peace in Palestine': a caveat that was to overshadow American policy in the coming years. At the end of August Truman forwarded a copy of the Harrison Report to Attlee with a covering letter expressing measured support for the expeditious admission of the 100,000. Attlee would not be moved. 'I'll send him a real stinker,' he told Harold Beeley, Bevin's adviser on Palestine and the Middle East. Couched in officialese, Attlee's 'real stinker' was firm, giving nothing away. The Jews, he told Truman, had yet to fulfil the quotas allotted to them; moreover, Arab and Muslim opinion (with India very much in mind) had to be taken into account; any other course would 'set aflame the whole Middle East'. Nor, he added, should the Jews be put 'at the head of the queue': it was not in their own interests that they should be treated as 'a special race category'. Attlee's hard-line tone reflected his government's decision of 6 September not to abrogate the May White Paper. Later that month the American press were informed at a White House press conference that the President's appeal to admit the 100,000 had fallen on deaf ears.[5]

Hoping to annul the White Paper as a first step towards creating their state, the Zionists worked assiduously to secure the immediate admission into Palestine of 100,000 immigrants: this magic figure came to symbolise the Zionist struggle, the focal point for a formidable propaganda campaign to win world sympathy and destroy Britain's Palestine policy. It was given an unexpected fillip when Truman formally announced his support for it at the end of September, leaving the British bitterly resentful at his infuriating public intervention. For an increasingly irritable Bevin, the Americans seemed to take a delight in stirring the British pot.

In April 1946 newspaperman Isadore ('Izzy') Feinstein Stone* was called away from covering a Security Council session to answer a phone call. His caller, 'a mysterious friend', asked him: 'How would you like to meet some boys who volunteered to serve as seamen for the illegal immigration?'[6] So began a journey that made Stone the first journalist to come into contact with the Jewish underground in Europe and to arrive in Palestine on a vessel crammed with so-called illegals. That night he met 'two dozen American Jewish boys' who had volunteered to man an 'illegal' boat, run the British blockade and land the 'illegals' in Palestine. Having arranged to meet them somewhere in France at their departure point, Stone travelled to Europe to survey the displaced persons (DP) camps. In Salzburg he came across 'Camp New Palestine', housing some four hundred and fifty refugees: over it flew the blue-and-white *Magen David*, the flag of the Zionist movement (and later of Israel). He visited a kibbutz, implanted, as fate would have it,

*Described as an 'iconoclastic American investigative journalist', Stone is best remembered for his self-published newsletter, *I. F. Stone's Weekly* (later biweekly). At its peak, in the 1960s, it had a circulation of about 70,000, and was required reading for the Washington political circuit.

Writing in *The Nation* (which he served as Washington editor in the 1940s), he was prophetic about the holocaust, which in 1942 he called 'a murder of a people so appalling . . . that men would shudder at its horrors for centuries to come'. In the immediate post-war years he fervently supported many of the Zionists' positions; and he strongly defended the State of Israel at its inception. His book, *Underground to Palestine* (New York, Boni & Gaer, 1946) is dedicated 'To Those Anonymous Heroes, The *Schlichim* [Emissaries] of the *Haganah*'. Later, in the sixties, he became sympathetic to the Palestinian cause.

See also, Robert C. Cottrell, *'Izzy'. A Biography of I. F. Stone* (Rutgers, NJ, 1992).

on a farm once owned by Julius Streicher, the notorious anti-Semitic Nazi pornographer. At Lansberg – where Hitler was imprisoned after the abortive 1923 Munich beer-hall putsch – he met a typical group of DPs, 'the second class of mankind', as one of them wryly put it. They were a mixed bunch: 'black marketeers and petty speculators' mingling with those of 'natural leadership and ability'. For the overwhelming majority, Palestine was their only goal: on cue, they would break out in song, 'Pioneers Prepare Themselves for Palestine'.

Time and again Stone heard from the refugees that they would never return to their homes. Everywhere they went 'they felt themselves unwelcome, despised, and hated in an atmosphere of virulent anti-Semitism'. One Polish Jew, who had fought throughout the war, first with the Red Army, then as a soldier in the Polish army, and who had participated in the liberation of Warsaw, met an ordinary – perhaps typical – Polish woman. He was in full uniform. She knew he was Jewish, but she couldn't hold back. 'The one bad thing about Hitler', she raged, 'is that he didn't kill all the Jews.' The DPs perfected a charged mantra: 'The Polish government is not anti-Semitic, but the Polish people are . . . We have no future in Poland. We see only more pogroms ahead.'*

Typical of the ships carrying the 'illegals' were the *Haganah* and the *Sir Josiah Wedgwood* (named after the pro-Zionist Labour radical), 750-ton vessels, veterans of the Canadian or American navies, due for the scrapyard. Their crews were made up of the oddest collections of would-be seamen: a few professional sailors were included, but also 'a Jewish hobo who had become a member of the Jehovah's Witnesses', an 'ex-Ranger' in the American army, and a number of 'ex-Wobblies'. Some were gentiles, others non-religious Jews with 'little Jewish

---

*It was an apposite comment. In the immediate post-war period pogroms broke out across Poland, Hungary and Slovakia. It has been estimated that, between September 1944 and September 1946, 327 Jews were killed in Poland, innocent victims of mass killings – and that by the summer of 1947 this figure had jumped to 1,500. Pogroms erupted in Krakow, Lodz, Lublin, Warsaw and other urban centres. The most notorious incident occurred in July 1946 at Kielce in central Poland, where a medieval-type anti-Semitic blood libel culminated in forty-one Jews being killed and many more seriously wounded. The Kielce massacre initiated a panic flight of Polish Jews to allied-occupied Germany, putting additional pressure on the displaced persons camps and the desire to escape to Palestine. (Figures from Yad VeShem Holocaust Research Department; also Marrus, pp. 335–6, and *WL*, XXII, no.192, n2).

upbringing and no Jewish education'. Many spoke 'a thick Brooklynese', heavily seasoned with GI expletives, and were as 'sore as a – boil' about the treatment the Jews received in Europe. Most of the crews had seen active service during the war. Some signed on because they were pro-Zionist; others were American *chalutzim* (pioneers) who intended to settle in the kibbutzim in Palestine.

Before boarding one of these ships, Stone explored the French and Italian coastlines, moving from port to port, harassed by the local authorities, particularly the French, careful to steer clear of overly inquisitive British intelligence officers. He was accompanied by 'a gentle, slender, dark-haired woman', Ada Sereni,* who acted as his Italian translator. 'Jake', the chief *Haganah* emissary in the area, one of Stone's 'Anonymous Heroes', was a particular favourite of his: 'an adventurous intellectual whose escapades, when they can be told, will rival anything in Dumas'. Having fought with the partisans during the war, the resistance fighters paid 'Jake' the greatest of compliments, dubbing him 'a Jewish Garibaldi'. When Stone finally rejoined the SS *Haganah* – as a security precaution the port of departure was not recorded – he was greeted with cries of 'Izzy, you lucky blankety blank son of a blank, you're back just in time'. Before setting sail eight crates of lifebelts, enough for a small passenger liner, were loaded on to the ship by a company of German prisoners of war (probably 'conscripted' by soldiers of the Jewish Brigade), an unforeseen helping hand for which Stone could find no logical explanation.

Loaded with canned foods, powdered eggs, an oven to bake bread, and separate cooking utensils for kosher and non-kosher food, the ship was ready to sail. Escorted by *Haganah* undercover operatives, the refugees arrived in open trucks: men, women and children, ultra-orthodox and secular, *chalutzim* and petit-bourgeois, partisans, Revisionists and members of *Hashomer Hatzair* ('The Young Guard', an extreme left-wing Marxist group), ages ranging from ten to seventy-eight. 'Linguistically, the ship was a floating Babel', the 'illegals' having made their way to the Mediterranean port from sixteen different countries. On board they would congregate socially in 'national colonies'. 'The embarkation was very orderly,' Stone recalled. At a

*The widow of Enzo, an Italian Zionist pioneer who parachuted into northern Italy in the latter stages of the war. Captured by the Germans, he was shot at Dachau in November 1944.

pinch, the *SS Haganah* could accommodate approximately one thousand passengers. Altogether one thousand and fifteen 'illegals', including five gentiles, were stowed below deck, each one assigned to a bunk by number.

As befitted a working journalist, Izzy Stone talked to as many of the refugees as he could, soaking up their 'human interest' stories, listening with a sense of wonderment at their hair-raising adventures, ordeals shockingly at variance with their current feeling of harmony 'under the starry sky, the lonely Mediterranean, the happy singing, the crowds of Jews milling about on deck as they might on Delancy Street or Petticoat Lane', furnishing the poignant circumstances with an agreeable romantic twist.

Some of the refugees' ordeals in Europe bordered on the fantastic. One Polish Jew from Krakow, a printer by trade, was put to work with 140 other printers, counterfeiting foreign currency and documents for the Gestapo. By chance, on the printer's birthday, Himmler arrived to inspect the workshop. On seeing the birthday decorations the *Reichsführer-SS* enquired whose birthday it was. 'Mine, Herr Commisar, I am a Polish Jew,' responded the printer. Delighted at the high standard of forgeries being carried out in this underground press, Himmler shook hands with the printer and wished him a happy birthday. 'What would you like for your birthday?' he asked. *'Freiheit,'* replied the printer. *'Es kommt,'* answered Himmler, 'with an odd smile'.

Stone also met Rudy from Poland, who grew up in Havana, became a 'rum-runner' during Prohibition, served a term in a Federal penitentiary, turned professional wrestler and later joined a European circus as its strongman. He ended up in Auschwitz, by now in his fifties. Owing to his strength and size – he was described as 'a sort of Jewish Man Mountain Dean' – and lasting power – he had survived a severe lashing – Rudy was made a head *capo*. He exploited his position to run a Black Market racket, bribing guards with cigarettes, brandy, meat, valuables and other luxuries that he had filched from the storerooms, aiming all the while to establish underground connections between the various camps for rescue work. In this way Rudy achieved a strange ascendancy in the camp, including over some of its commanders. In the course of his 'duties' he met Ruth, a young *chalutzah*, who was due to be hanged the next day. 'When I first set eyes on her I loved her as if she were my own daughter. She was such a sweet child. I couldn't let her go to her death. I had to find some way to save her.' He immediately approached the responsible SS officer, a client of his, armed with a bottle of schnapps. Having loosened him up, Rudy applied some emotional blackmail – 'I can't live without her' – and, perhaps more practically, pandered to the SS commander's fondness for fast women, promising to keep his mistresses happy with a ready supply of valuable jewellery. 'You're a crazy Jew,' he shouted at Rudy, but eventually yielded to the 'Mountain Man's' plans. He procured a false death certificate and fake Aryan papers for Ruth, who was then sent to a labour camp for Polish girls. Rudy had saved Ruth's life. When they next met it was on the deck of the *Haganah*, bound for Palestine.

The first eight days of the journey were uneventful. There were some discomforts: overcrowding, little ventilation below deck, stale air, seasickness, lack of adequate sanitary conditions, the tiresome tricks of hypochondriacs – including one habitual nicknamed 'Sleeping Beauty'.

Whenever another ship was sighted the passengers were quickly herded below. Every night at eleven a curfew was called. The food was 'not too bad', if a little monotonous: plenty of bread, stew and soup for the non-kosher, a thick vegetable soup for the kosher; occasionally, cigarettes and chocolate were passed round. 'There was never a gayer ship on the high seas,' ruminated Stone.

Below us one day three caps and one *yarmulka* were eating hardtack smeared with butter while they carried on a voluble conversation. A girl played a concertina on top of a pile of life rafts, surrounded by admirers. A fat red-head with a purple head ribbon sat by herself on a hatch, happily singing a Hebrew song and rocking back and forth to the rhythm. Two lovesick calves held hands as they sat along the rail: she plump, he thin with horn-rimmed spectacles. They kissed soulfully. An unshaven little man with a red Turkish cap wandered around in search of something, looking like an organ grinder's lost monkey.

Big, fat Rudy, the ex-circus strong man, dressed only in white shorts with a towel wrapped around his head like a turban, sat on a ventilator, swarthy, fierce, and bearded as a wild Mongol chief or galley slave-master. A group of *chalutzim* were dancing the Palestinian *hora*, holding hands in a great moving circle as they leaped and sang.

The first mate sat on the railing of the bridge, contentedly smoking a cigar as he looked on.

'Yes,' he said, as if after profound reflection, 'it's the old Hudson River Day Line all over again – next stop Bear Mountain.'

This idyllic scene was topped off with a traditional orthodox wedding, the guests celebrating the occasion by singing a Hebrew song set to the tune of 'Onward Christian Soldiers'.

The *Haganah* had been at sea for a week; normally, it would have reached Haifa in four days. Added precautions were now taken as they approached the British blockade. If captured by the British, the ship's (nameless) *Haganah* commander instructed his wards how to react. Tell them 'you are already citizens of *Eretz Israel*', he ordered, providing them with false certificates to prove the point. At this juncture, about a hundred miles from Palestine, the *Haganah* high command, fearful that the *SS Haganah*, a seaworthy boat, would be impounded by the British, decided to transfer the 'illegals' at sea to a Turkish-registered 250-ton freighter, *Akbel II* (a relic from the days of Abdul Hamid II). Conditions in the sixty-year-old wreck beggared description: the holds were 'dark, dank, and fearfully hot, much more like a den for wild animals than a habitation for human beings': only one water closet was serviceable. Fights broke out over who would go down into the holds, or rather who would remain on deck. Stone took his turn. Descending into the murky, polluted atmosphere, he decided that the most 'sensible thing was to sit and sweat and keep quiet' among these 'snarling, irritable shipmates'. A kind of fierce Darwinian struggle ensued: 'men seemed to become less than human. It was like living in a den of wolves': it reminded the refugees of the concentration camps from which they had only just escaped. Given one packed lunch and only sips of water to survive on, morale quickly dropped.

Finally, rather than risk a disaster – the *Akbel* being so unseaworthy it was feared she would capsize – the *Haganah* chief put out an SOS distress signal. Sooner than risk a tragedy – perhaps with the *Struma* catastrophe in mind – he was prepared to surrender his charges to presumed British goodwill. Off Cyprus, the *Akbel* was intercepted by a British destroyer, HMS *Virago*. A boarding party threaded its way through the mass of 'illegals' strewn on the deck, 'dazed, sleepy, tired, and resentful . . . too sick or exhausted to move'. It was brutally hot. And with a storm blowing up, there was a constant risk that the derelict hulk would overturn. Negotiations began. The *Haganah* spokesmen wanted food and water; in return, although still in international waters, they were prepared to submit to British authority and allow the *Akbel* to be towed into Haifa. After some humming and hawing, HMS *Virago* moved off, denying the 'illegals' the most basic of necessities, food and water. The *Akbel* too limped off, painstakingly steaming at seven knots towards Palestine, tracked all the while by the British destroyer. Eventually Mount Carmel was sighted. The cry went up, 'It's *Eretz Israel*': the Zionist flag, the *Magen David*, was raised, the Zionist anthem, *Hatikvah*, sung. But the British navy lay in wait and took possession of the ship – and of the 'illegals' – the moment the *Akbel* entered Palestinian territorial waters. Now under British protection, the conditions of the 'illegals' improved. Transferred to a larger, more sanitary ship, they remained holed up in Haifa Bay until the authorities decided upon their fate. Meanwhile, Haifa's Jewish community sustained them with fresh rolls, tomatoes and green peppers, cream cheese, pint bottles of cool *leben* (thick sour milk) and big bunches of grapes. After a few days, the 'illegals' were sent to the Athlit detainees camp and eventually released (under the quota system). It remained only for them to disappear into the anonymity of the *Yishuv*.

Others were not so fortunate. From August 1946 the British modified the 'rules of the game'. Now, 'illegals' trapped by the British blockade were dispatched to Cyprus to be detained in camps (prepared for them by German POWs). Some boats still successfully ran the blockade; many did not. The SS *Paducah* was one of the latter.[7] An ageing US gunship of 900 gross tons, it had been sold off as surplus after the war, having served its apprenticeship on the Great Lakes in the 1920s. It sailed from New York in May 1947, the starting point for a six-month voyage. Its captain, Rudolph Patzert, was not Jewish, nor were several of his crew. What moved Rudolph – and many like him – to embark upon such a hazardous adventure was embodied in the question he asked himself: whether

> I would ever rest easily again, or if for the rest of my life I would be haunted by guilt for what had been done to these people. It seemed to me as clear as the thin, bright sunshine that the crimes committed against the Jews had not left any of us untouched, and the guilt, somehow, was upon all of us.

American and Canadian Jewish volunteers made up the rest of his crew, joined by some Spanish exiles from Franco's Spain.

When the ship docked at Bayonne to take on supplies, some of the crew took pity on a 'poor girl' who told them that she'd been incarcerated at Dachau, that her parents had been killed and that she desperately wanted to go to Palestine. The chief *Haganah* operative on the *Paducah*, Mordecai 'Moka' Limon (later Commander-in-Chief of the Israeli navy), put the gullible sailors right. 'Your destitute girl is an old acquaintance of ours,' he revealed. 'She's a British agent', intent on discovering the *Paducah*'s true destination. 'I must warn all of you again to be on guard and to be very careful. Stay away from that girl.' After all, 'Our ships, these poor old tubs, are a lifeline for all our people. They sustain themselves with these symbols of a new life.'

At Varna, a Bulgarian port on the Black Sea, the *Peducah* took on 1,388 refugees. Moka not only assigned them by number to their bunks, he also organised them into 'special function' squads: 'Fire Squad', 'Food Squad', 'Cleanliness Squad' and so on: civic duties that were meant, Moka explained, to revive a sense of social obligation, of responsibility, virtues that had been largely cast aside in the camps. As the *Paducah* entered the Aegean sea the crew noticed it was being shadowed. When the British warship approached, 'a silent smell of hate, so intense it could almost be smelled, rose from them [the 'illegals']. With bitter eyes and grim faces they stared at the destroyer.' After ramming the *Paducah*, the British, shielded by a tear-gas attack, boarded the vessel. Resistance was minimal. Some British soldiers visibly showed their dislike of this detail, unhappy at having to man-handle the refugees, particularly women and children. In retaliation, Patzert and Moka ordered the ship's engines to be disabled, thereby leaving the British no alternative but to tow her to Palestine. In the event, they ended up in Cyprus. Loaded on to trucks, they were driven out of Famagusta. As they passed crowded cafés, the clientele waved at the refugees, pumping their fists in salute, crying out '*Shalom*'. These were Greek Cypriots also seeking independence from British rule.

The 'illegals' were detained in a complex of several camps known collectively as 'Xylotymbou' (named after a village in the Lanarca district). There they regrouped according to their various religious and political beliefs. With the aid of *schlichim* from Palestine – who appeared and disappeared almost at will – the detainees settled into a daily routine, preparing themselves for the rigours of life in Palestine with lectures on Zionism and Jewish history, study circles, discussions, Hebrew lessons, rudimentary military training. Gradually, the crew of the *Paducah*, masquerading as 'illegals', were released. Included in the regular monthly quota of 750 'illegals' who were officially allowed to enter Palestine (this number being deducted from the May White Paper figure of 1,500), the *Haganah* rationalised that in this way further ships could be manned to bring in more immigrants. After being sent to Athlit, and surviving the stringent interrogation techniques of the British, they were set free. Most of the crew, including Rudolph Patzert, when released returned to America, some to serve in other ships; others stayed in Palestine.*

Shortly after becoming Foreign Secretary Bevin briefed Attlee: 'Clem, about Palestine. According to my lads in the office we've got it wrong.' In late August 1945 a Cabinet committee on Palestine concluded: 'If partition is ruled out as impracticable or undesirable, a system of local autonomy emerges as the almost obvious solution.'[8] By early September, succumbing to the conventional wisdoms of the Foreign and Colonial Offices, and backed by the military establishment, the Cabinet, fearing repercussions in the Arab and Moslem world, decided to persevere with the White Paper policy. One concession was offered: Jewish immigration into Palestine would be allowed to continue on a limited basis of 1,500 per month.

On 13 November Bevin outlined the government's new policy to the House. He told a receptive audience that an Anglo-American Commission of Inquiry (AAC) into the problems of European Jewry and Palestine had been agreed upon: a diplomatic coup which, it was hoped, would neutralise American mischief-making. But Bevin also spoke of a compromise solution for the DPs not restricted to Palestine, which, he noted, did not 'by itself, provide sufficient opportunity for grappling with the whole problem' – a judgement echoed by a

---

*In all, approximately 50,000 'illegals' were incarcerated in camps in Cyprus. Life there took on a certain normality. Bar mitzvahs, family gatherings, weddings – 2,000 children were born. The majority of the 'illegals' made their way to Israel when the state was proclaimed in May 1948.

The fate of the *Paducah* was less uplifting. She was so badly damaged by British boarding tactics that she was sold to the Italians for scrap.

majority of members. In reply to a parliamentary question Bevin, impulsive as ever, staked his political future on solving the Palestine problem, reiterating a point often forgotten: 'but not in the limited sphere presented to me now' – a remark made plainly with the Zionists and the Americans in mind. Now clearly trapped in an impetuous mode, Bevin later stated at a press conference that 'if the Jews, with all their sufferings, want to get too much to the head of the queue, you have the danger of another anti-Semitic reaction'.[9] To stigmatise the Jews as 'queue-jumpers', as pushy troublemakers, in the prevailing atmosphere of post-Holocaust Europe was the height of insensitivity: such careless phrasing – and there would be other instances – helped fashion Bevin's image in most Jewish eyes – particularly in the United States – as a dyed-in-the-wool anti-Semite, even as Hitler's heir.

It has been pointed out that a man of sixty-five, of known strong prejudices and opinions, is hardly likely to become an anti-Semite overnight.[9] And Bevin's record on behalf of Zionism was better than most: both Weizmann and Ben Gurion counted him among Zionist sympathisers. As Foreign Secretary, he was certainly guilty of tactlessness, of adopting a hectoring tone, of unleashing a coarse tongue, of articulating unfortunate phrases with anti-Semitic connotations. Unknown to most outside observers, Bevin was suffering from a serious heart condition, which at times caused him to black out and often left him thoroughly exhausted, a complaint that helps explain his short temper and violent outbursts. Having foolishly staked his reputation on solving the Palestine issue, he vented his anger and frustration at those he believed were wilfully thwarting him. A street fighter, he paid back intemperate Zionist slurs on his person in the same coin. An old-style workers' leader, Bevin was roused to indignation by another consideration. 'I cannot bear English Tommies being killed,' he told Weizmann. 'They are innocent . . . I do not want any Jews killed either, but I love the British soldiers. They belong to my class. They are working people . . .'[11] There is no reason to doubt his sincerity.

There were more grievous defects in the government's Palestine policy than the fault lines in Bevin's character. Above all, there was a failure to evaluate correctly the temper of nationalist forces in the Middle East, and in particular in the Jewish world. Bevin, together with Attlee and many others, argued that Jewish survivors from the Holocaust still had a future in Europe. Churchill told the House in August 1946 that he did not believe that the Jewish problem could be resolved by 'a vast dumping of the Jews of Europe into Palestine'. He would not give up on 'the idea that European Jews may live in the countries where they belong'. For the Zionists, this was akin to sacrilege. Nearly six million Jews had been slaughtered in europe; and even after the end of hostilities Jews were still being massacred in eastern Europe by anti-Semites. Only Palestine could offer them a safe haven, they held. This message was promoted as a new commandment, graven in stone. Weizmann told a questioning Richard Crossman 'that Europeans are sick, and it will take a long time to get rid of the sickness. The presence of Jews in Europe today might exaggerate the sickness.[12]' If, in retrospect, this view may be judged as simplistic, at the time it resonated strongly, projecting a firmness of purpose and boldness of spirit that won the day, helped along by a heavy-handed British policy.

No doubt Bevin, relying on his experience as a trade union boss, believed that two sides to a dispute, no matter how far apart at the outset, would gradually draw together in mutual compromise, prompted by common sense and joint interests. But the Zionists were demanding that 'the gates of Palestine be opened . . . and that Palestine be established as a Jewish Commonwealth', while the Arabs were threatening a 'new crusader's war'.* This unbridgeable gap defeated Bevin, as it had others before him. One thing was crystal-clear: the halcyon days of the Anglo-Zionist concord of November 1917 were over. Times had changed: the same conditions no longer held. British and Zionist interests were at variance, pulling in opposite directions. Britain – virtually bankrupt, her economy run-down, dependent upon American largesse, saddled with added responsibilities in Europe, her Empire rent by belligerent nationalisms – sought stubbornly to maintain her position in the Arab and Muslim world, a desperate holding action in view of her shrinking resources. The Zionists figured marginally in this dismal story, their demands for justice merely aggravating an already complicated situation.

*At the beginning of 1945 the Lebanese minister in Paris met Duff Cooper, the British ambassador. He declared, Palestine should be 'an entirely Arab state'. 'How about the Jews?' asked Duff Cooper. 'If the British would only close their eyes for a few minutes,' the minister replied, 'the Arabs would soon settle the Jewish question.' See John Julius Norwich, ed., *The Duff Cooper Diaries* (London, Phoenix Paperback, 2006), p. 353.

Nowhere was this more evident than in the formation of the United Resistance Movement (URM), an attempt to coordinate, at times with mixed results, the actions of the *Haganah*, the *Irgun* and the Stern Gang. Established in October 1945, its aim was to 'persuade' the British government by deeds, not words, to take Zionist demands seriously. This was a *mariage de convenance*: profound ideological differences separated the three groups, differences that spilled over to divide mainstream Zionist leadership. Ben Gurion, who carried a majority opinion with him, was a determined advocate of the *mariage*; while Weizmann, resolutely opposed to any contact with terrorist organisations, maintaining that it would corrupt the movement as a whole, was shunted aside. This unholy alliance lasted ten months.

The first 'persuasive' actions occurred in early October. At Kfar Giladi, a settlement close to the Lebanese border, *Haganah* forces, covering Jewish 'illegals' crossing the frontier, engaged British units. At Athlit, a transit camp on the coast south of Haifa, the *Palmach* broke into the guarded site and freed 200 'illegals', an operation lauded by the *Yishuv*. On the night of 31 October, in a joint *Palmach–Haganah–Irgun–*Stern Gang operation, Palestine's railway system was sabotaged: 153 separate incidents were reported, paralysing all railway traffic. The *Yishuv* was delighted. The High Commissioner took note: 'Widespread sabotage on night of 31st October failed to elicit even customary formal expressions of deprecation. Dominant note was satisfaction at display of organisation and strength of *Yishuv*'s armed forces. *Palestine Post* signalised episode as evidence that Palestine Jewry had gone over to offensive.'[13] Shortly afterwards the *Irgun* and Stern groups attacked British police headquarters in Jaffa Road, Jerusalem, killing four British soldiers.

If this upturn in activism was meant to pressurise the British government into concessions, it failed. Bevin would not be intimidated. Speaking with 'great anger and tension', he told Weizmann and Moshe Shertok (later Sharett), head of the Political Department of the Jewish Agency, that these actions 'amounted to a declaration of war'. He derided the Jewish Agency's reservations, not as a condemnation, but a 'condonation'. Equally bitter at American waywardness, he dismissed Truman's irresponsible call for the immediate entry of a 100,000 as an electoral ploy, as 'impossible today'. Furious at this turn of events, perceiving self-serving American and Zionist politicians ganging up on him, Bevin appeared to his interlocutors as 'shocked, and stunned'.[19] A few days later he announced the government's new policy regarding the AAC to an amenable House of Commons.

Cunningham sent this message to London:

> On Jewish side statement is universally stigmatised as cynical and treacherous device to postpone decision on mass immigration until displaced Jews in Europe in despair accept rehabilitation in Diaspora. Insinuation that prospect of solution by mass starvation in Europe during coming winter is part of H.M.G.'s intention has also been voiced. Propaganda that Palestine is sole solution of Jewish problem followed usual lines. Press featured prominently resolutions in favour of Jewish state by bodies in U.S.A. together with other evidence of pro-Zionist activity in that country.

Ben Gurion fine-tuned Cunningham's communique. 'I am bitter and excited because of the shameful cruelty of Fate,' he told an emergency meeting of the Jewish Agency Executive, 'and because of the treacherous and shameful behaviour of the British Government towards us and because of the most anti-Zionist and anti-Semitic statement of Bevin.' He laid out a programme for 'our struggle'. Concentrating on land settlement and bringing in 'illegals', he advocated 'useful and constructive opposition'. It would include 'strong press articles and legal and illegal publications, violent speeches, strikes and days of fasting', but not terrorism, 'a waste of power and energy', although he warned, 'we may be unable to prevent certain groups from doing it'. As the 'ultimate step', he turned to 'civil disobedience', an 'open struggle': 'the non-payment of taxation, boycotting of Government offices, severing contact with officials, etc.'. Ben Gurion also made abundantly clear to a generally acquiescent Executive who was running the show. Certainly not Weizmann, the defeatist, 'the symbol of blind confidence in Great Britain', Ben Gurion told his colleagues, continuing: 'My opinion is that Weizmann's policy is bankrupt and that he must resign.'[15] Ben Gurion's cry for 'civil disobedience', an 'open struggle', did not go unheeded. Ivan Lloyd Phillips reported in a similar manner to his father how the *Yishuv* was reacting to Bevin's remarks in the Commons: violent demonstrations, police stations and government offices going up in flames, security forces shooting to repel the rioters. Bevin's comment that if the *Yishuv* 'had decided on war, they should be straight about it' contained more than a grain of truth, at least from the British point of view.[16]

The Arab reaction to the AAC was no less fierce, if more tactfully put. Hands were raised in despair at the prospect of yet another pointless inquiry, especially with American participation, which they reckoned was tantamount to surrendering to the Zionists.

> Killing a man and walking in his funeral is a known proverb, but harming a man and inquiring from his people about the cause for their sorrow is a case which no vocabulary has yet known . . . There is nothing more strange on behalf of the English than appointing committees of inquiry as though they do not know the causes and remedies . . . as though they are not . . . responsible for our difficulties.

Representative Arabs held that reopening the immigration issue – with the May White Paper restrictions still operative – was akin to opening a Pandora's box. Khalil al-Sakakini took a slightly different tack. By offering the Jewish refugees a sanctuary outside Palestine he detected a genuine humanitarian gesture in Bevin's statement. But the real sticking point, thought al-Sakakini, was that if the Jews were allowed to establish their National Home they would surely expel all the Arabs from their homeland.[17]

Immediately after Bevin's Commons statement a protest strike and riots broke out in Tel Aviv and Jerusalem. Jerusalem was quickly brought under control but in Tel Aviv the situation deteriorated rapidly. High-ranking officers, attached to the 6th Airborne Division, witnessed 'a huge anti-British Jewish crowd' rioting 'in time-honoured fashion, by tearing up paving stones on the street and smashing British, Arab and moderate Jewish property'. These 'hooligan elements' inflicted casualties on their troops. 'I [Colonel Corran Purdon] was hit by a rock thrown by a woman who had her skirt tucked into her knickers, revealing a pair of thighs worthy of an Olympic shotputter!' The order was given to open fire. One officer was credited with having 'personally shot three ringleaders'. The mob withdrew but then attacked the Post Office and Income Tax offices and other government buildings, which they set on fire, throwing 'a quantity of home made grenades'. Shots were fired in anger, killing and wounding a number of

Jews. 'We had a trained sniper in each section and it was possible to indicate a ring leader to him and have the man shot in the leg. When this happened the crowd would draw back.' Eventually a curfew was declared for some days, restoring a semblance of order.[18]

Ten days later, the *Palmach*, 'covered by heavy fire from automatic weapons', penetrated the defences of two coastguard stations at Givat Olga (near Hadera) and Sidna Ali (near Jaffa) and blew them up. According to the British, these raids were 'well planned, well executed'. The raiders were traced to outlying settlements that in turn were raided by British security forces. Confrontation was inevitable. Hundreds, possibly thousands, of Jewish *chalutzim* descended on the British lines circling the settlements, battering the armed cordons with 'stones and clubs'. As Colonel Purdon recorded, British troops 'were forced to open fire . . . In one case a crowd of about three thousand Jews approached a platoon in the outer cordon led by a man on horseback. The situation was restored when this gentleman was shot.' Eight Jews were killed in this head-on clash. Between the riots in Tel Aviv and those at Givat Olga, in less than two weeks, fourteen Jews had been killed. None of this deterred the URM: Ben Gurion's brand of 'activism' still held sway. In February 1946 the *Palmach* struck at four Police Mobile Force stations, inflicting severe damage and incurring four casualties. Sir Alan Cunningham reported to George Hall, the Colonial Secretary: 'You will appreciate the implications of a situation in which on the day of arrival of Dr. Weizmann in Palestine Jewish terrorists of *Palmach*, who had been shot *in flagrante delicto* while attacking a police camp with arms and explosives, were buried as national heroes.' A crowd of 50,000 attended their funeral in Tel Aviv. Some days later the *Irgun* and Stern Gang, with URM approval, destroyed twelve British aircraft, damaging eight more: the total cost to the RAF, £750,000.[19]

From late December to late March 1946 the twelve members* of the AAC had convened in Washington, London, Cairo and Jerusalem, hearing and cross-examining witnesses. As the commissioners' ship

*Sir John Singleton, a High Court judge, 'of Pickwickian boyishness and simplicity combined with judicial precision', presided (as joint chairman) over the British contingent. It included: Major Reginald Manningham-Buller, a Conservative MP; Richard Stafford Crossman, a former Oxford philosophy don – among the new crop of Labour MPs who entered the House in 1945, considered by some as a self-

drew into New York harbour, at the outset of their inquiry, Richard
Crossman noted in his diary:

> We start with a blankness towards the philosophy of Zionism which is
> virtually anti-Zionist. We have a feeling that the whole idea of a Jewish
> national home is a *dead end* out of which Britain must be extricated; that,
> whereas it is obvious that Arab independence in the end must be
> granted, we have not a similar obligation to permit the Jews in Palestine
> the fulfilment of Zionism.

Put this way, most of the commissioners tended 'to define the problem
as one of finding homes somewhere for the surplus Jews in Europe in
order to cut away the Zionist case for an impossible immigration into
Palestine'. Crossman drew no such hasty conclusions. 'We must
consider the Zionist case on its merits,' he argued. A Jewish national
home 'exists now in miniature, and we are pledged to assist it . . . *We
must in fact either accept or reject Zionism as such* [Crossman's italics],
putting the awkward incompatible alternatives clearly before our
Governments.'[20] These contrasting perspectives would plague the
Commission until its very last days.

---

opinionated left-wing intellectual; Sir Frederick Leggett, recommended by Bevin,
well experienced in the workings of international organisations and a skilful mediator
of industrial disputes; Wilfred F. Crick, an economist and adviser to Midland Bank, as
well as a don at the London School of Economics; and Lord (Robert Craigmyle)
Morrison of Tottenham, a career politician, previously a Labour MP.

Joseph ('Texas Joe') Hutchinson, a district court judge and one-time mayor of
Houston led (as joint chairman) the American delegation. It was said of him that on
the bench he was 'an absolute monarch', though he had little experience of international affairs. The remaining American commissioners included: James G.
MacDonald, who had previously acted as League of Nations Commissioner for
Refugees from Germany and had gained much experience in handling Jewish refugee
problems; William Philips, a career diplomatist; Frank Aydelotte, a former Rhodes
Scholar and Director of the Institute for Advanced Studies at Princeton, and a
practising Quaker; Frank Buxton, a journalist and Pulitzer Prize winner, appointed on
the recommendation of Supreme Court Justice Felix Frankfurter; and Bartley C.
Crum, a lawyer from Sacramento, California, who had acted as counsel to the US
delegation at the United Nations conference at San Francisco in 1945; and owed his
appointment to David Niles, a trusted Truman adviser. Crossman said of him that he
'Reads nothing, drinks too much and changes his mind according to the last
newspaper he received from the States'. See Nachmani, pp. 65–79.

Working in subcommittees, the commissioners also travelled throughout Europe, gauging opinion in the DP camps and main refugee centres. While in the Middle East they had explored current Arab opinion in Egypt, Palestine, Transjordan, Lebanon, Iraq and Saudi Arabia. During their stay in London, Bevin saw Crossman – for three minutes: 'conversation confined himself to asking me whether I had been circumsized'. But Bevin deigned to meet all the commissioners at a formal luncheon at the Dorchester Hotel, where, yet again, he made a far-reaching pledge. After proposing the health of the Committee, he unexpectedly launched into a personal statement: 'slowly but emphatically', he gave his word 'that if we achieved a unanimous report he would personally do everything in his power to put it into effect'. This promise 'very much influenced' the commissioners, recalled Evan Wilson, the American secretary to the Committee.[21]

As expected, in Washington the Committee was subject to Zionist pressure; in London the voices were more muted, except perhaps for the rantings of the rabid anti-Zionist, Sir Edward Spears. Leo Amery, a staunch gentile Zionist, favoured partition, while Sir Ronald Storrs, although opposed to a Jewish state, did not want to dismantle the Jewish National Home. Phil Piratin, the Communist MP, pleaded 'a straight anti-Zionist case', resentful that the Soviet Union had been left out of the picture. He was joined by Colonel [Major] Montague Gluckstein, Chairman of J. Lyons and Co., 'a Pukka Sahib anti-Zionist British Jew'. The Jewish case was put by Selig Brodetsky, a Zionist activist and mathematics professor at Leeds University, and Simon Marks, Chairman and joint Managing Director of Marks & Spencer, who, Crossman observed sourly, behaved 'like a small greengrocer in his Sunday clothes'. Spouting their 'propaganda pieces', they 'made a very bad impression'.[22]

In Europe, they met face-to-face the Jewish remnants of the Holocaust. However much they had mentally steeled themselves for such an encounter, the appalling reality of the camps, the desperate condition of the refugees, the mood of hopelessness that smothered them, came as something of a shock to these well-fed, comfortably off, middle-class Anglo-Saxons. 'The abstract arguments about Zionism and a Jewish state seemed curiously remote after this experience of human degradation,' remarked Crossman. Every straw poll they took indicated that the overwhelming majority of these wretched people saw a safe haven only in Palestine. Certainly, they saw no future in Europe, where anti-Semitic bloodbaths were still being reported. Nor even in America. Tearing up an entry visa to the United States, one Polish Jew exclaimed that 'he could never trust a Christian again'. Another, a young Polish boy of sixteen who had survived six years of his life incarcerated in Nazi camps, was asked whether he had any relatives in America. 'Yes,' he replied, 'my mother is there.' Were they in contact? 'His handsome face contorted in passion: "I have cut her off root and branch. She has betrayed my nation. She has sold out to the Goy. She has run away to America. It is the destiny of my nation to be the lords of Palestine." '[23] Undoubtedly, such encounters left an indelible imprint upon the minds of the commissioners – and would return to haunt them when composing their final report.

In Vienna, referring to the *Bricha*,* Crossman asked, 'How is it organised?' The answer soon became apparent. 'American Jewish Relief Agencies', who provided the financial muscle, channelled the funds into the hands of 'local Jews who are all Zionists' and who then 'organise the trek into Austria and Germany'. Once there the refugees make directly for the American zones 'where they are looked after as displaced persons by the Americans until they are ready for the illegal journey through Italy to Palestine . . . Not only is the trek to Palestine organised, but it is done with the specific connivence of the American military who have built and organised transit camps . . . and who wink at the illegal entry into Bavaria.' Meanwhile the British, Crossman noted, pursue an entirely different policy. They refuse to give Polish Jews displaced persons privileges and have closed the route to Italy across the mountains. 'The result of course is that there are no Jews in the British zone.'[24]

In Jerusalem, the commissioners, housed at the King David hotel, soaked up its hothouse atmosphere. Politely informed by the British authorities that their telephones were being tapped 'so that all our conversations were overheard', they were all too mindful of the 'private detectives, Zionist agents, Arab sheiks, special correspondents,

---

*Literally, 'escape': the organised illegal immigration movement of Jews from eastern Europe across the occupied zones in Germany and Austria, from there to Italian and French ports, and then on to Palestine.

and the rest all sitting discreetly overhearing each other'. Outside, the city appeared as 'an armed camp', barbed-wire roadblocks in abundance, tanks stationed at various intersections, while special pillboxes had been erected to guard the routes leading to the hotel.[25] The hearings were heard at the YMCA building, an architectural delight, positioned opposite the hotel. Leading the Jewish witnesses were Weizmann, 'who looks like a weary and more humane version of Lenin', and Ben Gurion, 'a tiny, thick-set little man with white hair – a Pickwickian cherub'.[26] Both called unequivocally for Jewish independence, a Jewish state. Weizmann: 'To expect that they [the Jews] will settle among the tombstones of the past and amongst the hatred of the present is really asking too much from flesh and blood.' 'The land, the book and the people are one for us for ever. It is an indissoluble bond,' claimed Ben Gurion.

Representatives of the *Ichud* (Union) group were also called. A group of intellectuals led by Judah Magnus, President of the Hebrew University, and Martin Buber, the distinguished philosopher, they advocated a bi-national solution, 'a common motherland for these two Semitic peoples'; but also 'large Jewish immigration'. Would you change the name of the Hebrew University to the University of Palestine? Magnus was asked. No, he replied, 'it was to be the university of all the Jewish people, established to fructify and revive Judaism'. Would you bring in the 100,000, if necessary by force? Yes, replied Magnus, adding cagily, 'but that is not the only way'. Crossman, a philosophy don himself, swiftly concluded 'that what he said represented nothing real in Palestine politics', a judgement upheld also by Sir Richard Catling, Assistant Inspector-General of the Palestine Police, who thought Magnus 'a man of high ideals but somewhat lacking a sense of reality'. On the other hand, Susanna 'Espie' Emery, an English teacher from Haifa, thought otherwise. 'The only really sound witness . . . really fair-minded,' she declared. 'I think that plan might work if the Jewish Agency could be abolished, and its members sent out of Palestine for ten years on probation.'[27]

Catholic, Protestant, Orthodox and Coptic clerics were also summoned, as were soldiers, whose evidence was presented in camera. Lieutenant-General Sir John Convers D'Arcy, the General Officer Commanding Palestine, was disarmingly frank. Crossman thought him 'completely honest and objective'. Earlier D'Arcy had described the

Haganah as well-armed, well-trained, highly disciplined, confessing that
he could see 'no precedent and little help in our long history of imperial
policing' for combating such a nonpareil organisation.[28] Speaking as a
soldier, D'Arcy told the commissioners he could enforce a pro-Jewish
solution 'without much difficulty', aided, needless to say, by the 'highly
efficient' *Haganah*. But to execute a pro-Arab outcome he would require
'an extra three army divisions, for at least four to six months, to break
the back of the [Jewish] opposition': even then underground resistance
would persist. Should the British withdraw, D'Arcy was adamant: 'the
Haganah would take over all of Palestine tomorrow', and they could
hold it against 'the entire Arab world'. 'You cannot disarm a whole
people,' the general warned the Committee. 'I rather think the world
will not stand for another mass murder of Jews.' Crossman chipped in:
'we're dealing with a genuine Maquis movement'.

Sir John Shaw, the Chief Secretary of the Palestine Administration,
offered a different perspective. Fiercely hostile to the Jewish Agency, 'a
state within a state', he felt that either it or the administration had to go.
Partition, he argued, was 'almost' impossible. And as for the 100,000,
that could only be countenanced after the disbandment of the Agency
and the decommissioning of the *Haganah*. (Crossman, when taking
informal soundings from other high-ranking officials, had heard the
same gloomy story: dismantling the Agency, even if it involved the use
of force, and disarming the *Haganah* were necessary prerequisites
before any further immigration could be sanctioned.)[29] Sir Alan
Cunningham, the High Commissioner, Shaw's master, begged to differ;
but then he too was a general. 'No,' he told Bartley Crum, 'I shouldn't
want to see the Agency disbanded. I am not one of those who
underestimate it. The Palestinian government may not like it, but it
cannot ignore it: it is a force to be reckoned with, and my own feeling
in this matter is that it really cannot be destroyed – even if the
government should wish to do so.' Unlike Shaw, Cunningham, perhaps
faute de mieux, was turning to partition as the only viable solution. A
curious situation had arisen: while the civilians were all for wielding the
iron fist, the military inclined towards a policy of relative restraint.

Arab witnesses were heard mainly in Cairo and Jerusalem. Azzam
Pasha, secretary to the Arab League, 'tall and melancholy', gave an
'impromptu and moving speech', temperate in language, but clear in
its message: 'We are not going to allow ourselves to be controlled

either by great nations or small nations or dispersed nations.'
Revealing great sensitivity to the plight of the Jewish refugees, he
reconciled himself to the 100,000, their absorption to be spread over
three years.[30]

Jamal al-Husayni, the Mufti's cousin, was less restrained when he
presented his case at the YMCA. Representing the newly reconstituted
AHC, a sure sign of Haj Amin's growing ascendancy over Palestinian
politics, he berated the Zionists, 'these pampered children, these spoilt
children of the British government'. To attain a just resolution of the
Palestine imbroglio he laid down five conditions: abrogation of the
British mandate; termination of the Jewish National Home; the creation
of a sovereign Arab state in Palestine; the immediate cessation of all land
sales to Jews; and no further Jewish immigration. Strong language that
failed to impress the commissioners. Instead, Jamal was grilled
relentlessly about the wartime record of his cousin, whom he had
introduced as the one man who 'could speak truly for the people of
Palestine'. Brushing aside the documentation revealing the full extent
of Haj Amin's collaboration with the Nazis, Jamal insisted that his
leader 'had always acted in the interests of his people, and that when he
was in Germany that is just what he was doing'.[31] Such testimony was
entirely self-defeating. To justify the actions of a suspected war criminal
barely a year after the end of the war, when the details of the Holocaust
were fresh in everyone's mind, damned his statement. Jamal only
succeeded in ruffling the feathers of the commissioners: his truculent
manner, his all-or-nothing demands, his defence of the indefensible,
ultimately damaged the cause he was sent to promote.

A far more positive impression was made by Albert Hourani, the last
witness to present the Arab case. Born in Didsbury, Manchester, of a
Lebanese family, Hourani was urbane, articulate and of a scholarly
disposition (an Oxford graduate and a former student of Crossman).*

*Hourani went on to follow a most distinguished academic career, teaching at
Magdalen College, Oxford, the American University of Beirut, and the Universities of
Chicago, Pennsylvania and Harvard. He ended his academic career as a Fellow of St
Antony's College, where he was one of the founders and Directors of its Middle East
Centre. Today many of his graduate students can be found on the faculties of Oxford,
Cambridge, Harvard, Yale, Columbia, MIT, the Hebrew University and the
University of Haifa, among others. Hourani's most popular work, *A History of the Arab
Peoples* (1991), an international best-seller, is still a most readable introduction to the
history of the Middle East.

Giving evidence on behalf of the newly formed Arab Office,* he put the Palestinian case moderately, though without conceding any points to the other side. Hourani elaborated on 'the unalterable opposition of the Arab nation to the attempt to impose a Jewish state upon it. This opposition is based upon the unwavering conviction of unshakeable rights.' He dismissed the idea of partition: only 'a self-governing state, with its Arab majority, but with full rights for the Jewish citizens of Palestine' would suffice. He also gave short shrift to the proposal to bring in the 100,000. 'The Arabs can never acquiesce in any immigration imposed upon them.' Nor would he subscribe to Magnus's dream of a bi-national state, repudiating it in words that are still apposite today. 'Again, a binational state of the kind that Doctor Magnus suggests can only work if a certain spirit of cooperation and trust exists and if there is an underlying sense of unity to neutralise communal differences. But that spirit does not exist in Palestine. If it existed, the whole problem would not have arisen in this form . . .' He warned of 'a violent reaction in some parts of the Arab world' should an attempt be made 'to continue the Zionist policy in Palestine'. As for the Jewish Agency, 'there can be no lasting peace in Palestine until the teeth of this monstrous organization are drawn.' In closing, Hourani elevated the Palestinian case to a higher plane. 'Ultimately, this is not a political or an economic problem to be decided only by political or economic criteria; ultimately and inescapably it is a moral question. There is a question of right and justice involved.'

For Crum, Hourani was the 'most persuasive' of the Arab witnesses, his evidence elegantly put. Jewish observers thought his testimony 'able and brilliantly presented', particularly when compared with the 'fanatical blood-and-thunder oratory' of Ahmed al-Shukeiri (later first chairman of the Palestine Liberation Organisation). Hourani was clearly ill at ease with Shukeiri's (and others') brand of sabre-rattling. Over dinner with his ex-tutor Crossman, he remarked 'that he and his friends are highly critical in a tolerant sort of way of the present Arab leadership and its methods of

*Formed in March 1945, after the Alexandria Conference. Under the direction of Musa Alami it ran offices in Washington and London providing information about the Palestinian Arabs and conducting a propaganda campaign on their behalf. The Arab Office was responsible for preparing the written evidence to be presented to the AAC.

propaganda'.[31] Style can be seductive; but in substance Hourani was no less intransigent than Jamal al-Husayni.

Towards the end of their stay in Palestine the commissioners began to feel the strain of working overtime in such a hothouse atmosphere. 'These hearings, 7 hours a day, are a bit trying and the Committee is getting very testy and bored,' Crossman grumbled to his wife, Zita. 'Their only interest is to get the Hell out of Palestine and to start finishing the job in Lausanne.' By now rather 'anti' the Committee, Crossman held the two chairmen, Singleton and Hutchinson, largely responsible: they were 'really too crotchety and uninterested for words . . . I hesitate to think what will happen when we get to Lausanne and start trying to agree on a report, with two such chairmen in charge.' To Zita, he summed up his experiences in Palestine. His unremitting grilling of Jamal al-Husayni had rendered him *persona non grata* with the Arab party, an untenable position that he was desperately trying to rectify – though without much success. Much of his invective was reserved for the British officials serving in Palestine. Crossman indicted them as 'utterly nauseating. They are snobbish, cliquey, second-rate and reactionary. They like the Arabs because they are illiterate, inefficient and easy to govern. They dislike the Jews because the Jewish leaders are ten times as able as they are.' As for the Jewish Agency, it

> runs the Jews of Palestine with a pretty good disregard for the government officials. It is really a state within a state, with its own budget, secret cabinet, army, and above all, intelligence service. Whatever you may think about it, it is the most efficient, dynamic, tough organisation I have ever seen, and it's not particularly afraid of us. It is a sort of socialist state set up inside and in defiance of us and despising and being constantly humiliated by a set of smug, autocratic officials.

Convinced in his own mind that partition was the only solution, Crossman doubted his ability to persuade his fellow commissioners, particularly the English contingent: 'Heavens, how the average fair-minded Englishman hates a tough realistic solution.'

Why, he finally asked Zita, must 'my last few days in this lovely and fascinating country be wasted mostly on hearings?' Determined to rectify the situation, he announced that he was soon 'off to Haifa', and to other engaging places.[32]* Many of his fellow commissioners followed suit.

Before the AAC left for Lausanne to draft their report, they toured the length and breadth of Palestine, taking in Arab villages and townships, Christian, Druze and Beduouin settlements, the Samaritan colony in Nablus, kibbutzim and Jewish towns, industrial and agricultural enterprises, social and educational projects, and finally the (Jewish-run) Potash Works by the Dead Sea. They left Palestine still debating various scenarios. But throughout this protracted, at times highly charged investigation, two factors in particular influenced them: first, the haunting, wretched scenes from the DP camps in Europe; secondly, and in vivid contrast, the achievements of the Jews in Palestine. If the utterly miserable state of the refugees, barely surviving in a state of limbo, proved virtually impossible to shake off, then conversely the vibrancy, unity of purpose and homogeneity of the *Yishuv* left a deep and lasting impression on the AAC. Richard Crossman visited Mishmar Haemek, a kibbutz in Emek Israel (the Vale of Esdraelon). Its turfed gardens, fountains, flower beds, vineyards, its collective ethos, captured the Labour MP's imagination. 'If I were a Jew I would like to live my life as a member of *Mishmar Haemek*. I have never met a nicer community anywhere.' For Frank Buxton, the

*Crossman's thoughts appear prominently in these passages simply because his *Palestine Mission* (1947), containing day-to-day extracts from his diaries, appeared close to the events related here. He has been described as 'among the most dazzling of Labour intellectuals'. His intellectual pedigree was impeccable: a Wykehamist, a double first at Oxford, from 1931 a philosophy don at New College and the author of *Plato Today* (1937) and *Socrates* (1938). During the war he served in the Pyschological Warfare Department, responsible for anti-Nazi 'black' propaganda. Later he worked under General Eisenhower at SHAEF (Supreme Headquarters of Allied Expeditionary Force) and was one of the first British officers to enter Dachau. While unquestionably the intellectual powerhouse of the Commission, it should not be inferred that his opinions dominated its proceedings – as can be seen from his failure to convince the commissioners of the rewards of partition. Considered by some to be wayward and erratic in his views, Crossman's own self-imposed high standards at times spilled over into a faintly disguised arrogance laced with intellectual bullying.

Crossman was captivated by Weizmann's personality. The last of Weizmann's gentile conquests, he considered as eminently sensible the more moderate policies the elderly Zionist leader advocated. Later, he became identified with *Mapam*, the left-wing Israeli party.

American journalist, the *chalutzim* conjured up remote but golden memories of the pioneer spirit of his forefathers: 'How my Vermont father, who used to glory in the land cleared by him and his brothers would have been amazed at the greater deeds of the Palestinian Jews! . . . I came away from those farms less cocky and more humble and not quite so certain that American pioneers left no successors.'[33] These perceptions worked very much to the advantage of the Zionists.

Minutes before he was due to board a plane to leave Palestine for Lausanne, Crossman was told by Mr Scott, the Financial Secretary to the Adminstration, 'You must produce a big idea which will pull Arab and Jew together.' Crossman listened, unimpressed. 'Not that Scott is a stupid man. He and Shaw [the Chief Secretary] are the brains of the government, extremely able and conscientious civil servants, but just with no political sense or vision. They see every sapling, but have never once seen the wood – and they detest the Agency like sin.'[34]

On 20 April 1946, at Lausanne, the members of the AAC, after much bargaining, managed to compose a unanimous report.[35] A short distance away, at Montreux, the Zionists had set up a monitoring unit. Known as 'Kibbutz Montreux', the scraps of information reaching it from the deliberations of the AAC suggested that the commissioners had reached 'an impasse'.[36] It turned mainly on whether or not the decommissioning of the illegal (Jewish) armies should be a prerequisite to sanctioning large-scale immigration – the 100,000. At first, Judge Sir John Singleton and Major Reginald Manningham-Buller put foward this demand as an ultimatum. The American delegation lined up against them. Crossman joined in, taking the American side, accusing his chairman of 'precipitating a war in Palestine': 'Unwisely, probably, I stated that if I were a Jew in Palestine today with a ban on my relatives in Europe coming to my National Home, a ban in complete violation of the Mandate, I should be a member of the illegal army.' Outnumbered and outmanoeuvred, the Judge and the Major backed down.[37]

The compromise formula that was hammered out called for the immediate admission of 100,000 immigrants and the annulment of the land sales restrictions. But it rejected the case for partition – despite Crossman's and Crum's advocacy – nor did it offer 'a self-governing state, with an Arab majority', as Hourani had urged. Instead, it proposed that the Palestine mandate make way eventually for a United

Nations trusteeship. But if the Committee had not awarded the Jews their state, it had in effect quashed the hated May White Paper, a considerable moral and practical windfall – despite Ben Gurion grumbling about its 'double elimination of both the White Paper and Zionism'. No similar gain was conferred upon the Palestinian Arabs: after four months of speechifying, they had emerged empty-handed. The AHC, naturally, rejected the report. In protest, a token strike was called; otherwise, they would wait upon events, leaving any violent resistance to it to the Jews. From the al-Ahliyah College in Ramallah came a feisty reaction. Wadi Dides wrote to Crossman, damning the machinations of 'Nazi Jews'. Angry demonstrations, however, were recorded in surrounding Arab capitals. At an all-Arab conference in Cairo in late May came a call to halt Zionist immigration, to stop land sales to the Zionists and to establish an independent Palestinian state. It went further: 'Any adoption of the resolutions of the AAC in a manner prejudicial to the Arabs of Palestine would be considered as a hostile act directed at the Arab states themselves.'[38]

British officialdom gave the report short shrift. The Chiefs of Staff thought it 'disastrous', as it mortgaged invaluable British assets throughout the area: imperial communications and defence requirements, oil resources, friendship of the Arab states, who would inevitably gravitate towards the Soviet Union. A senior, and highly influential, British official in Cairo, Sir Walter Smart, Oriental Secretary at the embassy, was 'much struck by the superficiality and intellectual dishonesty' of the report. Many Palestine government officials took a jaundiced view of it. Typical was Ivan Lloyd Phillips, District Commissioner for the Be'er Sheva region. The report, he wrote to his father, had been 'dictated by Jewish financial interests in America'. Hoping it will be 'stillborn', he thought it would be 'a blunder of the first order to attempt to implement it'. Lloyd Phillips explained: 'It gives the Jews the substance if not the shadow of their demands and certainly creates the opportunity for the ultimate realization of their goal, a Jewish state. This to my mind would be morally wrong, politically disastrous. If we persist in it we will throw the Arabs into the arms of Russia.' Reflecting further, he felt that 'nothing would come' of the AAC's handiwork, noting that he now understood 'why Hadrian adopted particularly drastic methods in Palestine'.[39]

Would the British government implement the report? Or would it, as the cynics would have it, suffer the fate of those two well-known types of committees, the 'Doing Nothings' or the 'Nothing Doings'?[40]

The answer was not slow in coming. Initially, subtle differences divided Bevin from Attlee. The Foreign Secretary was all for accepting the report in its broad outlines, banking on practical American cooperation in implementing it; the Prime Minister, more in tune with reality, suffered no such illusion regarding American intentions. At the time, the United States was disengaging from Europe, not seeking new responsibilities elsewhere. The Joint Chiefs of Staff urged that no American troops be committed to impose the Committee's findings – advice that Truman could hardly ignore. Consultations would continue, however. Where Truman squared with the AAC report was in his immediate acceptance of the 100,000 recommendation, without any firm commitment as to how this was to be realised in the face of widespread Arab opposition. This uncalled-for initiative left Attlee and Bevin fuming. Attlee responded accordingly. Fortified by his own intuition – and reflecting official opinion in Palestine and Whitehall, and that of his military advisers, all of whom rejected the report and were lobbying for a showdown with the Jewish Agency and the *Haganah*, even without the Americans – his statement to the House was unyielding.

> It is clear, from the facts presented in the Report regarding the illegal armies maintained in Palestine and their recent activities, that it would not be possible for the Government of Palestine to admit so large a body of immigrants unless and until these formations have been disbanded and their arms surrendered . . . Jews and Arabs in Palestine alike must disarm immediately . . . HMG regard it as essential that the [Jewish] Agency should take a positive part in the suppression of these activities.

When pressed further on the fate of the DPs festering in camps in Europe, Attlee refused to be drawn: 'I am unable to make any further statement.'[41] Though Susanna Emery thought it a highly 'sensible and timely' statement,[42] it spelled confrontation with 'the illegal armies', something the military authorities were preparing for and many welcomed. In May 1946, General Sir John D'Arcy, of a more accommodating mind, was replaced as GOC Palestine by General Sir Evelyn Barker, a hardliner with a careless tongue.

Was Attlee open to persuasion? Crossman, who many in government service thought had made 'a ghastly *gaffe*' in signing the report, made an effort. They met in early May. For Crossman the encounter was 'desultory and unsatisfactory'. The report, remarked Attlee, was 'grossly unfair' and he had 'let them down'.[43] Apparently he said little else. In a manner replete with classic Pinteresque pauses, the interview dragged on.

> Crossman expatiated on the Haifa refinery, the pipeline, the Holy Places, and the Stern Gang and so forth, and paused . . . Silence. Crossman then moved over to the Jordan Valley, the potash and the Gulf of Aqaba, and paused again. Silence. Somewhat nettled, Crossman passed on via the Suez Canal and tanker fleets back to the Haifa Refinery and after twenty-nine and a half minutes obstinately fell silent. After nearly half a minute's pause, Attlee commented, 'I saw your mother last week.'[44]

Crossman responded angrily to this performance, taking umbrage at being accused of having unfairly let the side down. In a strongly worded letter he defended the report's findings, particularly the need to admit the 100,000; otherwise, he asserted, a bloody war would break out between the Jews and the British. 'My dear Dick,' apologised Attlee, 'I certainly did not intend to be "unfair" to the AAC . . . my annoyance is with the Americans who forever lay heavy burdens on us without lifting a little finger to help.'[45]

If the Prime Minister was impervious to rational argument, Crossman tried Ben Gurion, who had also censured the report, though from a different angle. They met at Crossman's 'cottage', Prescote Manor, near Banbury, Oxfordshire, an estate of some 500 acres. They talked for six and a half hours, raking up the same points. Crossman reported back to George Hall, the Colonial Secretary. 'As you well know, it is not easy to stop Ben Gurion from making propaganda speeches even at the supper table, and for the first four hours we really got nowhere . . . On no point could I find any basis of discussion or possibility of agreement between himself and you . . . On partition he continued to say that he thought it the best solution if imposed by the British.' Frustrated, Crossman found Ben Gurion 'tiresome' and dismissed him with the comment: 'It is really a waste of time discussing anything with you.' Towards midnight the atmosphere warmed up. Ben Gurion insisted that immigration – the 100,000 – was the key, 'for the sake of that, he would of course be willing to make almost any sacrifice. He could not, however, nor could his people, formally renounce the Jewish state under duress. But he would forgo it for the time.' Crossman pressed him about a possibility of an Arab-Jewish Development Board, bankrolled by American money and staffed by foreign experts, whose dual purpose would be to find profitable ways of absorbing the 100,000 while at the same time raising Arab living standards.

> To this he emphatically replied that he would be willing and eager to back such a plan. He argued, as I thought sensibly, that both Jew and Arab would like to see positive proof that the British Government was really interested in development and to do something about it. 'We want deeds and not words. If you really do something serious in the next two or three years, and show you really mean to develop the country, then we and the Arabs will be equally interested. If we all work together on these plans for a time, then later on the insoluble political problem might not seem so insoluble.' I said that what he had just said was something I had wanted to say for a long time, and we both laughed.[46]

Ben Gurion's eagerness 'to back such a plan' had a long-drawn-out history. As noted, it had been traditionally held in some Zionist circles that raising Arab living standards would soften their opposition to Zionist political aims. The turbulent history of the mandate unequivocally proved otherwise; and there was no reason to believe that it would change in the immediate future. This was a classic case of self-deception. In any case, Attlee's intractable remarks killed off any chance of realising such a compromise.

It has been argued that had the British acceded to the demand of 100,000 it would have taken the sting out of Zionist demands: 'the problem would have lost its unendurable tension, and it is doubtful if the state of Israel would have arisen'.[47] This is highly speculative. Quite the contrary, it might well have whetted the Zionist appetite for another 100,000, a point Hourani had put convincingly in his evidence to the AAC.

In any case, events in Palestine were soon to overtake the report. Only three days after it had been signed, Cunningham was informed that the army would seek to impose law and order in its own way: it would take 'drastic action against the Jewish Agency and the *Haganah*'. Contingency plans were being finalised. Once the government gave the word to go ahead, the army would move into action. These plans were picked up by Zionist intelligence agents. Left in no doubt of the 'strong-arm policy' by which the government proposed once and for all to end the *Yishuv*'s powers of resistance, the Jewish Agency made its own preparations for the inevitable showdown.[48]

6

Black Sabbath

The British government's refusal to implement the AAC's recommendation regarding the 100,000, except as a package deal – together with the decommissioning of the *Yishuv*'s 'illegal armies' – brought an immediate response from the Jews. On the night of 16–17 June 1946 the *Palmach*, in an operation dubbed the 'Night of the Bridges', isolated Palestine from its neighbouring countries. Ten frontier road and rail bridges were blown up, without casualties; an eleventh bridge remained intact, British forces fighting off the *Palmachniks*, inflicting upon them a number of fatalities. The following day the Stern Gang attacked the railway workshops in Haifa, causing much damage. The Gang, however, paid a very high price: eleven killed, twenty-three taken prisoner.[1] Soon afterwards the *Irgun* kidnapped five British officers while they were taking lunch at their club in Tel Aviv, holding them for ransom for two of their own men, under sentence of death. (This affair was frowned upon by the Jewish Agency, claiming that it exceeded the boundaries of an authentic national struggle.) Official military estimates recorded '47 incidents of a major nature' between November 1945 and June 1946, resulting in the deaths of eighteen officers and men, one hundred and one wounded, and acts of sabotage valued at four million pounds' damage.[2]

Many in the *Yishuv*, particularly those bodies aligned with the Palestine (Jewish) Labour movement, viewed the indiscriminate character of the tactics employed by the *Irgun*, and especially the Stern Gang, with extreme distaste: these fine distinctions were not always apparent to the uninitiated. Overall, most of these operations were greeted by the *Yishuv*, and informed observers, as a telling indication of the organisational capabilities of the Jewish Agency, and particularly of the lethal striking power of the *Haganah* and the

Palmach. But no less, they were interpreted as a humiliating reversal for the British security forces, severely denting their reputation and pride.

How to respond? Plans for drastic action against the Jewish Agency and the *Haganah* were already in an advanced state of preparation.[3] Unlike D'Arcy and Cunningham, who had argued before the AAC that 'you cannot disarm a whole people', that the Jewish Agency 'is a force to be reckoned with . . . it really cannot be destroyed – even if the government should wish to do so', the newly appointed Chief of the Imperial Staff, Field Marshal Sir Bernard Law Montgomery, was in gung-ho mode: he instructed Sir Evelyn Barker, General Officer Commanding Palestine, to 'crack about' with his troops, 'to be aggressive' in Palestine, 'to turn the place upside down'.[4]* His philosophy prevailed; and it fitted in well with Barker's general outlook.

Barker laid out his ideas in a memorandum, dated 22 June 1946, entitled 'Military Action to be taken to Enforce Law and Order in Palestine'.[5] He went about his business with a no-nonsense, soldierly bluntness. But even for a top-secret internal paper, expressions such as 'Holocaust', 'Final Solution', or 'Extermination' were deplorable turns of phrase to employ when detailing how to enforce law and order in Jewish Palestine. First, the *Irgun* and Stern Gang: although they came within his remit, he did not propose to deal with them 'since our intelligence regarding them is insufficient', a startling admission of incompetence. Considering the *Haganah*, he thought it needed 'reorganisation and not disbandment', recognising it 'as necessary for settlement protection'. What followed was the result of muddled thinking or faulty intelligence, or a combination of both.

---

*Montgomery's 'gung-ho' outlook did not always please his military colleagues or his political superiors. General Sir Harold English Pyman, Chief of Staff to General Sir Miles Dempsey, C-i-C Land Forces, Middle East, noted in September 1947 that 'The Cabinet regards Monty as irresponsible. Monty is only happy when visualizing himself as "THE LEADER". He doesn't realise that a considerable part of the people of England is sick of his publicity, and goes about muttering, "we must not have another Cromwell".' (Pyman Papers, 7/3/1–13, LHC).

Cunningham also complained bitterly of Montgomery's aggressive, self-advertising behaviour, observing that 'bees buzz in berets, however eminent'. (Cunningham's Notes . . ., and his letter to *Daily Telegraph* [undated, but 1958], GB165–0072, Box 4/2 and Box 5/4).

In considering the guilt of the *Haganah* in outrages which have taken place over the last few weeks, it can be definitely accepted that the work has really been that of the *Palmach* who, we know, form the 'regular army'. The *Haganah* proper has a defensive role and in that, as I have already said, there is much to support their retention in some capacity. The *Palmach*, on the other hand, is used as an offensive weapon and is the real enemy of law and order. The *Palmach* receive their orders from GHQ *Haganah*, so the latter also is fully compromised. The chief responsibility, however, must ultimately rest with the Jewish Agency who have made a state within a state, and have built up this illegal army. Furthermore their inflammatory propaganda has helped turn the minds of the youth of the *Yishuv* into ways of violence and sedition.

It seems therefore that . . . action must be taken against those primarily responsible, and in this category I place the extreme element of the Jewish Agency, the GHQ *Haganah* and the whole of the *Palmach* force. Doubtless such action by us will close the ranks of the Jews, and there may then follow outrages by the *Haganah* proper. However, we will have so disrupted the organisation that there is no reason to believe that we cannot deal with them.

It is to be hoped that the distinctions made between the *Palmach* and the rest of the *Haganah*, implying as it does the fundamental right of the Jews to hold arms for self defence, will allow the more moderate elements to raise their heads and take control.

Targeting the more radical elements in the *Haganah* and the Jewish Agency, Barker continued, would also have the beneficial effect of 'pleasing the Arabs and may keep them quiet, anyhow for a period'. In addition, and on a more practical level, it would also 'result in certain documents falling into our hands and may produce information about arms caches which will enable us to carry out searches for arms to a limited extent'. Ultimately, Barker admitted, however 'drastic' the action, 'the great bulk of the rank and file and the majority of illegal arms will, however, remain and will continue to remain a major problem'. Barker's solution to this problem, fanciful to an extreme, was somehow or other to integrate the *Haganah* into the Palestine Police Force: 'they must be brought under the complete control of the I[nspector] G[eneral] P[olice]'. He concluded: whatever 'the decisions of HMG . . . it is essential that we get rid of the extremists now, whether more outbreaks occur or not'. There was a caveat, however, a rather obvious one: 'I would point out that it is impossible to subjugate a country by force, especially a virile and intelligent people like the Jews. The ultimate solution must depend on a satisfactory political answer.'

Seven days later, on 29 June 1946, Barker's army descended upon the *Yishuv* in a belated attempt to restore its self-esteem and battered prestige; and, no less, to repair the damaged authority of the Palestine administration. Code-named 'Operation Agatha', the action, committing close to 20,000 soldiers, had been under active consideration by the military for some months. The Jewish Agency building in Jerusalem was occupied, its Executive Committee confined to a camp at Latrun; other *Yishuv* leaders were sent to languish in an army installation in Rafah. In all, some 2,700 suspects were interned. (Two prominent leaders escaped capture: while their comrades were under lock and key at Latrun, Ben Gurion and Moshe Sneh, Chief of the *Haganah* Command, were photographed sipping coffee at a Parisian pavement-side café.)* The military extended its activities. Curfews were imposed; low-flying planes buzzed Jerusalem; trains and buses were flagged down; extra roadblocks set up, disrupting normal day-to-day civilian communications. Twenty-seven kibbutzim were raided, arms caches confiscated, members arrested. The most notorious case occurred at Yagur, a settlement to the north of Haifa. Barker himself led the sweep on the kibbutz. Here a major *Haganah* arms cache was unearthed. 'Great ingenuity had been used in siting and constructing the caches,' he reported, 'such as false backs to cupboards, window sills which pull out leaving a recess below, "coffins" let into the floor of the nursery over a veranda, circular concrete or metal containers let into the ground underneath footbridges' – 325 rifles, 96 mortars, 5,200 mortar shells, 78 pistols, 425,000 bullets, 5,000 grenades and 800 pounds

*Details of 'Operation Agatha' had been leaked to the *Haganah* by a pro-Zionist British officer. A week before the army went into action, *Kol Israel* ('The Voice of Israel': the clandestine radio station of the *Haganah*) broadcast the main objectives of the operation: to disable the Jewish Agency; to cripple the *Palmach*; to arrest *Haganah* leaders; to search for documents implicating *Haganah* leaders in terrorist activity. Richard Crossman enlightened the House of Commons about the efficiency of 'The Jewish Intelligence Service, among the best in the world'. One senior British military commander had told him 'that every order of his was in Jewish hands within 24 hours'. See *PD*, vol. 426, c.1872–73, 1 July 1946; and *WL*, XXII, no. 193, n.6, p. 171.

of explosives were ferreted out. A contemporary official report
recorded how the soldiers, a battalion of the Cheshires, had 'a devil of
a time with women trying to hold on to the men to prevent them being
taken away . . . After collecting them all into the main dining hall they
had to use tear gas in order to get them out on to vehicles. The heavy
oil projectors were very useful also in this.'[6]

At Na'an, a kibbutz lying to the south-east of Rehovoth, things
were not much better. Rifle butts were used to round up the
Palmachniks hiding out in the kibbutz; but also on those women
members trying to defend them. When the detainees refused to
identify themselves – a tactic designed to provoke the squaddies – the
soldiers, some of whom were allegedly the worse for drink, threatened to open fire on their prisoners as they lay spreadeagled on the
ground. Left standing in the scorching sun from early morning till late
evening, they were eventually taken in open trucks to Latrun. On the
way, in another provocative demonstration of defiance, they began to
sing the 'Internationale'. Told to 'shurrup' by the soldiers, they
rebelliously raised their voices, only to be met by the strains of the
'Horst Wessel': the 'Socialists' drowned out the 'Nazis' (or so it is
recorded). But goading the soldiers had a price. More than ever they
felt justified in retaliating, aiming blows at their tormenters, as they
often did. From Latrun the *Palmachniks* were transferred to Rafah.
Overcome by boredom, they relieved the tedium by endless games of
chess, or by solving crossword puzzles – with an occasional (futile)
hunger strike thrown in for good measure. After some weeks they
were released.[7]

'Agatha' triggered memories of the Holocaust in the minds of many
Jews. Women ripped their clothing to expose concentration camp
tattoos. Settlers taunted the soldiers with shouts of 'Heil Hitler' or
'Gestapo' or 'English Bastards', implying they were no better than
Nazis. Kibbutz children were well organised. Egged on by their elders,
they were lined up in front of the troops and indulged in a vulgar form
of spitting drill, interspersed with the singing of patriotic songs.
Swastikas were chalked or painted on walls and pavements, an
offensive reminder to the soldiers of the Jews' former persecutors.
There were fatalities: three Jews and one British soldier.[8]

Exposed to abusive taunts, and subject to extreme provocation, the
soldiers reacted in kind. Incidents of verbal and physical brutality were

recorded. Slogans – 'What we need is gas-chambers!', 'Hitler didn't finish the job!' – were routinely yelled at the Jews as the furious soldiers went about their business, betraying deep-rooted prejudices. One senior officer summoned an impromptu press conference to vent his feelings. After referring to the Jews as 'a despicable race' who ate too much carp and whose women bulged in all the wrong places, he told the astonished journalists: 'These bloody Jews – we saved their skins in Alemein and other places and they do this to us.' The GOC Palestine, Sir Evelyn Hugh Barker, was credited as saying that he would like 'to uproot every Jew in Palestine'. (A story, perhaps apocryphal, perhaps not, tells of Barker, as he departed Palestine, urinating on its soil, 'as if in symbolic disgust'.)* A senior British intelligence officer, Lieutenant-Colonel Martin Charteris, observing these events, though conscious that some measures had to be taken against the Jewish Agency, found the mood of his fellow officers highly offensive. 'At parties,' he said – probably thinking of Katy Antonius's soirées, at which Barker was a welcome guest – 'anti-Semitic remarks were recklessly bandied about, betraying a deep well of antagonism towards the Jews.'[9]

On 17 July the *Va'ad Leumi* (the National Council of the *Yishuv*) proclaimed a general strike in protest 'against the continued detention at Rafah of 1,650 men taken from their settlements during the military searches 19 days ago'. Simultaneously, in a demonstration of solidarity, the 450 prisoners of Latrun went on hunger strike. Weizmann, as he saw his British-orientated policy crumbling around him, was mortified at this turn of events. 'Palestine today', he recorded, 'is not merely a police state: it is the worst form of military dictatorship . . . Anybody may be arrested by any soldier or officer, without warrant, without reason given . . . He has no redress. In Palestine today the writ of *Habeas Corpus* does not run.'[10]

*For Barker urinating, see Louis, 'British Imperialism . . .', p. 14.

To put these incidents in a wider perspective, see Ronald Hyam, *Britain's Declining Empire. The Road to De-Colonialisation, 1918–1968* (CUP, 2007), p. 40, and Piers Brendon, *The Rise and Fall of the British Empire, 1781–1997* (Jonathan Cape, 2007), p. 505, for the behaviour of British soldiery, and the language they employed, during the period of decolonialisation. Punishments, or more accurately, torture methods, such as 'wall-standing, hooding, excessive noise levels, bread-and-water diet, deprivation of sleep', were commonplace; while terms of abuse, 'wogs, niggers, nig-nogs, Gypos, Chinks', were in common usage; and expressions such as 'That's another cunt getting fucking done' were not unknown.

As the general strike began, Weizmann left for London to continue negotiations with the government. He left behind a message for the *Yishuv*, commending it for its disciplined behaviour,

> the *Yishuv* knows it must continue in its restraint and not permit itself to be provoked from whatever quarter. There is a hard struggle ahead of us, both in Palestine and other centres. The terrible experiences of recent years, down to the massacre at Kielce, have apparently not yet demonstrated to the world where the only solution to this problem lies. But whichever way the present consultations may lead, whether of this or succeeding phases, my hope remains firm that justice will triumph and that our tortured people will be enabled to make their home here.

He warned, however, that no meaningful consultations were possible until the detainees at Latrun, 'the elected leaders of the *Yishuv*', were released. This, Weizmann asserted, was 'a necessary preliminary to the renewal of confidence in the intentions of Great Britain, a renewal which we all so much desire'.[11]

The events of 29 June 1946 have gone down in Zionist historiography as 'Black Sabbath'.

'Black Sabbath' was debated in the Commons on 1 July. Sidney Silverman, a Jewish MP representing Nelson and Colne, with the DPs in Europe very much on his mind, ended his speech on an emotional high. Describing the operation of Saturday 29 June as tantamount to a 'declaration of war', he refused to contemplate that Attlee and Co. 'mean to commit an act of betrayal or treachery'. The Labour government was 'a new hope,' he went on, 'an unexpected hope, to all the tortured, persecuted and oppressed of the world. I believe they are the last hope of those people. Do not let them down.'

Richard Crossman also intervened. One of two members of the House with direct and immediate experience of the Palestine imbroglio (the other was Major Reginald Manningham-Buller), he informed the House, as though to establish his objective credentials, 'I am not a Jew and not even a Zionist.' Then, with great authority, he proceeded to point out to the House just how badly the government had misread the situation. It seems to believe 'that there are just a small handful of wicked men in Palestine who are causing all the trouble and that if these men can be hand picked out of the Jewish community war can be averted'. To impose on the Jewish community by force 'a re-imposition of the White Paper is something which no Jew in Palestine accepts as law or order'; it merely alienates moderates, such as Weizmann. The *Haganah*, he argued, is a genuine resistance move-ment and it is 'impossible to crush a resistance movement which has the passive toleration of the mass of the population'. 'We are not Nazis,' Crossman asserted, 'and we are not prepared to take the step of liquidating the Jewish community, which would be necessary in order to crush the resistance movement.' He challenged the House: is our motto to be *'Oderint dum metuant* – Let them hate as long as they fear'? Accepting 'in principle' the AAC report, he argued, was the way out of this impasse. And then 'work out with the American Government and with the Jewish Agency the way to implement all those ten Clauses of the Report which hang together and without which we can have no peace in Palestine and no peace in the Middle East'.

In his reply Attlee brushed aside Silverman's pleas and Crossman's arguments. In the face of 'a long series of outrages', of 'terrorist and illegal actions', his government had shown 'the very greatest possible patience and forbearance'. Nor can one deny 'that these activities are part of a wide-spread plan' linking the *Haganah*, the Jewish Agency, and the *Irgun*. We have the evidence to prove it, he claimed.[12] 'No Government worthy of the name will yield to that kind of pressure, and certainly this Government is not going to do so.' 'Black Sabbath' was 'forced upon us', he insisted. As for the AAC report, Attlee reminded the House that so far no one had endorsed it 'with acclamation . . . It has not been accepted by the Zionists or by the Arabs.'

Despite the emotion and passion these exchanges generated, the protagonists, perhaps unwittingly, found common ground on the basic essentials. Attlee clarified: the government was intent on making a new start by 'getting together with America'.* Ongoing consultations

*At the time Attlee's government found itself in a most delicate position. Negotiations were in progress for a life-saving $350m American loan. But with American Jewry inflamed by the events of 'Black Sabbath', Jewish activists were calling to 'Kill that loan'. In fact, the pressure eased. But it was only after acrimonious debates in Congress, fuelled by traditional American 'anti-(British) imperialists' aided by Zionist sympathisers, that Truman was finally able to authorise the loan on 15 July. See Bullock, *Bevin*, p. 272, and Bethell, *The Palestine Triangle*, pp. 255–6.

were proceeding as to 'how to go ahead'. Although he considered the report 'a very good basis for discussion', it can only be implemented after exhaustive and fruitful discussions with the United States as its implications 'are very far reaching'. This was not too far removed from Silverman's or Crossman's concluding judgements. Attlee surely knew that 'getting together with America' rendered the AAC report a dead letter; but by his carefully couched phrases he had forced his government's severest critics on to the back foot – at least, for the time being![13]

Despite their display, in equal parts, of bravado and *savoir faire* – business as usual at Latrun* – Jewish leaders were stunned by the ferocity with which 'Operation Agatha' was carried out, by the destruction it caused, by the disruption it wreaked on the day-to-day business of life. It plainly indicated that the authorities had the capacity, if not to dismantle the *Yishuv*, then to cripple it at a decisive moment in its history. To persist in large-scale operations such as the 'Night of the Bridges', or for the Jewish Agency to maintain links with the terrorist organisations – ties well known to the British – would be akin to playing dice with history.

Serious doubts were raised about the advantages to be gained by the Jewish Agency and the *Haganah* in continuing to cooperate with the *Irgun* and the Stern Gang. Weizmann was the most prominent public figure in favour of disbanding the URM. His political clout in the *Yishuv* was marginal. But should he resign his position as President of the World Zionist Organisation over this issue, as he was threatening to do, it would have major adverse effects on Zionism's moral probity and international standing, considerations not to be dismissed out of hand. He sent word through his confidant, Meyer Weisgal, to 'Committee X' (the body responsible to the Jewish Agency and the *Va'ad Leumi*, which coordinated activities with the *Irgun* and Stern groups) that he would resign forthwith unless all violent actions against the British military and police installations were suspended until the Agency could meet to decide on an agreed policy. His ultimatum carried considerable weight. It was sufficient to convince a majority of the 'Committee' – some of

*Later, Shertok told 'Baffy' Dugdale that 'the British are quite unfit to run a police State. His mail (uncensored and unknown to the authorities) was delivered to him every morning punctually at eleven. His lonely evenings were spent in writing political directives' *Dugdale Diaries*, 7 December 1946, p. 242.

whom had already concluded that cooperating with the URM was counter-productive – though some hardliners, such as Moshe Sneh and the *Palmach* commander, Yigal Alon, were unhappy with the decision. Major operations were to be postponed, including a projected strike at the British Army and Palestine Administration headquarters located in the south wing of the King David Hotel. Not only fundamental ideological differences separated the *Irgun* and the Stern Gang from the Jewish Agency–*Haganah*. With bitter memories of the *saison* still fresh in everyone's minds, no love was lost between these three groups. Mutual suspicion was rife. Repeated messages were relayed to the *Irgun* to postpone planned actions. Perhaps faulty communications also played a role. At any rate the patience of their leader, Menachem Begin, finally ran out. Enthusiastic for the operation, he gave the green light to go ahead to attack the King David.

On 17 January 1946 George Hall contacted Cunningham. Take all necessary precautions to secure key buildings, he implored, in particular the King David Hotel, the heart of the Palestine Administration, against probable terrorist acts. Cunningham replied: 'steps already taken should be adequate'.[14]

On 22 July, evading roadblocks, barbed-wire barriers and armed sentries, seven members of the *Irgun*, masquerading as Arabs, led by Israel Levi, disguised in a Sudanese uniform (similar to those worn by workers in the hotel), penetrated the kitchens of the hotel as far as the hallway outside the Regence Café: they carried with them seven milk churns containing 250 kilos of explosives. The main aim of the operation, Levi later explained, was to destroy incriminating documents relating to the *Irgun* – not the most convincing of excuses. There were immediate casualties: one British officer killed, another wounded, while two of the *Irgun* assault party escaped suffering minor injuries. At 12.37 p.m. officials deliberating in the Jewish Agency building, within walking distance of the hotel, 'were startled by a tremendous explosion which rocked the neighborhood . . . A huge cloud of smoke spiralled upwards into the sky in the near distance.'[15] The south wing of the King David had collapsed, reduced to a pile of rubble and dust. The *Irgun* 'hit-and-run' attack resulted in ninety-one deaths: twenty-eight British, forty-one Arabs, seventeen Jews and five of other nationalities; forty-five others were wounded.

The Chief Secretary (and Acting High Commissioner), Sir John Valentine Wistar Shaw, was trapped in his room on the first floor. His door had jammed. It was broken open. He emerged shaken but unhurt, and immediately took charge of the rescue operations. A thin, stately, Gothic figure, with a slight bulge under his armpit where he kept a gun, he stood at six feet seven inches. Known as 'Long' Shaw, he once quipped to some journalists, 'They could hardly miss a man my size. Could they?' Some days later, Shaw wrote to Crossman – who had been closeted with Weizmann in his suite at the Dorchester Hotel when news of the tragedy came through – and had tried to make intelligible the subtleties of the political background to the disaster. More in sadness than in anger, Shaw countered Crossman's fine-drawn inferences harshly: 'My own police escort, who had been my inseparable companion and friend for 20 months, my own Armenian chauffeur, and many other humble persons of this type were among the dead. I helped to dig out their stinking putrefying bodies and I attended about 14 funerals in 3 days. In these circumstances I find the niceties and refinements of political argument and discussion rather hard to digest.'[16]

Peter Duffield, a *Daily Express* journalist, was sitting in his room, no. 105 on the second floor of the hotel, typing a feature article entitled 'Date Line, King David'. He had just reached the phrase which read, 'a country in which it is always a close season on sweet reason', when he heard bursts of machine-gun fire from under his balcony. A few moments later the hotel roof rocked, the windows blew in, debris and dust filled the corridors. He scrambled to safety. Hours later Duffield cabled his office: 'a lot of the hotel I was writing about is not standing up now – but maybe the feature will'.[17] Ivan Lloyd Phillips was sitting in the bar of the hotel savouring a pink gin when the room imploded. 'There was the most appalling roar . . . Everything went completely black & there was the noise of smashing glass & wrecking furniture & through the blackness one could feel the atmosphere was full of smoke & dust . . . from above came the most terrifying sound I have ever heard: the sound of falling masonry, & we could only assume that we were about to be crushed to death.' He managed to escape into the garden, unhurt. But not his Arab driver, who was killed. 'It will be grand when I leave Palestine never to have to speak to another Jew again – they have murdered too many of my friends.'[18]

Not far away, at the Christchurch Hostel in the Old City, the English teacher, Mary Burgess, heard the explosion. 'It is a most dreadful thing,' she told her family,

5 stories have been sliced off as with a knife . . . Never have I heard of such a city of mourning. Anglican, Orthodox, Muslim and Jewish funerals are going on all day long . . . The shops are shut most of the time & the streets are lined with silent crowds. As the coffins went by, there was silence from all the Arab crowds (no Jews!). Their sympathy with the British is very real. 1000 Arab families have themselves been affected. The Arab hatred of the Jews is at boiling point. So what will happen now, no one knows. This is such a wonderful land, it is awful to think of the strife which defiles it.

In Haifa, Susanna (Espie) Emery, another teacher, wrote to her mother:

We have all been unutterably shocked by the outrage at the King David Hotel. I think everyone of the dozen or more women killed were people whom I had taught in Jerusalem, and whose families I know well, and many of the Englishmen were my friends . . . Then came the revelations of how completely the Jewish Agency was mixed up with the terrorist organisations which they pretended to deplore. Their faces are blackened for ever, and I sincerely hope that (Moshe) Shertok and Ben Gurion and (Bernard) Joseph will be shot, but I expect they will wriggle out somehow. I suppose the good Jews are very shocked and regretful, but I think that most of them have been so poisoned by propaganda that they think murder for political reasons quite justifiable; just like the Germans.[19]

Later, the *Irgun* commander Israel Levi rationalised the outrage: 'What with the shootings and smoke grenades [diversionary bombs – 'petards' – had been set off prior to the explosion], and the telephone warnings, something should have clicked with the British that something was about to happen to King David.'[20] Were warnings actually given? Sir John Shaw denied categorically that he had received any such warning. But one (*Irgun*) account has a 'phone ringing in his office, him picking it up and barking down it: 'I am here to give orders to the Jews, not to take orders from them'. It is not a story that can be substantiated by any reliable source (Shaw later won a libel suit against a newspaper that published the allegation), though it continues to burden some histories. Adina Nisan, an *Irgun* courier, has testified that she indeed made three phone calls, to the King David, to the *Palestine Post* and the French consulate: 'This is the *Irgun*. We have placed explosives in the hotel. Clear out! This is a warning!' A police investigation later substantiated that warnings had certainly been sent, only that, tragically, they had arrived too late. Mr Hamburger, manager of the King David, affirmed that as he was being informed the hotel blew up.

Would even a thirty-minute warning have made much difference? It might have caused even more casualties, with panic-stricken hotel guests, officials and visitors cramming the corridors and stairways, jostling and pushing, desperately seeking a way out to safety. And why, it might equally be asked, didn't the *Irgun* carry out the operation after office hours, thereby reducing to a minimum potential fatalities, instead of at lunchtime, thereby guaranteeing the maximum number of deaths? These questions remain unanswered.

Khalil al-Sakakini described the bombing as 'a Holocaust'. In the Commons, Attlee condemned this 'dastardly outrage', the worst of all the 'brutal and murderous crimes' yet committed in Palestine. The elected representatives of the *Yishuv* followed suit, readily condemning this wilful act of murder (even though the *Haganah* was implicated in pinpointing the hotel as a legitimate target). The Jewish Agency expressed 'their feelings of horror at the base and unparalleled act perpetrated by a gang of criminals'. *Davar*, the organ of the Palestine Labour Movement, editorialised: 'The entire *Yishuv* has been shocked to the core by the criminal and abhorrent distortion given yesterday to the struggle of the Jewish people by a gang of dissidents. This criminal massacre has no reason and no atonement . . . It is a crime not only against the many dead but against the Jewish community and its future.' The *Palestine Post* also took a firm stand, condemning the outrage as an 'unqualified evil and will be judged as such by honest men in every part of the world'.[21]

Begin himself was genuinely shocked at the needless loss of life, but the blame, he insisted, lay with the British authorities for failing to heed the warnings.[22] He could hardly say otherwise. But after weighing all the available evidence, Begin's *Irgun* must be held fully responsible.

* * *

In the aftermath to the King David outrage a horrified Cunningham, who was in Scotland on leave, wrote to George Hall evaluating the deteriorating situation. Disturbed at the low morale of British troops and the local British community, he thought it necessary to take action, though he doubted it would yield positive results, hinting broadly that faulty intelligence and insufficient troops would hinder any effective operation. As an immediate response he proposed halting immigration and sequestering Jewish funds, knowing that such measures would only exacerbate relations with the *Yishuv*. Clearly at a loss how to react adequately, he floated an idea, rarely spoken out loud but often whispered in dark corners: 'I consider we should now be prepared to accept the risks of scuttling, etc., which has prevented me from advising this course in the past.' Apart from the option of 'scuttle' – that is, to cut and run – Cunningham placed the same ideas before the Cabinet on 25 July. Owing to ongoing talks with the Americans, they were not taken up.[23]

Matters were further aggravated by General Barker. A letter to his troops, clearly meant to stiffen their resolve, backfired when its text became known. Demanding non-fraternisation 'with the Jewish community of Palestine', he made clear – in phrases that have since become notorious – that by so doing 'they shall suffer punishment and be made aware of the contempt and loathing with which we regard their conduct . . . [and you] will be punishing the Jews in a way the race dislikes as much as any – by striking at their pockets and showing our contempt for them'. One senior officer thought that Barker had expressed himself 'rather strongly when he mentioned our loathing for the Jews': but who can blame him, he added, 'not anyone on the spot'. Cunningham found Barker's language 'unfortunate', explaining that it was intended only for senior officers.[24] An embarrassing blunder on the part of one of Barker's staff officers cannot justify the racist overtones of his fiat. Barker later admitted that he had erred in writing it. But the damage had been done. It tarnished Britain's image, causing her grave political harm, particularly in the United States.

Despite Cunningham's initial reservations, the British reacted to the King David bombing in hot fury. In the early hours of 30 July 20,000 troops, led by the 6th Airborne Division, descended on Tel Aviv with instructions to seal off the city. It was the largest-scale operation – or 'stunt' as the soldiers preferred to call it – of its kind ever to take place in Palestine. Naval and police launches patrolled Tel Aviv's seaboard. Under cover of darkness a continuous outer cordon was put in place, isolating the city. Telephone and telegram communications were cut off. Curfews were imposed and inner cordons set up, effectively splitting the city into a number of separate independent sections. Loudspeakers informed the residents that anyone caught infringing the curfew was liable to be shot on sight. The High Command's instructions were clear: to search every house, attic, cellar and basement in Tel Aviv for arms caches and to screen every person, young or old, healthy or infirm, for suspects. Armed with a list and photographs of suspected terrorist leaders, by the evening of the first day 25,000 persons had been interrogated. But, clearly, applying such an order in a city of approximately 170,000 resentful inhabitants was in essence an impossible task.

'Operation Shark' extended over three and a half days. As was only to be expected in a massive 'stunt' of this kind, 'tempers frequently frayed', but journalists also noted 'genuine cooperation by both searched and searchers', who, on the whole, 'were civil and polite'. The prime suspects, however, escaped capture. Begin, who headed the wanted list, moved into a 'special compartment' at his home on Bin-Nun Street, a kind of 'Priest's Hole', where he remained until his pursuers gave up the chase.[25] Five arms dumps, however, were uncovered, including a major *Haganah* cache discovered at the Tehkemoni school, and a Stern Gang stockpile, in the basement of Tel Aviv's Great Synagogue. Nearly eight hundred Tel Aviv residents, who were unable, or unwilling, to give a satisfactory account of themselves, were detained and incarcerated in a detention camp by Rafah. In a colder but no less menacing mood, the authorities stepped up their campaign against the 'illegals', the government approving Montgomery's recommendation to transfer them to camps in Cyprus.[26] These were nightmarish days for the *Yishuv*.

Hopes for a political outcome were also fading. Since the issuance of the AAC Report, Anglo-American contacts had been maintained and, despite the repercussions of 'Black Sabbath', King David and 'Operations Agatha and Shark', had not been suspended. In late July, the so-called Morrison–Grady plan was put on the table. Drafted by Herbert Morrison, the Deputy Prime Minister, and Henry Grady, the American ambassador to London, it laid out a scheme for provincial autonomy under British trusteeship; it also proposed admitting the 100,000 within one year – an intriguing about-face on the part of the British. The plan was rejected by both Jews and Arabs. Some Zionists were tempted, but they would go no further unless a viable partition proposal was placed on the agenda. The Palestinians rejected it as yet another dead end: they would accept nothing less than the terms first endorsed by the AHC in November 1935.

The Jewish Agency accrued some marginal benefits from this volatile state of affairs. With the British targeting the *Irgun* and the Stern group as their prime targets, the *Haganah*, now under less pressure, was granted more room for manoeuvre. It did not abandon strikes against (self-defined) legitimate British military targets, radar stations or detention camps for 'illegals' and suchlike. But at the same time it stepped up more compelling forms of 'activism', establishing new settlements, ensuring that the so-called 'illegals', running the British blockade, found a safe haven in the *Yishuv*: creating facts on the ground. In August, in Paris, the Jewish Agency Executive reconsidered its strategy. Talking and acting tough had not brought the desired results; quite the contrary, it had exacted from the *Yishuv* a high price, perhaps endangering its very existence, or so it appeared to many of its acknowledged leaders. As a result, the Executive confirmed the break-up of the URM, recognising the damage it had inflicted, not only on Zionism's image, but also on realising Zionism's long-term aims. It also reiterated in less ambiguous terms its commitment to partition, a position the movement had first adopted (in principle) in August 1937. It was the return to more moderate policies; it was the resurrection of 'Weizmannism', if not of Weizmann himself.

The 6th Airborne Division's tour of duty in Palestine covered almost the entire post-war period, from October 1945 until April 1948. Its reputation stood high, having distinguished itself during the war from the D-Day Normandy landings to the conquest of Germany. Known jocularly to the *Yishuv* as *Kalanioth* (or 'Poppies', referring to their distinctive red berets, but also the name of a popular Hebrew song) the Division spearheaded the military response against the *Haganah*, the *Irgun* and the Stern group, regarding the two latter with bitter hostility, but reserving its particular venom for the Sternists whom it considered as little more than cold-blooded murderers. But what of the Palestinian

Arabs? Were they any longer a threat to the authority of the mandatory power?

A staff officer at Division headquarters, Major R. Dare Wilson, ventured an opinion:

> From the end of the war until the closing stages of the Mandate . . . the Arabs by their exemplary behaviour caused neither the Government nor the security forces the slightest embarrassment . . . the Palestinian Arabs, though united in their desire for independence and the cession of the Mandate, were so absorbed in evils of tribal faction that the demands of national unity were relegated to the status of minor importance.

They never presented the same problem as the Jews, Wilson claimed. Many held, rightly or wrongly, that Britain was indirectly supporting the Arab cause. Not as the Arabs would have wished. But for various and obvious reasons the British government had generally adopted policies inimical to Jewish aims, particularly over immigration. Nor were they organised to make trouble, even if, like the Jews, they would have liked to back their threats with force. Finally, Wilson continued (with tongue in cheek?), neither the British soldier nor the Arab used to take each other too seriously. 'Both have a wonderful sense of humour, and on occasions when trouble was developing, this invaluable asset very frequently saved the day.'

Of course, 'a wonderful sense of humour' might, at times, have had a bonding effect. Sometimes, however, things slipped out of control. Pilfering was rife. Army camps, temporarily vacant, proved to be of great temptation to Arab marauders 'who would descend on it by day and night and carry off every moveable fitting'. Even fully operational camps were not immune. Working 'by stealth', the Arabs very rarely attacked sentries. 'He was a specialist at penetrating the best defences undetected and after visiting one or more tents occupied by sleeping soldiers, left lightly with his loot.' Often soldiers would wake up in the morning to find their bed and blankets over them the only articles left in the tent. 'Pistols would disappear under pillows, and even tents themselves, if unoccupied, would vanish without a trace on a dark night.' The Jews were no better, only more focused and less subtle. They would brazenly enter a camp, prepared and equipped to shoot it out if necessary with the camp guards. What interested them were mainly arms, uniforms, and military equipment, 'although they occasionally devoted time to stealing large quantities of NAAFI cigarettes, of which any surplus to their needs would then be sold on the Black Market to swell gang or party funds'.

Instances in which the Arabs caused trouble were infrequent, recalled Major Wilson, though occasionally amusing. One such incident, he recounted, occurred in July 1947 near Gaza when an Arab car was checked by the security forces and found to contain a load of land mines which, according to the Arab driver, he had contracted to transport for some Jews. The driver was immediately arrested, together with another Arab who at the time was trying to buy the consignment for his own use with counterfeit five-pound notes.[27]

Humorous instances aside, compared with the growing militancy of Jewish resistance, the Arabs at this stage did remain remarkably passive. But the cause is not difficult to ascertain. Bereft of authoritative, viable and credible leadership, the Palestinian national movement lacked cohesion. And the appearance of the Mufti, Haj Amin, much acclaimed by the masses and his own faction but loathed by many of the notables and their followers, only worsened matters. Internecine violence flared up again, perpetuating the ruinous legacy of the Arab Rebellion of 1936–9. Feuding political clans, conflicting personal ambitions, all fuelled by long-standing family (tribal) rivalries, steered the Palestinian national leadership into a cul-de-sac, into a chronic state of disintegration that prevailed until the last days of the Mandate and beyond.

At the Alvin Theatre, 250 West 52nd Street, NYC, a new production premièred on 5 September 1946. A Flag is Born boasted a star-studded company. Written by Ben Hecht, the renowned screenwriter and playwright, with music by Kurt Weil and directed by Luther Adler, the well-known war journalist, Quentin Reynolds, served as narrator. It starred the Academy Award-winning actor Paul Muni, Celia Adler, known as the 'First Lady of the Yiddish Theatre' and an up-and-coming twenty-two-year-old actor, Marlon Brando.

A Flag is Born was blatant propagandist melodrama. The play is set in a graveyard (a metaphor for Europe at the time) and featured three characters: Tevye (Muni) and Zelda (Adler) – elderly survivors of

Treblinka – and David (Brando), an angry young concentration camp escapee. The narrator sets the tone: 'Of all the things that happened in that time – our time – the slaughter of the Jews of Europe was the only thing that counted forever in the annals of man. The proud oration of heroes and conquerors will be a footnote in history beside the great silence that watched the slaughter.' Zelda, remembering that it is Friday night, lights candles on a broken tombstone. Tevye begins to chant the traditional prayers, and as he does so he dreams about his home town synagogue before its destruction; of King Saul at the battle of Gilead; and of a conversation with King David. He makes an unheard plea to a 'Council of the Mighty' (a reference to the Security Council). Tevye wakes up to find that Zelda has died. Preparing for his own death – he recites the Kaddish and bids a final farewell to David. Abandoned, David contemplates suicide before three Jewish soldiers rescue him and promise to take him to Palestine. As David leaves the graveyard for his new homeland, the play reaches its climax. He berates Anglo-American Jewry, harshly, brutally:

> Where were you – Jews . . . when the killing was going on? When the six million were burned and buried alive in lime, where were you? Where was your voice crying out against the slaughter? We didn't hear any voice. There was no voice . . . You Jews of America! You Jews of England! Where was your cry of rage . . .? Nowhere! Because you were ashamed to cry as Jews! A curse on your silence . . . And now, now you speak a little. Your hearts squeak – and you have a dollar for the Jews of Europe. Thank you. Thank you.

Brando's impassioned, heart-rending speech capitalised on a known theatrical device. Beginning softly, his voice rising to a crescendo, he repeated the accusation 'Where were you?' again and again. The impression was overpowering. Overcome with emotion, young Jewish girls were seen to leave their seats to crowd the aisles, screaming and crying in sadness.

A Flag is Born was not just an impassioned cry censuring the apathy of Anglo-American Jewry. Of no less consequence, it struck a pitiless anti-British note: Tevye at one point claiming that 'the English have put a fence round the Holy Land. But there are three things they cannot keep out – the wind, the rain and a Jew.' And, in an arresting

symmetry that was bound to appeal to the American ethos, *A Flag* . . .
bracketed the American revolutionaries of colonial America in the
1770s, battling the British despot, with the Jewish resistance movement
in Palestine, conjuring up Thomas Jefferson's memorable phrase,
'Resistance to tyranny is obedience to God'. Just to emphasise the
point, the programme booklet for the show featured an illustration of
three young Jews, one with a gun, one with a hoe and one bearing the
Zionist flag, parading against the background of three figures from
the American revolution playing the familiar drums and fife. The
analogy resonated.

At the end of the opening night, Hecht stepped onstage to appeal for
donations: 'Give us your money and we will turn it into history',
meaning that 'history' would eventually rule in favour of Jewish
statehood. The play ran for a full ten weeks, 120 performances. It then
went on to tour six North American cities – Washington, Detroit,
Philadelphia, Baltimore, Chicago and Boston – and raised more than
$400,000 (some estimates put the sum at one million dollars) for its
producers, the money financing pro-Zionist causes.

Most American reviews were generous. *Life* magazine reported that
it served with 'wit and wisdom an uninterrupted 105-minute mixture of
bitter attacks on rich and powerful Jews, on world diplomats in the
U.S., Russia and, with greatest malice, England'. The London *Evening
Standard* replied in kind, inveighing against 'A Flag . . . as the most
virulent anti-British play ever staged in the United States'. Concerned
British consular officials in New York reported back to London that
large crowds were flocking to Hecht's play, soaking up its anti-British
message. Worse was to follow. Later, in the wake of a daring rescue
raid on Acre prison by the *Irgun*, Hecht wrote a 'Letter to the Terrorists
of Palestine'. It read:

> The Jews of America are for you. You are their champions. You are the
> grin they wear. You are the feather in their hats. In the past 1,500 years
> every nation in Europe has taken a crack at the Jews. This time the
> British are at bat . . . Every time you blow up a British arsenal, or wreck
> a British jail, or send a British railroad train sky high, or rob a British
> bank, or let go with your guns and bombs at British betrayers and
> invaders of your homeland, the Jews of America make a little holiday in
> their hearts.

Quoted on the front page of the *New York Times*, it was circulated widely in many other publications. The British government was outraged. In a vigorous protest, it described Hecht's letter as thoroughly 'disgusting' and as plain incitement to murder British officials and soldiers. It was quite 'intolerable', it said, that such pernicious agitprop should appear in the press of a friendly country. Bevin exhorted the Truman administration to take 'effective measures' to ensure there would be no repeat of these Hecht-style calumnies.[28]

Hecht's unbridled criticism of British policies in Palestine, and his open encouragement of the most extreme of Jewish militants, led to his credits – he had been nominated six times for an Academy Award, winning twice – being removed from all his films shown in England for some years. On the other hand an *Irgun* ship running 'illegals' and arms was named *Ben Hecht*.

The guiding hand behind *A Flag* . . ., by any reckoning a barefaced piece of anti-British propaganda, was one Hillel Kook, (aka Peter Bergson), a prominent *Irgun* activist. Persuasive, inventive, with a wide range of influential contacts, keyed-in to wide (headstrong) circles among American Jewry, he set up the 'American League for a Free Palestine' (ALFP), among other committees.* Such were his connections that he conscripted to his ventures many noteworthy political, judicial, cultural and show-business celebrities – Eleanor Roosevelt, Leonard Bernstein, New York City Mayor William O'Dwyer, Bob Hope, Jimmy Durante, Groucho and Harpo Marx, Paul Robeson, Frank Sinatra, among others – high-profile names that lent added punch to his propaganda campaigns.

The responses to Kook's initiatives, aided skilfully by Hecht, were interpreted, rightly, by the British government as an extreme manifestation of the growing militancy of American Jewry, feelings that also touched wider sections of American society. One such indication occurred during Bevin's November 1946 visit to the United States, when New York dockers defiantly refused to handle his luggage; and later, at a football game, the British Foreign Secretary suffered further loss of face when he was booed by the crowd who

---

*Kook's activities were not well received by the official American Zionist establishment. In particular Rabbi Stephen Wise – an intimate of Presidents Wilson and Roosevelt, and President of the American and World Jewish Congresses – made every effort to protest Kook's uncalled-for projects and to limit the damage they caused to mainstream Zionism.

remembered his comment that the American campaign for 100,000 Jews to be admitted to Palestine 'was proposed from the purest of motives. They did not want too many Jews in New York' – a remark quoted unforgivingly by the media worldwide.[29]

The wave of anti-British feeling in America, feeding off the Palestine issue, was a factor not to be dismissed out of hand in the months leading up to the Congressional and Presidential elections. There were other circumstances, imperial and strategic, that Britain had to take into account when adjusting to the new realities of the post-war world. But Britain, so dependent on American aid and support in these years, also had to calculate how much humiliation, international criticism and tension with the United States it was willing to endure, before it reached the conclusion that holding on to Palestine, thereby alienating the powerful American Jewish lobby, was not worth the cost.

Britain was presented with a stark reminder of this dilemma at the beginning of October 1946. Frustrated by the Democrats' humming and hawing over their Zionist commitments, a newly formed, militantly inclined 'Zionist Actions Committee' (ZAC) ran advertisements in the New York City newspapers: 'We do not seek new promises or new planks. The old ones are good enough. What we ask is that our administration fulfill old promises now.' 'Now' referred to the impending Congressional elections scheduled for 5 November. Other leading Zionists – Stephen Wise – and the ladies of Hadassah (Women's Zionist Organisation), Democrats by conviction, less assertive than the ZAC and unhappy at this brazen attempt to exploit the Jewish vote – were at the same time discreetly petitioning the President to make a favourable announcement regarding partition. Truman hesitated. But he eventually succumbed, his close advisers, Bartley Crum and David Niles, prodded forward by Eliahu Epstein (later, Eilath, Director of the Jewish Agency's office in Washington), pressing him to go ahead.[30] Nor is it surprising that he decided to do so. Although as yet untested as a president, Truman was an experienced politician, having served a long apprenticeship in the Senate. Obviously, he was alert to the potential political clout of American Jewry, particularly in key states such as New York. Equally, he was mindful that lobbying, that ethnic politics, were legitimate and long-standing traditions in American electioneering practice.

On 4 October, in the so-called 'Yom Kippur' speech, Truman elaborated upon the Jewish Agency's proposal to establish 'a viable Jewish state in control of its own immigration and economic policies in an adequate area of Palestine'.[31] He casually mentioned the Morrison–Grady provincial autonomy plan, hoping it could be taken into account in any eventual settlement. But Truman and his advisers must have known perfectly well that Morrison–Grady was a non-starter, having been given short shrift by both Arabs and Jews. Lastly, he proposed 'the immediate issuance of certificates for 100,000 immigrants'. A solution along these lines, Truman held, 'would command the support of public opinion in the United States'. No less controversially, he urged other countries to press the British to sanction more generous immigration quotas for Palestine.

Truman, artlessly, denied his speech was politically motivated. But even the most naive of observers would not have been fooled by his pretence at even-handedness. In effect, Truman had sanctioned his administration's backing for the Jewish Agency's programme, relieving the Zionists of any need to make concessions. *The Times* drew the obvious conclusion: 'Last Thursday's statement from the White House may well compel people in Britain as well as Arab countries to the reluctant conclusion that no solution to the Palestine question will satisfy the President unless it goes the whole way to meet Jewish claims.'[32]

Attlee was certainly not naive. Having been forewarned of Truman's démarche he had tried to block it, pointing out to the President that joint consultations were in progress with the Jewish Agency and that any precipitate move would be likely to wreck them.* Unfazed, Truman went ahead. An incandescent Attlee responded:

---

*Bevin and George Hall had met Weizmann and other Jewish Agency leaders on 1 October. The meeting was conducted in a workmanlike, at times bantering, atmosphere. When told by Rabbi Fishman that Palestine had been given to the Jews by God, Bevin replied that God moved in mysterious ways. In a more serious vein, Bevin made clear that the feeling in Britain was that the 'Jews had declared war'. If no settlement could be reached, the only alternative was for Britain to turn to the United Nations. Meanwhile, he proposed 'a transitional period' on the basis of a bi-national state, though what it would lead to was left hanging in the air. Once again, he refused to accept the view that Jews had no future in Europe. One constructive result of these talks was the release of the Jewish internees at Latrun. More meetings were scheduled. But serious talks did not get under way until the beginning of 1947 (see Bullock, *Bevin*, pp. 303–4).

I have received with great regret your letter refusing even a few hours grace to the Prime Minister of the country which has the actual responsibility for the government of Palestine in order that he might acquaint you with the actual situation and probable results of your action. These may well include the frustration of the patient efforts to achieve a settlement and the loss of more lives in Palestine . . .

In a pointed riposte, Truman chided the mandatory power for neglecting its duties. Concerned with the fate of the DPs in Europe, and their American sympathisers, he felt it only right that on the Jewish Day of Atonement, a day of contemplation, he should remind the world that the main purpose of the British mandate for Palestine was the development of the Jewish National Home, which had no meaning without Jewish immigration and land settlement. Hence, there should be 'immediate and substantial' Jewish immigration: otherwise the refugees in Europe would spend another winter in camps in Germany and Austria without hope for their future.[33]

Not surprisingly, there is no mention in these exchanges of the link between the 'Yom Kippur' declaration and the forthcoming Congressional elections in November, even though the elections were very much on both Truman's and Attlee's minds at the time. Thomas Dewey, the Republican Governor of New York and his party's front runner for presidential candidate, was due to make a major speech to the United Palestine Appeal Fund on 6 October, with the Palestine issue very much on his mind too. He outbid Truman, calling for Jewish immigration not of a 100,000 but 'of several hundreds of thousands'. Other Republicans outbid Dewey, urging that Palestine become a sanctuary 'for millions'.[34] Jewish-Zionist votes were up for sale to the highest bidder. These ploys were entirely transparent. Abba Hillel Silver, Chairman of the American Section of the Jewish Agency and a Republican supporter himself, highly sceptical of Truman's lasting good faith, drew the self-evident conclusions:

The need of the Administration forces it to counteract the widespread resentment and indignation of the Jews of the United States in the face of the Administration's political inaction prompted them to issue this statement. Mr Crum and Mr Niles [Truman's advisers] seemingly persuaded the President to issue the statement as a smart pre-election move.*

The danger now is, of course, that having cashed in on whatever goodwill this statement may have produced among the Jews of America, the White House will be content to let the matter drop – as it has done time and again in the past after similar manoeuvres on the eve of elections.[35]

Unlike British and Arab sources, who attacked Truman's statement, the Jewish Agency welcomed it. Its spokesman – one must assume with a sharp sense of irony – stressed that American policy was funda- mentally bipartisan: it took fully into account both Arab and Jewish viewpoints; and, most crucially, it was not concerned with cornering election dividends.[36] Whatever Truman's motives, and they seem abundantly clear, his desire to secure Jewish votes – surely a politician's prerogative – does not necessarily diminish his genuine concern for the fate of the Jewish refugees in Europe, for which there is abundant evidence.[37] The two are not mutually incompatible.

Attlee and Bevin, maddened by the infuriating American habit of preaching to them how they should behave, about what they should or should not do, had no real cause to complain. It was they who had invited American involvement in the Palestine quagmire in the first place. They, or at least their advisers, should have been aware of the complexities of American voting patterns, of the efficacy of highly sophisticated political lobbies, of the role 'ethnic voting' played in determining the outcome of borderline elections. Surely, the 'Yom Kippur' affair, taken together with the widespread enthusiasm with which *A Flag is Born* was received, must have reinforced the perception in British government circles of the political leverage the Jewish lobby was capable of wielding. Equally, British politicians and officials should have been painfully aware that American foreign

---

*If it was intended as a 'smart pre-election move', it sadly misfired. A largely untried President, Truman's approval rating had sunk to thirty-two per cent, a verdict that influenced the November elections. The results have been termed a 'Republican avalanche'. In New York State the Democrat candidates, the former Governor, Herbert H. Lehman and Senator Mead, were swept away. Nationwide, the Democrats lost twelve Senate seats, losing control of the Senate to the Republicans for the first time since Herbert Hoover's administration in 1928.

policy was undergoing a process of retrenchment from overseas commitments, mainly in Europe, and was not seeking new adventures abroad, particularly in unstable regions. Given these easily available facts, Bevin and Attlee could hardly reproach Truman for choosing to follow an agenda different from their own. In supporting partition and the 100,000, Truman could reasonably claim that he represented American opinion.

Were these British misperceptions the result of faulty intelligence? Or of wishful thinking, a vain hope that the Americans could somehow be inveigled into active participation in resolving the Palestinian impasse? Whatever the explanation, one thing was clear. With the United States opting out of any firm commitment – apart from campaigning for the 100,000 – and the situation in Palestine deteriorating day by day, the prospect of 'scuttle', first whispered in dark corners, assumed for many British policy-makers a distinct, if painful, likelihood.

7

Confrontation

At the beginning of October 1946, in a dusk-to-dawn exercise immediately following Yom Kippur, eleven kibbutzim were established in the Negev. It constituted one of the largest settlement undertakings since the founding of Petach Tikva in 1878, surpassing all previous records of the 'Tower and Stockade' period. It signalled a political decision of major consequence. While not directly linked to Truman's Yom Kippur speech, it relied very much on the President's much-publicised sponsorship of the 100,000 and a partition-style compromise. For the Jewish Agency, it now became urgent to establish facts on the ground as expeditiously as possible, before a political arrangement was agreed upon by the powers.

The scheme, audacious in concept but entailing huge risks, was the brainchild of Levi Shkolnik (later, Eshkol).* Some of his colleagues, nervous that the British would detect and scotch the action, and apprehensive as to how the local Bedouin would react, initially resisted the operation. Eshkol reassured them. The day after Yom Kippur, 5 October, fell on the Jewish Sabbath, another day of rest. The British, Eshkol argued, expected the Jews to abide by their religious commitments on such holy days, eschewing all physical activity. To this dubious assertion he added another: British soldiers and police would be recovering from – or still participating in – weekend binges, rendering them incapable of reacting. Whatever the reason, the operation

---

*At the time Eshkol acted as Director of Mekoroth Water Company, served on the Land Settlement Department of the Jewish Agency and was in charge of the Finance Department of the *Haganah*. A powerful figure in Israel's major party, Mapai, and renowned for his ironic (Yiddish) comments, he served as Israel's Minister of Finance, 1952–63, when he was appointed Prime Minister, a post he held until his death six years later.

proceeded smoothly, without interference from the authorities. When they woke up, the British faced a fait accompli.

Responsibility for drawing up the details of the project was handed over to a senior officer of the *Haganah*, Joseph Rochel (later, General Joseph Avidar). Under cover of darkness 300 trucks loaded with equipment and over a thousand *chalutzim* (pioneers) set out from six bases. By morning, the foundations of eleven kibbutzim – Kidma, Galon, T'kuma, Be'eri, Kfar Menachem, Shuval, Mishmar HaNegev, Orim, Nirim, Chatzerim and Nevatim – had been secured. 'These eleven settlements', trumpeted the *Palestine Post*, 'will revive the desert and provide a haven for refugees.'[1]

The scale of this enterprise, the logistics involved, the resoluteness of the *chalutzim*, the speed and efficiency with which it was carried out, clandestinely with no improper leaks, left an indelible impression upon outside observers, both political and military. It was, they concluded, a striking demonstration of the strength of character and of the organisational power of the elected bodies of the *Yishuv*, of the Jewish Agency – including its appendage, the *Haganah* – and the *Va'ad Leumi*, bodies that were supported by an overwhelming majority of Palestinian Jews.

It has become a well-worn cliché to classify the Jewish Agency as 'a state within a state', controlling its own cabinet, ministries, budget and army. Like most clichés it contains more than a grain of truth. Expressions like 'a state within a state', a 'genuine resistance move-ment', or the *Haganah* commands the backing of 'every adult Jew, male or female, capable of bearing arms' began to enter the common discourse. Drawing on two pertinent examples from recent British history, Richard Crossman reminded the House of Commons that 'as in Ireland and with the Boers in South Africa and as we shall find in this case . . . we are fighting against a people's natural rights' for national liberation: 'it is impossible', he went on, 'to crush a resistance move-ment which has the passive toleration of the mass of the population'. Some British policy-makers, perhaps even a majority, including Bevin, realised that the *Yishuv* could not be browbeaten into obedience. Nor could Britain continue to maintain indefinitely its current obligations in Palestine, a continuous drain in blood and money on its dwindling resources, its reputation under unremitting fire from a generally hostile world public opinion, particularly where it counted most, in the United States. Cunningham had spoken of 'scuttle'. Others began to air the same notion, though less bluntly.[2]

If in some British political circles judgements about the Jewish Agency–*Haganah* were being revised, to encourage its so-called moderate elements, the same was also true of some military thinking. Even Barker – to say nothing of D'Arcy and Cunningham – had discovered that the *Haganah* possessed some positive qualities. The same could not be said for their attitude towards the dissident groups, the *Irgun* and the Stern Gang. Both factions flaunted a casual disregard for human life, in particular the Sternists. Their record spoke for itself. In July 1938 the *Irgun* planted bombs in Arab market places in Haifa and Jerusalem, exacting heavy civilian casualties. During the war the Stern Gang, defying all rational calculation, flirted with the Axis powers: its proclaimed doctrine of 'personal assassination' as a political tool, as the ultimate sanction to coerce the occupying power into submission, culminated in the execution of Lord Moyne in November 1944 (and later of Count Folke Bernadotte, the United Nations mediator, in September 1948). In February 1944 Begin called for a revolt against the British tyrants. 'Our people is at war with this regime,' he proclaimed, 'war to the end . . . There will be no retreat. Freedom – or death.' For the *Irgun* the British regime, bereft of any 'moral basis whatsoever for its presence in *Eretz Israel*', had shamefully betrayed the Jewish people in its hour of greatest need. 'This, then, is our demand: immediate transfer of power in *Eretz Israel* to a Provisional Hebrew Government.'[3] Begin's call was the signal for his followers to engage the British 'illegal' occupiers in a continuous round of offensive actions. These patterns of behaviour extended well into the post-war years.

On 23 April 1946 the *Irgun* attacked the police station at Ramat Gan, killing a policeman and suffering a fatality themselves. One Dov Gruner – a name that would later attract many headlines – was seriously wounded and captured. Two days later, the Stern Gang attacked a 6th Airborne Division camp on Tel Aviv's seafront. Seven unarmed soldiers were shot down. The raiders carried off their booty: twelve rifles. 'It wasn't a fight, it was murder,' recorded Major-General James Cassell, the divisional commander. There was talk of retaliation. Nothing happened in Tel Aviv; but elsewhere, at Netanya and Be'er Tuvia, soldiers went on the rampage, wrecking property and injuring two settlers. On 17 June the Stern Gang raided the railway workshop in Haifa, causing some damage. But the assault turned sour for the raiders. Army roadblocks caught them making their escape, killing seven, wounding seven more and capturing twenty-six others.

The following day twelve *Irgun* militants entered the officers' club on HaYarkon Street, Tel Aviv, and kidnapped five officers – including an RAF flight lieutenant – while at lunch. Concurrently, botched attempts at further kidnappings were made in Jerusalem. It was intended that the captured officers be held as hostages to obtain the release of two *Irgun* men apprehended earlier during a raid on Sarafand army base and sentenced to death, sentences yet to be confirmed. Cunningham feared for the lives of his officers. Pessimistic about rescuing them, he was conscious of the serious effect that losing them would have on the morale of his troops. In what amounted to a knee-jerk reaction, he suggested suspending any further discussions on the 100,000, and taking drastic action against the 'Agency and illegal organisations', propositions eagerly supported by a bullish Field Marshal Montgomery. The Jewish Agency-*Haganah* distanced themselves from the kidnappings – a proscribed act in their view that stained the ethics of a genuine national struggle. After intervening with the British, they were given an undertaking that the death sentences would be commuted. Four days later the British officers were released, three of them dumped in a crate outside the officers' club in Tel Aviv. 'Most undignified,' remarked one of their fellow officers.[5]*

Between May 1945 and April 1947, British intelligence sources estimated that casualties suffered by the security forces – the army and Palestine Police – as a result of terrorist outrages stood at 103 killed and 391 wounded. The 6th Airborne Division, which bore the brunt of the fight against 'the illegal Jewish armed organisations', calculated its losses over a shorter period – November 1945–June 1946 – at eighteen officers and men killed and 101 wounded; the Palestine Police sustained proportionate casualties. Damage to property was put at approximately £4,000,000. Every means, the paratroopers' account went on,

*These actions of the *Irgun* and the Stern Gang were carried out within the framework of the URM. But they differed in kind from those of the *Haganah–Palmach*, as can be seen in the installations targeted on the 'Night of the Bridges' (see 'Black Sabbath', p. 104).

was tested to bring the extremists under control, 'but the situation far from improving, had in fact worsened'.[6] On 22 July the *Irgun* blew up the King David Hotel, with appalling casualties.

With the break-up of the URM, its constituent elements pursued their own preferred aims in their own characteristic way. First priority for the Jewish Agency and its attendant bodies, the *Haganah* and *Palmach*, was to ensure that the maximum number of so-called 'illegal' immigrants found a secure sanctuary in the *Yishuv*. In a spectacular incursion in October 1945, the *Palmach* infiltrated the Athlit detention camp and rescued over 200 'illegals': it would be the last operation of its kind. But in view of the recent British decision to 'export' 'illegals' to camps in Cyprus, rescuing them became more than ever a national interest. Evading the British blockade, finding and safeguarding suitable disembarkation beaches sometimes involved attacking military targets such as radar stations, or waylaying troops on their way to stymie a landing. When the occasion demanded it, violence was not ruled out. Casualties were inevitable. Fierce resistance to the deportation to Cyprus of almost 4,000 refugees entombed in the *Knesset Israel* resulted in two Jewish fatalities and many wounded, including thirty British soldiers. Land settlement was also high on the list of priorities, an exercise in defining the future borders of the Jewish state. Between February 1940, when the Land Regulations of the May White Paper became operative, and May 1948, the month the state of Israel was established, seventy new kibbutzim were founded, together with twenty other rural communities.[7]

The dissident groups also went their own way, employing the same tactics as before. Throughout the autumn months of 1946 incidents were recorded of sabotage, arson, bank robberies, sniping, the mining of roads and bridges, attacks on the railway network, even local business people being 'persuaded' to contribute to the cause.[8] At the end of October an *Irgun* unit bungled an attempt to blow up the main railway station in Jerusalem. An ex-*Irgun* informer leaked the plan to the authorities. The police lay in wait and opened fire on the attackers, wounding several and capturing four. One constable was killed when the booby-trapped suitcase he was carrying exploded. In mid-November the *Irgun* blew up the central income tax office in Jerusalem.

Then, in December, two *Irgun* teenagers, Kimche and Katz, captured during a bank hold-up in Jaffa, were sentenced to eighteen strokes of the cat and eighteen years' imprisonment. The *Irgun* circulated a notice condemning this 'humiliating' punishment meted out by 'an illegal British military court', warning that retaliation in kind would follow should the sentence be carried out. It was: on 27 December Kimche was lashed. Two days later a major and three sergeants were kidnapped and flogged. What was all the fuss about, a bemused Cunningham asked members of the *Va'ad Leumi*? As a boy he had frequently been caned at school. 'One shouldn't take these things so seriously,' he counselled.[9] His administration did, however. An amnesty was declared for seventeen prisoners, including Katz. It was a humiliating climbdown for the Palestine government. The whip was never again used in mandatory Palestine.

On 27 January 1947 a district court judge, Sir Ralph Windham, was conducting 'a rather boring case' in his court in Tel Aviv when he was seized by an *Irgun* squad, hustled out of the building and frog-marched, still wearing his wig and gown, into a waiting car and driven into captivity. Windham was being held – together with a retired major, H. A. Collins – as hostage for the life of Dov Gruner, sentenced to be hanged on 28 January. He was treated well. Windham's aristocratic pedigree, a trump card, or so it was believed, in bargaining with the government, appealed also to Begin's overdeveloped sense of etiquette. Of his captors, Windham later recalled, 'We were quite friendly with each other.' They conversed in halting German. To pass the time, he was presented with a copy of Koestler's *Thieves in the Night*. Alternatively, his jailers would whistle themes from Beethoven's violin concerto, 'which I identified . . . they were very pleasant because I appreciated music, as they did . . . they were very musical'. Altogether it sounds like a rather jolly interlude after his 'rather boring' trial. Only hours after Windham's abduction the authorities decided to suspend Gruner's execution. Having achieved their immediate aim, Windham was set free on the outskirts of Tel Aviv. Collins was also released. Gruner's fate was less fortunate: he was hanged at Acre prison on 16 April, together with three others.[10]

The *Irgun* and Stern Gang did not confine their anti-British operations to Palestine. Headed by Eli Tavin (aka 'Pesach'), the *Irgun* set up a

European network based in Rome and Paris. It sited the British embassy in Rome as a prime target. On 31 October 1946 two loaded valises were smuggled into the embassy. The resulting explosion wrecked much of its lower floors. In Vienna the legendary Sacher Hotel, that served as British army headquarters and an officers' club, was bombed: only light casualties were reported; while in Graz, *Irgun* activity was also noticed.[11] Britain took note. Panic-stricken banner headlines, 'Irgun Threatens London', screamed at Londoners. Rumours circulated of public buildings selected for destruction and of an *Irgun* hit list headed by Sir John Shaw, the former Colonial Secretary, George Hall and Montgomery. Cabinet ministers were allotted special guards and troops were put on stand-by orders. Security checks at airports and ports were beefed up. In fact, there was no real threat: it was a pertinent example of press hysteria and frayed nerves.

Later, there would be more cause for concern. While on service in Palestine, General Sir Evelyn Barker, a favourite target of the *Irgun*, had escaped a number of assassination attempts. Barker was now back in Britain. In April 1947 the *Irgun* tried again: once more, without success. By one of history's curiosities one of the *Irgun* operatives was a former Royal Air Force pilot, Ezer Weizmann (later General Weizmann, Commander-in-Chief of the Israeli air force and subsequently the seventh President of Israel), the twenty-three-year-old nephew of Chaim. The police soon picked up the hit squad's trail, arresting and deporting its leaders. 'Be so kind as to return to Palestine,' the police advised Ezer. Often undone by his impulsive nature, Ezer now acted judiciously and quietly left the country. Soon after this fiasco the *Irgun* closed down its operations in Britain.[12]

The main threat to British targets, however, would come from the Stern Gang. Ya'akov (Yoshka) Eliav, impatient to open, as he put it, a 'Second Front', ran the Gang's network in Europe. Based in Paris, he procured arms and explosives with funds raised from local sympathetic sources. Some intellectuals rallied to his support, including, so he claimed, Jean-Paul Sartre. Scientists too were among his contacts, in particular bacteriologists based at the Pasteur Institute. His monthly bulletin, *L'Endependence* (sic), an agitprop newsletter, promulgated the Gang's world outlook. Attempts to coordinate with the French government an anti-British campaign failed miserably. Eliav naively believed that he could exploit French resentment at their being kicked out of Lebanon and Syria by the British. However, on 28 August 1946 Alfred Duff Cooper, the British ambassador in Paris, recorded in his diary: 'The Jews have threatened, anonymously on the telephone, to blow up the Embassy, so that we are now surrounded by policemen and detectives.' Three months later the situation had not improved: 'All getting rather worried about the threats of the Stern Gang and say I must have a guard in the front of my car. How a man sitting in the front seat of a car can prevent another man from throwing a bomb at it I cannot understand.' To protect his embassy, his security experts advised Duff Cooper 'to put a barbed-wire fence across the middle of the garden to keep the Stern Gang out'. The ambassador was not impressed: 'I never heard such nonsense.' Duff Cooper and his embassy survived intact.[13]

Eliav turned his attention to London. Letter bombs were sent to the War Office – Barker once again the target – and the Colonial Office: the first exploded causing minor damage, the second was successfully dismantled. Still, the colourful press reports only added to the general public's concern for their safety. Special guards were placed at London's railway termini and underground stations. In late April an explosion rocked a gentlemen's club near St Martin-in-the-Fields church, London. Frequented by the staff of the Colonial Office, one survivor attested: 'The room shook, lights went out and I felt the debris falling all round me.' A number of casualties were recorded, but no fatalities. Additional letter bombs, almost sixty in number, addressed to high-ranking government officials and Cabinet ministers, Sir Stafford Cripps and Sir John Shaw among them, were produced. To bamboozle the British authorities they were sent from various locations in and around Turin and Brussels. By now Eliav was based in Brussels from where he planned to sabotage a British destroyer anchoring off the Belgian coast and to blow up the British embassy in Brussels. All these schemes came to nothing. Picked up by Belgian security agents, he was grilled by them with a Scotland Yard anti-terrorist expert in attendance. As a result, the letter bomb plot was also foiled: none exploded. For his pains, Eliav received a short jail sentence.

On his release, and towards the end of his stay in Europe, Eliav began to think of more unconventional methods of forcing the British to their knees. In fact, he devised the most diabolical of schemes: to infect London's water supply with active cultures of cholera bacteria. For this purpose he exploited his contacts at the Pasteur Institute, among them some Holocaust survivors, and 1,000 concentrated cultures were prepared. An emissary, a Parisian water engineer, was sent to London to discover where its water reservoirs were located and how best to pollute them to induce a mass cholera epidemic. Others, those who would actually execute the outrage, were briefed and equipped with detailed maps of London showing the locations of the main water supplies. The plot hung fire. By the winter of 1947 it was called off, the United Nations decision to partition Palestine – together with the earlier British ruling to evacuate the country – rendering it defunct. The Stern Gang wound down its activities in Europe. As for Eliav, he returned to Palestine to press on with his crusade.[14]

Towards the middle of January 1947 armed camps began to appear in strategic locations in the main towns of Palestine. Enclosed by barbed-wire fences and heavily fortified, they were intended to provide greater security for the armed forces. Dubbed by the locals as 'Bevingrads', it reminded many of those it was meant to protect of a 'Concentration Camp'. Here we are, grumbled Rex Keating, Deputy Director of the Palestine Broadcasting Service, 'confined to a small uneasily fortified area, going home only to sleep. Not allowed to move except on official business – and then only with heavily armed escorts.'[15] The main 'security zone' in Jerusalem centred on the 'Russian Compound' in downtown Jerusalem and included the Anglo-Palestine Bank and the central Post Office: others were located at the upmarket residential quarters, Talbieh and Rehavia, along sections of King George Street, a main thoroughfare, and the area surrounding the Schneller army barracks. Local people – mainly, but not only, Jews – were 'asked' to evacuate their shops and offices, without compensation. Those who wished to enter the 'Bevingrads' for whatever reason were required to show proof of identity, often after body searches were carried out. For the soldiers, police and officials, places of entertainment – which were all outside the security zones – were now strictly out of bounds. Fraternization with the civilian population gradually dwindled, though social contacts between the parties did not die out entirely. In the name of sound government official contacts between the administration and representatives of the Palestinians, both Jews and Arabs, continued. A conscious choice had been made to segregate as far as possible two communities: the ruled and their confused rulers.

A further step along this road was taken on 31 January when it was announced that British women and children, together with other 'non-essential' British nationals, were to be evacuated from Palestine. 'Operation Polly' – immediately reinterpreted by army families as 'Panic Over Lots of Lousy Yids' – was put into practice. David Tomlinson, an impressionable teenager at the time, recalled the 'mini convoy', escorted by 'lorry loads' of military police, that was drawn up on the parade ground of the Allenby Barracks in Jerusalem for their conveyance. Awarded a warm send-off by 'the band of the Black Watch playing the Skye Boat Song', the convoy made its way down the Judaean hills and along the winding valley road that led to the vast army base at Sarafand where they joined 2,000 other displaced persons. From there they travelled by train to Cairo, a tiresome twenty-four-hour journey. Eventually they were billeted in a tented camp by the Suez Canal. Guarded exclusively by German POWs, the 'Polly-style' waifs were treated to kibbutz-style communal eating and schooling. After five months of a collective lifestyle, they were shipped out on a White Star liner, the *Circassia*, 'literally packed to the gunwales', that docked at Liverpool in July. David and his family ended up in a guest house in Abingdon, near Oxford, their next door neighbour, one Klaus Fuchs, the notorious atom bomb spy.[16]

One of the severest winters ever recorded in England awaited the evacuees from 'Operation Polly'. 'Annus Horrendus', one observer called it.[17] Heavy snowdrifts, freezing temperatures, floods, thick fogs, icy roads crippled the national transport system. An acute shortage of coal and electricity supplies obliged the government to impose strict rationing for domestic and industrial use: factories were put on shift work, or on a shortened week; households spent their evenings by candlelight, well wrapped up against the biting cold. In February, the crisis month, unemployment peaked to 2.3 million, or fifteen and a half per cent of the insured workforce. There were those who didn't hesitate to relate the crisis to the struggle for Palestine. 'Stories of spreading floods all over the country,' recorded 'Baffy' Dugdale. 'The blizzard has moved North. Ghastly destruction of livestock, especially sheep, is being revealed. This poor country is undergoing afflictions like the Ten Plagues. Could the reason be the same?' she speculated. 'Too fantastic an idea to utter!' But she did: 'Let My People Go.' Ernest Bevin, indulging his taste for black humour, put it another way: 'All the lights have gone out except the Israelites.'[18]

After the Morrison–Grady plan was shelved, Britain was left with little room for manoeuvre. There would be other plans, variations on the same theme, but they would all amount to nothing. The choices were depressing: the British government could either negotiate on Arab terms, a position that would not only alienate the White House and American public opinion, but also lead to a full-scale revolt in the *Yishuv*; or it could agree to partition, to establish a Jewish state in a viable area of Palestine, thereby inflaming Arab and Moslem opinion and endangering Britain's imperial-strategic posture in the Middle East and India. Given this Hobson's choice, the only practicable option appeared to be to hold firm and urge concessions on both sides, not the most promising of outlooks. But for how long would this holding action be respected? The less charitable might say that this course of inaction was very much in keeping with the (assumed) traditional British way of muddling through in the hope that something constructive might materialise. A Micawber-like prescription.

February 1947 also proved to be a crisis month in Britain's imperial affairs. Revolutionary decisions would be made that would dramatically shift the balance of her worldwide strategic standing. India, Palestine, Britain's role in combating the Soviet threat in Europe and the eastern Mediterranean, her relations with the United States, all would be reviewed, not in isolation, but as overlapping parts of a remodelled design commensurate with Britain's rapidly shrinking resources and, inevitably, reduced role in world affairs.

India would be the key. Since the 1920s successive government commissions of inquiry and Cabinet committees had recommended degrees of greater autonomy for India, with the prospect of fully fledged independence at some time in the future. A major step was taken in August 1935 when the Commons ratified the Government of India Act. As in so much else, the war proved to be a catalyst also for the question of India. In 1942 far-reaching proposals were tabled. These new measures envisaged complete independence for India after the war; acknowledged India's right as a dominion to secede from the Commonwealth; and provided safeguards for the principalities and the dissident, that is Muslim, provinces to remain outside the new Indian state. In effect, the principle of the partition of the subcontinent into a Hindu Indian state and a Muslim Pakistan was recognised.[19] These were the most radical of notions, and the idea of partition as a solution to seemingly insoluble communal conflicts would crop up again.

This was Labour's inheritance. Attlee's government was firm in its resolve to discharge its obligations, to fulfil what had become a recognised fact in British politics. In a series of statements he made clear his intentions 'to help India attain that freedom as speedily and fully as possible'. On 20 February 1947 Attlee informed the House of Commons that 'it is our definite intention to take the necessary steps to effect the transference of power into responsible Indian hands not later than June 1948'.[20] As it happened events outran Attlee's statement. Religious and racial violence soon flared up, leading to ethnic cleansing and a refugee crisis on a scale without precedent in the history of the British Empire. On 15 August 1947 India and the Islamic state of Pakistan gained their independence.

Two days before Attlee's statement, on 18 February 1947, Bevin told the House that 'the only course now open to us is to submit the [Palestine] problem to the United Nations'. All attempts at reaching a compromise formula had broken down: the AAC proposals; the Morrison–Grady scheme; the abortive London discussions in the autumn. The last chance of a negotiated settlement occurred during a February conference, parallel 'unofficial' talks that the government conducted with the Arabs and Jews. As a last-ditch compromise, the so-called 'Bevin plan' was put to both sides. It called for a five-year trusteeship under the UN, a period intended to prepare Palestine for independence as a bi-national state. Jewish and Arab cantons, not necessarily contiguous and with restricted powers of self-government, were envisaged. Central government powers were to be equally shared. Finally, 96,000 Jewish immigrants were to be admitted in the course of two years. Both sides rejected this trade-off: the Arabs would not agree to any form of Jewish self-government or of increased immigration; the Jews would not agree to any plan that did not include a Jewish state. Weizmann, when he heard of it, rejected it as 'absurd and unpractical'. An oft-neglected provision of Bevin's plan made plain that if the two parties were unable to reach an agreement, the problem would be turned over to the United Nations. And this was precisely the import of Bevin's statement to the House on 18 February, which, for a change, benefited from across-the-board parliamentary backing. Only six months earlier, the Leader of the Opposition, Winston Churchill, had urged the government 'to lay the mandate at the feet of the United Nations'.[21]

Most Jews and Arabs, and many other commentators, thought the referral to the United Nations a crafty ruse, yet another example of that old bogeyman, Perfidious Albion, up to his tricks again. Britain had calculated, so the sceptics assumed, that the discussions at the UN would end in a deadlock, thereby compelling that body to request Britain to reassume its mandatory obligations. In this way, Britain would return to Palestine through the back door of the United Nations, thereby re-establishing its imperial standing. No evidence has yet come to light to support this conspiracy theory. But there were many who were willing to lend it credence. The Palestinian Arabs, still in thrall to the discredited Husayni leadership, had always suspected Britain of ulterior motives. The Zionists too were uneasy regarding British intentions. A new, more militant leadership, Ben Gurion and the hard-line Rabbi Abba Hillel Silver, had been voted into office; Weizmann, the moderate, tainted with a pro-British orientation, had been shunted aside, and was now living, semi-retired, in Rehovoth. The British were not being allowed the benefit of any doubt.

For all the suspicions of the interested parties, the British decision to settle for the UN option was entirely genuine, part of a wider pattern. Between 14 and 20 February 1947 Britain announced that it would not only withdraw from Palestine and India, but that it would also not renew aid to Greece and Turkey. There was talk of taking over the mandate for Cyrenaica, claiming that a British military presence there would cancel out the need to remain in Egypt and Palestine. Attlee and Bevin wanted to strike a bargain with the Russians to allow this. Clearly, wide-ranging strategic rearrangements in the eastern Mediterranean were in the air, and had been for some time. In March 1946, Hugh Dalton recorded in his diary:

Attlee is pressing on the Chiefs of Staff and the Defence Committee a large view of his own, aiming at considerable disengagement from areas where there is a risk of clashing with the Russians. We should pull out, he thinks, from all the Middle East, including Egypt and Greece, make a line of defence across Africa from Lagos to Kenya, and concentrate a large part of our forces in the latter. The Middle East position is only an outpost position. I am beginning to doubt whether the Greek game is worth the candle.

Bevin did not demur from Attlee's initiative. He concurred 'that the real line of the Commonwealth runs through Lagos and Kenya'.[22]

Other considerations also prompted the government to reappraise its position in the region, to scale down its direct responsibilities. Since the end of the war, propping up Iran, Greece and Turkey from Soviet encroachment had been a British prerogative. Greece in particular was an exacting burden on Britain's dwindling resources, tying down tens of thousands of troops, eating into what remained of its economic assets, all in an attempt to save Greece from a Communist takeover. Not surprisingly, Britain was anxious to rid itself of this financial and military liability. From the late autumn of 1945 the question of economic aid to Greece had been on the Anglo-American agenda. These talks picked up in the autumn of 1946, with Turkey now part of a prospective deal. The State Department finally recognised that Britain needed American support in the eastern Mediterranean, a standpoint endorsed by the White House. It may well be that British statements announcing the withdrawal of aid for Greece and Turkey were intended to quicken the American response. In the event, it came quickly enough. On 12 March Truman told a joint session of Congress that 'it must be the policy of the United States to support free peoples who are resisting attempted subjugation by armed minorities or by outside pressures', a policy that would be carried out 'primarily through economic and financial aid'. In its immediate context, the 'Truman Doctrine' clearly applied to Greece and Turkey.[23]

With India gone, a new strategic line to be drawn from Lagos to Kenya, a mandate for Cyrenaica contemplated, ongoing negotiations with Egypt to regulate Britain's position in the Canal Zone and increased American involvement, Britain had earned more elbow room to juggle its resources, obligations and options. On balance, it left Palestine more expendable in British calculations, provided an honourable way out could be devised.

The concept of a Jewish state was frowned upon by those traditional anti-partitionist bodies, the Foreign Office and the Chiefs of Staff, and for the most pragmatic of reasons: partition would alienate the goodwill of the Arab and Muslim world, endangering Britain's imperial-strategic position. But what was the alternative? Attlee and Bevin too would have preferred a unitary state – as in India – but would accept partition – again as in India – *faute de mieux*.* Moreover, there was growing support for partition in the Cabinet, including some heavyweights such as Hugh Dalton, Aneurin Bevan, 'Manny' Shinwell, Creech Jones and John Strachey. On the whole the Parliamentary Labour Party favoured it, as did Cunningham and many of his Palestine colleagues, civilians and generals. By now, partition was also the official line followed by the leaders of the Jewish Agency, although they did not speak about it too loudly in public. The Jewish dissident groups rejected it outright, trumpeting their disapproval throughout the world in word and deed. Did their actions – violent, bloody-minded, headline-grabbing – justify their declared aim to force the British government to abandon the mandate: Bevin's statement being the first stage towards its total withdrawal from Palestine? Set against the wider range of issues already noted, the ruthless measures of these splinter groups, painful and shocking though they were, could only have been marginal considerations. If anything, the government was more unnerved by the actions of the *Haganah–Palmach*, its full complement conservatively estimated at 65,000 (as compared to the *Irgun*, 3,000–5000, and the Stern Gang, 200–300). Regarded by most observers as a 'people's army', it acted under the auspices of the Jewish Agency, for whom that hackneyed expression 'a state within a state' was generally accepted as a truism among British policy-makers. As Sir John Shaw noted, 'you can't rule a country against the will of its people'. Colonel Martin Charteris – serving as a voice for many of his fellow officers – was in no doubt that the Jewish Agency-*Haganah-Palmach*, not the *Irgun* or the Stern Gang, posed the greatest threat to British authority in Palestine. Once neutralised, he held, 'it would be simple to deal with the dissident groups'. Impressed by the fighting efficiency and high morale of the *Haganah* and the *Palmach*, Charteris

---

*At the end of October 1946 Bevin, disillusioned with the Americans, put three choices before the Cabinet, the last of which spoke of the adoption of partition, the Arab part of Palestine to be merged with Transjordan. See Cabinet minutes, 25 October 1946, CAB.128/6, NA, quoted in Cohen, p. 203. See also, p. 126.

was utterly confident that any Arab-Jewish military showdown would end in a Jewish victory.[24]

Despite the clear signs that Britain's Palestine policy was moving towards eventual withdrawal, the dissidents refused to be convinced and remained faithful to their own perverse interpretation of British aims. Their actions continued. On 1 March the *Irgun* launched sixteen separate operations, the most spectacular of which was an assault on the Jerusalem Officers Club at the Goldschmidt House. Located in a 'Bevingrad' opposite the Great (Yeshurun) Synagogue on King George Street, an *Irgun* squad, under cover of machine-gun fire and tossing satchel bombs to clear their path, rushed the building, allowing sappers to place three rucksacks containing thirty kilograms of explosives against the supporting pillars. The resulting explosion left the building in ruins: seventeen officers were killed, twenty-seven injured.

Martial law was imposed on Jerusalem and Tel Aviv. Crippling cordon-and-search operations, code-named 'Elephant' and 'Hippo', paralysed normal life in these two urban centres,[25] but they had little effect on the activities of the *Irgun* and Stern Gang. Further attacks were carried out in Tel Aviv, Jerusalem, Haifa and Rehovoth; in Jerusalem, one operation gutted the heavily guarded Schneller building. Incidents of sniping, arson, land mines, hand grenade attacks were reported throughout mandatory Palestine. On 17 March martial law as well as 'Hippo' and 'Elephant' were cancelled, having produced negligible results. Two weeks later the Stern group bombed the Haifa oil refineries. Towering sheets of flame shot up into the air, while black clouds of smoke blanketed the city. It took almost three weeks to bring the raging blaze under control. Churchill spoke for many when he asked the House how long this 'senseless, squalid war with the Jews in order to give Palestine to the Arabs, or God knows who' will continue. He advised the government to pursue the UN option as expeditiously as possible.[26]

In Palestine the ultimate penalty, the gallows, was readopted to counter the upsurge in terrorist activity. At a security conference on 11 April Cunningham sanctioned four hangings, together with plans designed to foil any retaliatory kidnappings by the *Irgun* or Stern Gang: 'they should make the dissidents go off at half-cock,' he confidently asserted. Five days later Dov Gruner and three of his comrades were hanged at Acre prison. Since his imprisonment Gruner had become something of a *cause célèbre*. The streets of London and New York were strewn with the slogan 'Save Dov Gruner'. One story has Gruner reprimanding another condemned man who was brought into his cell, and who ordered a warder, in an off-hand manner, to 'get me a glass of water'. 'Look here,' said Gruner, 'when you speak to a British warder, call him "Sir", and I'll have you know that I'm the senior inmate here.'[27]

Ben Hecht responded to the hanging in typical style: 'As an American giving alms to Britain, I would like to know how much Dov Gruner's gallows cost.' In a chilling warning to the British authorities, so too did the *Irgun*:

> Our war of liberation shall continue in all its fields of activity . . . We will no longer be bound by the normal rules of warfare. War courts would accompany every combat unit of the Jewish Underground Movement. Every enemy subject who is taken prisoner will be immediately brought before the court, irrespective of whether he is member of the Army or Civil Administration. Both are criminal organisations . . . there will be no appeal against the decision of the people's court. Those condemned will be hanged or shot.

There were no 'enemy subjects' to save Meir Feinstein (*Irgun*) and Moshe Barazani (Stern Gang), due to be hanged in Jerusalem on 21 April. Sooner than go to the gallows they chose a Samson-like gesture, blowing themselves up with hand grenades concealed inside oranges.[28]

Two weeks later a number of dissidents, masquerading as British army personnel, mounted a spectacular assault on Acre prison, breaching the walls of the fortress. Explosives, smuggled earlier into the prison, were set off by their comrades, adding to the confusion. In the ensuing chaos, 214 Arab convicts escaped – many of whom were later recaptured – together with 29 *Irgun* and Stern Gang prisoners. In its daring and execution, it was a headline-catching operation. As one commentator saw it: 'An underground Jewish army had assaulted an apparently impregnable British citadel in the midst of an Arab city.' It inspired Hecht's notorious 'Letter to the Terrorists of Palestine': 'The Jews of America are for you. You are their champions. You are the grin they wear. You are the feather in their hats . . .' But the underground army paid a heavy price for its triumph. British roadblocks and ambushes killed nine dissidents and arrested eight more. For all that, Cunningham had no alternative but to admit that overall it was 'a bad show'.[29]

So the dissidents' actions continued unabated. Judged reckless and irresponsible by the Jewish Agency, its leaders sought to curb their activities. Ben Gurion broached this prickly question when he met Cunningham: how best to employ, in a circumspect manner, *Haganah* units against the terrorists, making clear it was essential to do so without conveying noticeable cooperation with the official security forces. The first feelers towards this 'mini-*saison*' had been extended in January. After much soul-searching, a special unit of 200 *Haganah* fighters was delegated to act against the dissidents. Passions ran high. They 'hated' the *Irgun* and the Stern Gang, regarding them as no more than 'fascists'. Their orders were precise: 'break bones, yes, but no "hits" '. Blunders were inevitable. An *Irgun* unit, looking for Yehoshua 'Shaika' Gavish, beat up his father and brother instead. Gavish (in time a major-general) sought out the culprits, found them hiding in Rehovoth and exacted retribution. Although some incidents of cooperation between the British and the *Haganah* were recorded, the 'mini-*saison*' soon deteriorated into a depressing sequence of mutual beatings-up and kidnappings. Relations between the Jewish Agency, the *Haganah* and the dissidents, in any case at a low premium, slumped even further.[30]

These never-ending, highly publicised actions of the *Haganah* and the dissidents reflected badly on a British army of some 100,000 personnel who had emerged from the Second World War battle-scarred but victorious. Captain W. C. Brown, to his disgust, found himself in a very different kind of war, waged against illegal immigrants and Jewish insurrectionary movements, 'mainly the *Haganah* who murdered our men whenever they could. Of course we received no help from the Jewish police!' His response was forthright, if nothing else: 'We set up an underground force, and whenever a soldier was killed, we shot one of theirs . . . an eye for an eye.' These military vigilantes were brought to heel only after embarrassing questions were asked in Parliament. One contemporary observer, John Watson, writing to his mother, noted the 'rampant anti-Semitism among the British troops in Palestine who seem to get a dreadfully Deutsch kind of Herrenvolk attitude out here . . . British people are becoming anti-Semites – How much more reason have the Jews to be anti-British?' He went on to report about 'the trigger-happy behaviour of some British soldiers which causes civilian deaths and which goes largely unreported'. In a case unique in British military history, Lieutenant Kenneth A. Gourley, an Oxford graduate, was put on a court martial libel charge for allegedly defaming the 6th Airborne Division. He had accused the Division of 'behaving badly', so much so that if known it would cause 'such an outcry'. Gourley called for the Division's removal from Palestine, together with Sir John Shaw and the entire Palestine administration, and for an inquiry to be held 'into their trusteeship'. The results, he confidently asserted, 'will no doubt be more revealing than the Nuremberg trials'. The libel case was dismissed, however; and no inquiry was ever held. As for Lieutenant Gourley, his fate remains unknown.[31]

The subject of the libel case, the 6th Airborne Division, including units serving under its command, suffered 169 fatalities during what it termed the 'insurgency'. Naturally, their angle on the actions of the 'Jewish underground armies' was quite different; as it was for those they were charged with protecting – other British citizens serving in Palestine. Some disturbing comparisons were drawn. Susanna Emery, as a teacher, was concerned for the well-being of her wards, Jewish and Arab. The behaviour of some of her Jewish pupils troubled her. She spoke of 'a crowd of [Jewish] school boys & other very young people, egged on by political agitators'. 'For years,' she went on, 'the minds of the Jewish school children have been poisoned, just as the Hitler youth were poisoned, with ideas just like those of the Hitler youth, only directed in this case against the British.'* Utter ruthlessness was another trait attributed to the 'insurgents', especially to the dissidents, who 'will stick at nothing' to attain their ill-conceived aims. These 'terrorists', pitched in Emery, are 'mostly gangsters', and are not 'driven by the suffering of their people in Europe'.[32]

Colonel C. R. W. Norman, Head of Military Intelligence in Palestine from October 1946 to July 1948, didn't mince his words, either on paper

---

*Emery's harsh criticism was levelled at the Zionist youth movements. An iron discipline was indeed imposed upon its members, but their main aims – at least for those movements obedient to the Palestine (Jewish) Labour movement – were to demonstrate against the May White Paper, to engage in land settlement and to bring in 'illegals'.

in a detailed memorandum or in a lecture he gave to his fellow officers, raking up raw memories from the Second World War. The Jews, he said, like the Germans, are 'very easily susceptible to mass hysteria', making clear that he regarded 'bestial hysteria' as 'really disgusting'. Like the Nazis, Norman decided, the Jews 'will go to any lengths to achieve a Jewish majority in Palestine'. The *Irgun*, he ruled, 'is organised on lines similar to Nazi organisations', equating its fighters with 'storm troopers', and *Betar* (the Revisionist youth movement) with 'the Hitler Jugend'. As for the Stern Gang, according to Norman it was 'essentially an assassin group', its members 'born criminals . . . the lowest types of humanity . . . though among [its] leaders there is a proportion of intellectual fanatics'. Nor did Norman spare another of his adversaries. Turning on the Mufti, 'a thoroughly disagreeable person', who would brook no argument and 'bumped off' those that dared to disagree with him. 'No one trusts him,' Norman concluded, 'not even the Arab states or his own henchmen.'

The *Haganah* and *Palmach* fared far better in the Colonel's survey. 'Well armed' and 'well organised', the average Palestinian Jew regarded

the *Haganah* as being the first really Jewish army and takes an inordinate pride in the fact . . . It is considered that 99% of the population are behind the *Haganah* in their efforts to bring immigrants to Palestine . . . In addition to its normal role of settlement protection and illegal immigration, the *Haganah* has tried with some measure of success to suppress the *Irgun* and Stern Gang, considering them with their gangster methods of extortion and assassination to be enemies of the Jewish people . . . some of their actions have prevented serious loss of life amongst the security forces.[33]

Norman was at a loss to propose a military solution to quell the insurgency. To judge from his comments, all he could offer was a holding action until something better turned up. Like many senior officers, he too reflected upon various political outcomes. Relying on his vast experience of local conditions, he dismissed talk of Britain retaining the mandate: employing an unfortunate phrase, he argued it couldn't be 'anything more than a temporary measure to a final solution'. What of a bi-national state? 'A utopian dream', he cautioned. Only 'partition' would provide an answer, not a perfect one, but in the prevailing circumstance the best of a series of bad alternatives. In fact, a political door had opened, slightly. Bevin had kept his promise 'to submit the [Palestine] problem to the United Nations'. On 28 April, at an extraordinary session of the General Assembly at Lake Success, a United Nations Special Committee on Palestine (UNSCOP) was set up. Entrusted with investigating the Palestine problem, it was ordered to report back to the General Assembly with a practical proposal for it to consider. On 15 June UNSCOP arrived in Palestine to begin its inquiry.[34]

8

Partition

UNSCOP arrived in Palestine on 15 June, twenty-three delegates representing eleven countries, the Big Five – Britain, the United States, the Soviet Union, France and China – compromised by their Great Power interests, being excluded from its ranks. The Commission spent six weeks in the region before retiring to Geneva to deliberate its report. They toured Palestine, visited the Lebanon and Transjordan, inspected the DP camps in Germany and Austria, held thirteen public hearings, listened to thirty-seven persons giving evidence on behalf of six Arab states and seventeen Jewish organisations, and participated in forty-three private meetings; four subcommittees and three working groups were formed. To cover its proceedings, two hundred correspondents from twenty different countries were accredited to the Committee, ensuring widespread publicity for the ailments that afflicted Palestine. The Colonial Office nicknamed it 'the Travelling Circus'. Its inquiry coincided with two notorious incidents – the '*Exodus*' affair and the hanging of two British sergeants – each equally dramatic in its own way, that shaped – again each in its own distinctive fashion – the political fate of Palestine in the immediate future.

The prospect of yet another commission of inquiry did not inspire great enthusiasm among the interested parties. The Arabs made their position clear. 'UNSCOP arrives,' noted Lloyd Phillips, '& the [Palestine] Arabs, with incredible folly, have decided to boycott the proceedings', apparently content to have their interests hijacked by outside Arab rulers.'[1] The Jews, instinctively wary of commissions of inquiry, swallowed whatever doubts they had, drawing some encouragement from knowing that the Committee was sponsored by the United Nations. But it was Andrei Gromyko's, the Soviet Union's representative at the United Nations, astonishing declaration of 14

May to the General Assembly, that brought them fresh hope. It amounted to something of a political thunderbolt. The Soviets had traditionally adopted an extreme anti-Zionist stand. According to classic Leninist-Stalinist theory, the Jews possessed none of the attributes necessary for genuine nationhood. The Zionist movement was condemned as a reactionary bourgeois institution, a lackey of the imperialist powers, a product of the minds of rootless, cosmopolitan Jews. Yet, considering past Soviet antipathy, here was Gromyko speaking like a born-again Zionist.

Recognising as an 'indisputable fact' the Jewish people's 'historical roots' in Palestine, he acknowledged that 'the aspirations of a considerable part of the Jewish people are associated' with that country. There can be 'no one-sided solution', he warned, that ignores 'the legitimate rights of the Jewish people'. The Holocaust, and the lessons to be drawn from it, played a large part in Gromyko's declaration. 'The Jewish people experienced exceptional calamities and suffering which defy description,' he explained. The fact that

> No single western European state proved capable of ensuring the defence of the elementary rights of the Jewish people, and of protecting it against violence on the part of the Fascist hangman, provides an explanation of the Jewish aspiration to create their own state . . . It would be unfair to . . . deny the right of the Jewish people to satisfaction of this aspiration, especially in view of everything it experienced during the Second World War.

'Almost completely exterminated', the survivors, 'deprived of their homelands, shelter, and means of subsistence . . . kept in DP camps, continue to endure hardships'. The time has come, he lectured the General Assembly, 'to render assistance to these people not by words but by deeds'.

What did Gromyko propose? He rejected a continuation of the 'mandate system', maintaining it had bankrupted itself, leaving Palestine as 'a kind of semi-military and police state'. One possible way out would be to create an 'independent, democratic Arab-Jewish state . . . based on equal rights'. But if it proved 'impracticable' for the two peoples to coexist peacefully in one state – as was clearly the case – Gromyko would accept partition as a legitimate alternative.[2]

The *Yishuv* received Gromyko's statement 'with a joy that required a conscious effort to moderate it'. To British officials it was baffling. To the Arabs it was an undeniable blow. Moshe Shertok called it 'the most revolutionary change in the political status of Zionism and of the Jewish people since the Balfour Declaration'. An 'extraordinary windfall', remarked Abba Eban, the Jewish Agency's liaison officer to the Committee, conscious that the Soviet volte-face shifted the balance of forces in the United Nations in favour of partition.* Partition was now formal Jewish Agency policy. Eban and David Horowitz, his fellow liaison officer, had been briefed beforehand by their masters – Ben Gurion and Shertok – to steer the Committee towards partition 'in a suitable area of Palestine'. The word partition, it was noted, 'has acquired almost the force of an incantation'. In this way the momentum for partition would build up, neutralising the anti-partitionists, located mainly in the British Foreign Office.[3]

In UNSCOP's public sessions, and in private meetings with its members, Jewish Agency leaders promoted a clean-cut partition as an outcome that would bring 'finality, equality, and justice'. Weizmann laid out the minimum territorial requirements for a Jewish state: the Peel proposals plus the Negev desert in southern Palestine. David Horowitz, present at the dinner parties Weizmann hosted for the Committee members at his estate in Rehovoth, described the deep impression the ageing leader left on them. 'Dr Bunche [the Committee's secretary], who was greatly moved, referred to his feelings as a Negro and the emotional identity that Dr Weizmann's description of Jewish destiny aroused in him . . . Driving back to Jerusalem they [Justice Emile Sandstrom and Justice Ivan Rand, the Swedish and Canadian representatives] sat silent and meditative, and only murmured: "Well that's really a great man."' Already convinced, Rand, articulate, persuasive, intellectually alert, assured Horowitz, 'I won't allow you to be placed in a territorial ghetto.'[4]

*Commentators have long puzzled over the change in Soviet policy. Were the Soviets aiming to acquire a territorial foothold in the region in the form of a joint trusteeship? Or were they simply mischief-making, stirring the pot, creating confusion, hoping to gain something from the ensuing commotion? Eban, perhaps more down to earth, thought 'its real objective in 1947 was to get British and French bases out of the Middle East' (see MSS Brit. Emp., s.527/10, vol. 1, RH). For a detailed discussion of Soviet policy, see Gorodetsky, op. cit.

However, not all the Committee members were as amenable as Rand and Sandstrom. Sir Abdur Rahman, the Indian representative, proved the most awkward of its members. 'He thought the Jews wanted to set up a springboard in Palestine to conquer the entire Middle East,' recalled Horowitz. Abba Eban remembered Sir Abdur displaying his feelings in picturesque style: he 'revealed himself with more valour than discretion as an upholder of the most extreme Arab case. Proceeding to Mosque every Friday in full Arab attire, he ostentatiously avoided any risk of contamination by contact with Jewish life.'[5]

At a top security meeting on 27 June, Cunningham made clear that his administration 'does not favour contacts between UNSCOP and the underground'. Three days earlier, Begin and two of his aides had convened with Sandstrom (chairman of the Committee), Dr Victor Hoo (representative of the Secretary-General of the UN) and Ralph Bunche. They squared up: Begin and his colleagues at the head of the table with their backs to the window, facing Sandstrom, flanked by Hoo and Bunche.

After it was agreed that there would be no leaks, the meeting began. Begin monopolised the conversation. 'What were the aims of the *Irgun* organization?' enquired Sandstrom. 'Its object is to bring about the liberation of the country from foreign yoke,' replied Begin, 'the attainment of freedom for the Jewish people and the restoration of Jewish rule in *Eretz Israel* [the Land of Israel].' Britain, he charged, 'wishes to steal the country for itself and to give it neither to Jews nor Arabs, keeping it as a military base for herself'. He sought 'to expose British perfidy'. Begin summed up his organisation's aspirations:

1. *Irgun* considers that *Eretz Israel* is the homeland of the Jewish people.
2. *Eretz Israel* means both East and West of the Jordan, including Transjordan . . . the forefathers of the Jews conquered Palestine from the present Transjordan . . . *Irgun* considers the whole territory as Jewish territory and aims at the creation of a Hebrew republic under a democratic government.
3. The immediate repatriation of all Jews wishing to be repatriated to Palestine . . . [they] would run into millions . . . Their return is prevented only by British illegal rule and by British armed forces, which should be removed.

4. We reject any statement made by the Labour Party as to the transfer of any Arabs from the country. There is enough room in Palestine for all, both Jews and Arabs. *

5. Since Britain has decided to keep the country under her own control by force of arms there is no other way to accomplish our aims than to meet force with force.

Begin explained that *Irgun*'s immediate aim was to establish 'a provisional Hebrew government' to secure 'the repatriation of all Jews who wish to be repatriated'. Once this had been attained 'the provisional government will resign and then free elections will be held, participated in by both Jews and Arabs, and a permanent government would thus be established. In this Government there could be Arab Ministers, perhaps an Arab Vice-President.'

What, Sandstrom asked, 'would the *Irgun* do in the case of partition'? Begin:

None of the *Irgun* members will accept any carving up of the territory they consider to be the property of the Jewish state of Palestine ... The Jewish claim was not based on the Mandate but on the natural rights of the Jews to their country, on the historical fact that Palestine has been Jewish territory for tens of generations. Already 3,000 years ago there was a Jewish state here. Therefore the *Irgun* rejects partition and will fight against it. First of all, as a matter of principle ... a country is a thing no one is entitled to trade ... no majority of this generation of the Jewish people has the right to give up the historic right of the Jewish people to their country.

Having disposed of partition, Begin then rejected a federal solution, for under it 'the door might be closed to repatriation to some parts of the country and this would be against one of *Irgun*'s basic principles'.

What about 'Arab resentment?' he was asked. 'The *Irgun* does not believe in such a phenomenon as independent Arab opposition to Jewish repatriation. All Arab opposition is instigated by the British themselves, to take a position of opposition to the Jewish state.'

*For the Labour Party resolution proposing the transfer of Palestinian Arabs, see 'The 100,000', pp. 71–72.

He believed that all Arab threats of 'war' were 'empty threats'. But if they do attack, Begin 'had no doubt the Jews would win the day . . . The Arabs never created an Arab government in Palestine. This was never an Arab country.'[6]

If nothing else, Begin had made a frank exposé of the all-or-nothing case, a mirror-image, in fact, of Arab claims.

On 7 March 1947, at a security meeting of the Palestine government, it was confidently reported that 30,000 'illegals' were 'strategically placed' in Europe and that a number of ships to transport at least 25,000 of them had been put on stand-by by the *Mossad L'Aliyah Beth*.

Three weeks later, on 29 March, the *President Warfield*, a Great Lakes and river steamer of some 4,000 tons, able to accommodate approximately 4,500 passengers, sailed from Norfolk docks, Virginia. Of squat, ugly appearance, its built-up decks topped by a preposterously high black funnel, it was manned by a crew of *Haganah* and *Palmach* members and American volunteers. In the evening of 9 July the *President Warfield* made its way from Port-de-Bouc, near Marseilles, where it had taken on supplies, to Sète, some sixty-five miles to the west. The British were aware of the *Warfield*'s movements and its intentions. Creech Jones, the Colonial Secretary, sent a top-secret telegram to Cunningham on 14 July.

> I consider that the successful return of the *President Warfield*'s immigrants to France is likely to have a most important effect on the whole future of illegal immigration. Not only would it clearly establish the principle of *REFOULEMENT* [driving, or forcing, back] as applied to a complete shipload of immigrants, but it will be most discouraging to the organisers of this traffic if the immigrants in the first ship for some weeks to evade the British 'blockade' end up returning whence they came.

The High Commissioner was assured that this was Cabinet policy, both Bevin and Attlee attaching 'much importance' to this plan of action. Three cargo ships were already on alert to re-transfer the 'illegals' back to southern France.[7]

In the early morning of 12 July the *President Warfield*, carrying some 4,500 'illegals', set sail for Palestine. She was soon picked up by British naval vessels: overhead, Lancaster bombers provided air cover. 'We were in fact prepared to outsmart the British Navy,' said Noah Klieger, a French Jew who served as first mate on the now newly named *Exodus*. Our plan 'counted on the surprise of speed'. The *Exodus*, when running all engines full blast, was capable of sailing at twenty knots. 'But we sailed ten to twelve knots to fool the British Navy.' On approaching Palestine's territorial three-mile limit, 'we would gear up to maximum speed and start a run', making for a beach before the British realised what was happening. 'Well,' Klieger recalled, 'the British in fact outsmarted us.'

Captain Stanley Brian de Courcy-Ireland commanded the heavy cruiser *Ajax*, the flagship of the British flotilla (which included four destroyers) that would shadow the *Exodus* across the Mediterranean. Apparently, a conventional stiff-necked naval type, he regarded the *Haganah* people as 'determined ruthless fanatics' who 'exploited, robbed and treated with ruthless callousness' the ill-fated 'illegals'. Nor was he an advocate of the United Nations, 'that modern Tower of Babel'. The *Exodus* headed towards the North African coast, navigating the shallows towards Alexandria, the *Ajax* tracking her all the way. 'This is the *Ajax*,' de Courcy-Ireland called out to the would-be immigrants, 'What Port are you making for?' His call was met by shouts of defiance and abuse.

As you will not tell me I must warn you that illegal entry of your passengers into Palestine will not be allowed; and your ship will be arrested if you try to do so. We do not want to hurt anyone, but if you resist force will be used . . . I repeat force will be used if our sailors are attacked. Your leaders and all sensible passengers must stop the hotheads from futile resistance. Resistance will not help your cause.

Back came the reply:

On the deck of this boat, the *Exodus*, are more than 4,000 people, men, women and children, whose only crime is that they were born Jews. We are going to our country by right and not by permission of anyone. We have nothing against your sailors and officers, but unfortunately they have been chosen to implement a policy to which we shall never acquiesce, for we shall never recognise a law forbidding Jews to enter their country. We are not interested in the shedding of blood, but you must understand that we shall not go to any concentration camp of our own free will, even if it happens to be a British one.

By now, the *Exodus* was positioned some twenty miles off the coast of Gaza. At 2 a.m. on 18 July, the destroyers *Childers* and *Chieftain* moved in, ramming the *Exodus* from both sides. 'The whole exercise was fraught with danger to life and limb,' recalled de Courcy-Ireland, 'and hazardous to the *President Warfield*,' an old, barely seaworthy, top-heavy river steamer. Boarding parties were sent in.

It was 'a terrifying experience' testified Mordecai Stever and David Kochavi, as they squared up to the boarders, at first wielding batons, but soon firing their guns. Kochavi, himself badly wounded, saw Bill Bernstein, the second mate, shot in the head (other versions have him severely coshed: Bernstein died later in hospital). Izzy Stone accused the British of murder and piracy on the high seas, pointing out that the *Exodus* had been attacked in international waters, that three 'illegals' (including Bernstein) had been killed and that many others had been wounded. In the face of this assault, the Jews retaliated. Having vowed they would 'never acquiesce', they turned on their tormenters. De Courcy-Ireland recorded:

> The boarding parties soon learned what they were up against. Those that got over were assaulted from all angles, steam jets were turned on them, the side decks coated in oil to make them slippery, smoke bombs, fireworks and a variety of missiles hurled at them and tear canisters thrown. An Ordinary Seaman reported back: 'I tried to get on board three times but there was too much opposition in the shape of big Yids. I was forced to draw my revolver and fired eleven warning shots. One of the last shots, however, I used to stop a lad of 17 or 18 from collecting my scalp with a meat axe. He got it in the stomach.

While this bloody confrontation was going on the crew of the *Exodus* were transmitting radio commentaries to the *Yishuv* to gain maximum publicity and sympathy. After about three hours the violence drew to a close. The British pulled off a minor success by seizing the wheelhouse, only to have it nullified by 'Ike' Aranne, the ship's captain, who continued to steer the ship, albeit erratically, from somewhere below deck. Aranne still believed, despite all the odds, that he could beach the ship and land the immigrants. Yossi Harel, in overall command as representative of the *Haganah* and *Mossad*, overruled him. Landing the 'illegals' was now of secondary importance. What was important, insisted Harel, was to make maximum political capital out of this sorry affair, to capture world public opinion for the Zionist endeavour. This was a difference of opinion without real meaning. Holed on both sides, leaking water badly, the *Exodus* was in serious danger of sinking. Saving innocent lives had to be Harel's first priority. Hence, at 5.15 a.m., de Courcy-Ireland spotted the 'white flag of surrender'. By mid-afternoon the *Exodus*, preceded by the *Ajax*, anchored at a Haifa quayside. Thousands of Jews, bunched up behind the gates and fences of the docks, greeted it, cheering and shouting. The 'illegals' responded by singing *HaTikvah* (The Hope), the Zionist anthem. By 9 p.m. that evening the cargo boat *Ocean Vigour*, loaded with 'illegals', set sail; early next morning the *Runnymede Park* and *Empire Rival* followed suit. All told, 4,429 'illegals' had been turned back from Palestine. It was thought they were heading for Cyprus; in fact they were being 'taken back whence they came', to Port-de-Bouc.

These harrowing events were witnessed by two UNSCOP members, Emile Sandstrom and Vladimir Simic (the Yugoslavian delegate). They saw the *Exodus*, battered and listing, dragging itself into port: they saw the seriously injured being stretchered off to hospital, the pregnant women in need of attention, the dazed children; they saw the bloodstained uniforms and bandages of British sailors and marines. These ghastly scenes were filmed and photographed. Eban recalled that the *Exodus* incident 'was crucial . . . it really moved them . . . [after that] the idea that the mandate could continue seemed absurd . . . they saw the hose pipes and the tear gas being turned on these very wretched people, who had escaped from concentration camps in Germany'. Simic was reported to have said: 'this is the best testimony of all'. Had they been brought by design to the port by their liaison officer, Abba Eban, to witness these heart-rending scenes? Nothing can be ruled out. Whatever the explanation, the timing was perfect.

The *Ajax* and two frigates were ordered to escort the cargo ships back to France. 'We had our problems,' continued de Courcy-Ireland. Not only hunger strikes, but 'the doctors had practically no instruments and few supplies. With many of the Jews suffering from

T.B. and other diseases and injuries, and *pregnant women*, they were up against it – particularly pregnant women. We had sixty births in four days!' Off Malta, *Ajax* was relieved by HMS *Troutbridge* (a T class destroyer). 'All I can say', sighed a weary de Courcy-Ireland, 'is that I was very thankful to get shot of that job. I had more than enough of Jews. But the repercussions were to last . . .' The 'illegals' reached Port-de-Bouc on 29 July.

Their arrival revived a simmering Anglo-French controversy about the fate of these Jews. Bevin had previously warned the French Prime Minister, Paul Ramadier, about the ramifications of allowing the *President Warfield* to sail. But it had, with some 4,500 potential immigrants on board. Duff Cooper, the British ambassador at Paris, thought 'the French have behaved abominably . . . they allowed five thousand Jews [sic] with obviously forged visas to sail in a ship that was unfit, by their own admission, to carry any passengers'. He broached the subject with Georges Bidault, the French Foreign Minister. Bidault 'felt as strongly as I did'; he thought the French government had been 'entirely in the wrong'. But the Cabinet was split. Edouard Dupreux and Jules Moch, the socialist Ministers of the Interior and Transport, egged on by Leon Blum, refused to toe the British line: the country could ill afford 'a government crisis', confessed Bidault. The same pattern repeated itself when the three cargo ships docked at Port-de-Bouc. The Foreign Office asked the French to give 'full assistance in landing the Jews by force'. But again the socialist ministers refused to budge. This time Duff Cooper agreed with them: 'and now we look silly as I told the FO we should. You can't forcibly land 4,500 people of all ages and sexes without great brutality, especially when there is no cooperation from the land.' He advised the Foreign Office 'to withdraw the ships immediately'. The Foreign Office refused. The normally urbane Duff Cooper exploded:

> It is astonishing and deplorable that a Government department can be so utterly ignorant, so entirely remote from realities, as to believe that such a thing is possible. This morning the French press is solid, from the extreme left to the extreme right, in attacking Great Britain, and the use of force now against the emigrants would produce an explosion. Nor would the [French] Government contemplate for one moment the possibility of assisting us in such a policy. I thought the only thing

to do was to send Ashley over to London, in the hope that he might be able to knock some sense into the addled pates of these ignorant bureaucrats.

As a gesture the French offered the 'illegals' asylum: only a handful, thirty-one, accepted. Despite the appalling conditions on board, the overwhelming majority refused. They stuck it out until 23 August when the Foreign Office finally capitulated and agreed that the ships could sail. But again, 'the addled pates of these ignorant bureaucrats' miscalculated. After almost three weeks at sea, the three ships anchored off Hamburg, Germany. They were met by 1,000 fully armed British troops backed by 1,500 German police. The 'illegals' from one of the ships – the *Empire Rival* – evacuated the ship without resistance, but only because they had planted a time bomb – later disabled – in its hold. On the other two cargo ships the 'illegals' fought back. Screaming defiance, they wielded clubs and hurled at their tormentors an array of assorted missiles. They were met by British water hoses and truncheons. Drenched and battered, they were dragged off to two ex-concentration camps, Poppendorf and Amstau near Lübeck, still hemmed in by barbed-wire fences and watchtowers, the grimmest of reminders of what they had only recently experienced in Nazi-run Europe. These squalid scenes were recorded by the world's press, shaming the British government for its obtuseness.[8]

The *Exodus* affair, which no dramatist could have elaborated upon, was enacted in the full glare of the world's newsreels, press and radio; and the well-oiled Zionist propaganda machine exploited it to devastating effect, offering it as decisive proof of British depravity, callousness and moral bankruptcy. The Zionists won a stunning victory in the eyes of the world; and the British, in their folly and anger and frustration, allowed them to do so. As Simic aptly commented: 'This is the best testimony of all.' For British policy, the *Exodus* episode was an unmitigated disaster.*

Exodus was the most sensational operation of *Mossad L'Aliyah Beth*, but it was not the only one that attracted worldwide attention. At La Spezia, a port located on the north-west coast of Italy, just south of Genoa, the *Mossad* orchestrated what turned out to be a trial run for the *Exodus* affair. From April to May 1946 all the essential ingredients later observed at Port-de-Bouc were first witnessed at La Spezia. Sympathy and cooperation of the local population and authorities; units of the Jewish Brigade

★ ★ ★

On 29 July the three *Irgun* fighters, Avshalom Chaviv, Ya'akov Weiss and Meir Nakar, captured after the Acre prison break-out and sentenced to death on 16 June, were hanged at Acre jail: they went to the gallows singing *HaTikvah*. In his monologue to UNSCOP Begin had explained that his organisation refused to recognise the legality of British military courts, accusing the British of 'maltreating' *Irgun* prisoners, of treating them in 'a barbarous way'. He then spelt out for his listeners *Irgun*-style legality. 'In the *Irgun* tradition if a British official is regarded as a criminal in his activities a court trial is held, with the defendant *in absentia* . . . A verdict is reached and the order is given to carry out the sentence.' Begin stated flatly that 'if the British execute *Irgun* men, *Irgun* will execute British men – also by hanging. No member of the *Irgun* ever asks for mercy,' he bragged. '*Irgun* is absolutely convinced that it fights not only for the independence of Palestine but for the right of free men.'[9]

Immediately after the sentence of death had been passed the *Irgun* began searching for suitable hostages, preferably high-ranking officers or public officials. But the heightened security precautions put in place frustrated their efforts. Second Lieutenant R. Hodges, a Transport Officer, was sufficiently bothered to tell a friend jocularly, 'I hear now that Joe Stern and his minions have threatened to take an officer hostage – so I am keeping my hand near my gun and practising quick draws.'[10] Not all military personnel were equally cautious. In the late evening of Saturday 12 July, two British Field Security sergeants, Cliff Martin and Mervyn Paice, accompanied by a Jewish War Department

---

furnishing logistical support; the single-mindedness of the 'illegals' to reach Palestine; all augmented by a vigorous, sophisticated public relations campaign. Over the entrance to the port hung the sign, 'the Gate of Zion', above which flew the Jewish flag. The 'illegals', all 1,014 of them, went on hunger strike that lasted seventy-five hours. If British soldiers would try to evacuate them forcibly, the *Mossadniks* threatened to blow up the ship, with its immigrants. Yehuda Arazi, head of the *Mossad* in Italy, aided by his deputy, Ada Sereni, directed this operation. He manipulated public opinion: he conducted daily press conferences, sent off telegrams to Truman, Attlee and Stalin, briefed the most influential press agencies. The Genoa port workers downed tools in sympathy. After thirty-three days, under pressure from home and abroad, embarrassed by the adverse publicity, the British government granted permission for the immigrant ships to sail for Palestine. On 13 May 1946, the *Eliyahu Golomb* and *Dov Hos* entered Haifa bay.

clerk, left the Gan Vered Café in Netanya to return to their base. The sergeants were unarmed, in mufti, and out of camp after hours. They were trailed by a black sedan: inside, a five-man *Irgun* kidnap squad waited. At an appropriate moment, the kidnappers surrounded the sergeants, clubbed them, bundled them into the car, and bound and chloroformed them; the Jewish clerk was set free. They were driven to a diamond factory in Netanya where an underground bunker, totally sealed, allowing no air or light to penetrate, had been carefully prepared to receive them. Provided with oxygen bottles, food for a week, a canvas bucket for a toilet, they were brought to the surface from time to time to breathe fresh air. Amichai 'Gidi' Paglin, the *Irgun*'s Chief Operations Officer, left them in no doubt what their fate would be should the death sentences delivered on his three comrades be carried out.

The British dilemma was acute: whether to give in to blackmail or to risk the sergeants' lives. They reacted in customary fashion, in what might be (perhaps facetiously) described as rounding up the 'usual suspects'. 'Operation Tiger' was set in motion. The morning after the sergeants were abducted troops cordoned off Netanya and its environs. Martial law was imposed. Searches were carried out; 1,400 suspects were interrogated, a number even arrested. Apart from combing Netanya itself, twenty surrounding settlements were raided. But apart from unearthing a few 'slicks', 'Operation Tiger' failed in its primary aim, even though soldiers had twice searched the diamond factory. Paice and Martin remained imprisoned in an airless bunker. On 27 July martial law was called off. Two days later the British, fearful of losing face, of parading their impotence, hanged the three *Irgun* men at Acre prison in the early hours of the morning.

Paglin favoured carrying out the execution, but formalities demanded that he should first confer with his Commander. Begin gave the go-ahead and the order was passed down to Yoel Kimche, in charge of the death squad. The sergeants would be strung up at the diamond factory and then removed to a suitable location. One of the sergeants, hooded and bound, was brought out of the bunker, placed on a chair, the noose round his neck attached to a hook in a rafter. 'Can I leave a message?' he asked. 'No time,' came back the reply and the chair was kicked from under him. The second sergeant was given the same treatment. The bodies were then loaded on to a jeep and driven to a eucalyptus grove just south of Netanya, where they were left hanging from two saplings, barely two metres from each other, their hands tied behind their backs, their heads wrapped in pieces of shirt. On the bodies were pinned notices that 'the Court' had found the sergeants 'guilty on all charges'. Beneath the dangling corpses the ground was mined.*

The *Irgun* broadcast that the sentences had been carried out. Still, the bodies were not traced. Fearful that the mine would be set off by a *Haganah* patrol, they called Netanya municipality and informed them of the exact location of the bodies, complete with a map reference. In turn, the Town Clerk directed the authorities to a eucalyptus grove at Umm Uleiqa, south-west of Beth Lydd. At about nine o'clock in the morning of 31 July a party of troops, police, civilian officials and journalists, armed with mine detectors, made their way to the death site. The accompanying Intelligence Officer's record read:

> Their faces were heavily bandaged so that it was impossible to distinguish their features . . . their feet were about 6 ins to 1 ft off the ground . . . They were wearing just their trousers and one wore a vest. One of them had a pair of shoes on, the other was wearing some thick socks.
>
> Their bodies were a dull black colour, and blood had run down their chests which made us at first think they had been shot.
>
> The sappers had swept a path up to the bodies, and the press were allowed to take photographs of the spectacle. When this had been completed it was decided to cut the bodies down . . . As the body fell to the ground, there was a large explosion . . . the two trees had been completely blown up and there was a large crater where the roots had been. One body was found horribly mangled about twenty yards away . . . the other body disintegrated, and small pieces were picked up as much as 200 yds away . . . The one remaining body was put on a stretcher and carried away. Any remains of the other corpse were also collected and put on a stretcher.

*A rumour later circulated that Cliff Martin 'was possibly Jewish or had a Jewish father'. Although a seemingly authoritative report appeared in the *Jewish Chronicle*, 28 August 1981, that Martin had a Jewish mother, which according to rabbinical law would render him Jewish, nothing was ever proved one way or the other. See file AR-0204, Begin Centre, Jerusalem. Some of the details for the above passage rely on the same source.

On the chests of the two corpses were pinned typewritten sheets in Hebrew, rationalising the hangings. The *Irgun*'s Kangaroo Court had charged Martin and Paice with 'illegal entry into our homeland' and of 'belonging to a British terrorist organisation known as the British Military Occupation Forces in Palestine'. They were accused of 'depriving the rights of our nation to live', of 'torture', of 'murdering women and children and prisoners of war', of 'driving out Jewish citizens from their country and homeland', of 'being in unlawful possession of arms for the purpose of enforcing despotism and oppression', of 'acting cunningly towards the Jewish Underground, soldiers, bases, and arms'. Found guilty on all charges, their appeal summarily rejected, they were sentenced to death by hanging. Leaflets to the same effect were distributed in the main urban centres of Palestine. Begin summed up the verdict. 'We repaid our enemy in kind. We had warned him again and again and again. He had callously disregarded our warnings. He forced us to answer gallows with gallows.'[11]

Cunningham was at a loss what to do. He suggested to Creech Jones, without much enthusiasm, 'the imposition of controlled areas', or the 'complete cessation of immigration and/or the introduction of a compensation bill [a collective fine to be imposed on the *Yishuv*] now in your hands', while fully recognising that these measures might well backfire on his administration. Eventually he fell back on already well-tried measures; though they had produced meagre results in the past and were bound to do so again. On 5 August some forty prominent Jews, mostly Revisionist politicians and *Irgun* suspects, but also the mayors of Netanya, Tel Aviv and Ramat Gan, were detained – and in due course released.[12]

If Cunningham felt helpless, many of those under his command felt otherwise. John Wells Watson, a senior announcer of the Forces Broadcasting Service in Palestine, bore witness to the reprisals. Twelve hours after the bodies had been found, 'a Palestine Police (British) armoured car-load of avenging (British) angels let loose hell into a bus load of ordinary Jewish civilians in the middle of Tel Aviv. 5 innocent people (including an eight-year-old girl) died and 70 were seriously injured.' And: 'There are days, weeks, sometimes months of six or seven o'clock curfews . . . people shot unwarned if merely seen behind unshuttered windows . . . soldiers dissatisfied with conditions and trigger-happy, firing at the slightest opportunity . . . A man looks out of his window, a soldier fires "over his head" and hits a woman in the eye (in a flat above, behind curtained windows) – she is blind now and her face horribly mutilated.' Watson goes on: 'Do people at home say, "the only thing to do about the Jews is to have them shot 'en masse'. The Germans were quite right of course, I suppose we can be thankful they wiped out as many Jews as they did?" My only reaction to these remarks (which are not usually meant as jokes, and are pretty universal) is to feel like getting a Bren gun in the mess of the typically clottish British uncultured soldiers.' Cunningham was more under-standing. His soldiers were young and inexperienced, working in an atmosphere of 'constant danger and increasing tension, fraught with insult, vilification and treachery; and it can be understood that the culminating horror of the murder of their comrades, Sergeants Martin and Paice, in every circumstance of planned brutality, should have excited them to a pitch of fury which momentarily blinded them to the dictates of discipline, reason and humanity alike'.[13]

Virtually everyone, everywhere, registered unqualified disgust at this barbaric act. (Even Ben Hecht had nothing to say – at least in public.) The mainstream Jewish leadership of the *Yishuv* inveighed against 'the dastardly murder of two innocent men by a set of criminals'. Moshe Shertok, Head of the Political Department of the Jewish Agency, spoke for many: 'It is mortifying to think that some Jews should have become so depraved by the horrible iniquities in Europe as to be capable of such vileness.' His deputy, Golda Meyerson (later Meir), assured the Palestine government that 'the *Haganah* had been doing their best to find the men', hinting strongly at 'an offer of co-operation against terrorism in some form'. Ivan Lloyd Phillips reported to his father: 'A dismal week here, which has demonstrated that political Zionism when carried to its logical conclusion will stick at nothing – even the most cold-blooded and brutal murder – to attain its ends. Such is the measure of Jewish achievement.' Sickened by this bloody affair, he resolved to quit Palestine as soon as possible. 'I never had any sympathy with Zionist aspirations, but now I'm becoming anti-Jewish in my whole approach to this difficult problem; and it is very difficult to keep a balance and view matters objectively.'[14]

In Britain, naturally, the reaction was extreme. Over a photograph of the two hooded, hanged sergeants, the *Daily Express* splashed the headline 'Hanged Britons: Picture that will shock the world'. 'They were kidnapped, unarmed and defenceless; they were murdered for no offence,' proclaimed *The Times*. 'As a last indignity their bodies were employed to lure into a minefield the comrades who sought to give them a Christian burial. The bestialities practised by the Nazis themselves could go no further.' 'Take the gloves off,' advised the *Daily Telegraph*.[15] Anti-Semitic incidents were recorded throughout the country: in Birkenhead, Liverpool, Manchester, Derby, Glasgow and London. Jewish shop windows were smashed, defamatory slogans smeared on synagogue walls, Jewish cemeteries desecrated, some Jews were set upon. In Parliament, Creech Jones deplored the 'cold-bloodied and calculated murder of these innocent young men . . . I can only express what I know to be the deep feelings of horror and revulsion shared by all of us here at this barbarous crime.' Sidney Silverman and Barnett Janner, both Jewish and both devoted supporters of Zionism, felt 'a sense of deep shame and humiliation that this (just) cause should have been so stained with innocent blood'.[16] Churchill, another friend of Zionism, addressing a Conservative rally at Blenheim Palace, expanded upon the same theme.

> Our sympathies go out to the British soldiers who have endured these unspeakable outrages with so much fortitude and discipline . . . No British interest is involved in our retention of the Palestine Mandate. For nearly thirty years we have done our best to carry out an honourable and self-imposed task.
>
> A year ago I urged the Government to give notice to the UNO that we could and would bear the burden of insult and injury no longer. But the Ministers only gaped in shameful indecision and they are gaping still.[17]

This was a choice example of Churchillian rhetoric. Apparently overcome by the barbarous nature of the hangings, he had conveniently forgotten that the government, only five months earlier, had done precisely his bidding.

Convening in special session, the Commons interrupted its summer recess to debate the Palestinian troubles. The House displayed a rare unanimity. Speaker after speaker condemned the brutal murder of two innocent soldiers; equally, there was all-party regret at the anti-Semitic demonstrations, 'deplorable and un-British', that had disgraced Britain, perpetrated by 'minnow-like fascists'. Creech Jones made himself abundantly clear: 'there is obviously a limit with which Britain can burden herself overseas'. And as Palestine was clearly a burden in the opinion of the House, the subtext was self-evident. 'Partition or evacuation', called out Oliver Stanley, a former Colonial Secretary under Churchill, underlining the only practical alternatives. Michael Foot, a left-wing Labour MP, elaborated. Our Palestine policy has left Britain 'morally isolated', he contended, referring to the *Exodus* 'illegals', still trapped at Port-de-Bouc. Keeping our soldiers in Palestine is both 'wasteful' and 'inhumane', Foot carried on. He urged the Government to 'declare now that whatever decision is arrived at by U.N.O. we are going out of Palestine, that we shall play our part on an agreed U.N.O. basis so long as others make their contribution'. All this was pretty much in line with government opinion.[18]

The *Daily Express* had got it right. The picture – that 'monstrous publication', in Michael Foot's words – it published of the two sergeants did shock the world. The pitiless manner of their execution was truly a traumatic event. But was it the last straw that broke the mandate's back, as some have suggested? In essence, the decision to abandon Palestine had already been made, for that was the thinly veiled reality of referring the Palestine question to the United Nations. If one discounts conspiracy theories of the Perfidious Albion variety – as one should – no evidence has yet been brought to light to suggest that the government had changed its mind. If there were any doubters, it may have finally convinced them that the original February decision had been the correct one, particularly as the government's ruling now commanded popular backing. The combination of the *Exodus* débâcle and the tragedy of the two sergeants, one feeding off the other, made it abundantly clear that it was too costly in blood and treasure, too humiliating, too discreditable to retain the mandate, and that the decision to refer the Palestine bugbear to the United Nations was the right one from which there should be no return.

At midnight on 1 September UNSCOP handed over its completed report to the Jewish liaison officers in the Palais des Nations at Geneva. It proved to be an authentic turning point. Its conclusions were a triumph for Zionist lobbying; and consequently a drubbing for the Palestinian political leadership, still dominated by the intractable Haj Amin. In

September senior British officials travelled to Cairo to see whether the Mufti would compromise on a partition-like settlement. The answer was an uncompromising 'No!': Palestine was sacrosanct Arab territory and was not a subject for bargaining; all Arabs, he pronounced, were vehement in their refusal to countenance Jewish statehood.* Having spoken, Haj Amin's edicts received wider backing at a meeting of the Arab League in Lebanon. Yet the termination of the mandate (by unanimous vote) and the partition of Palestine (by a majority of seven to three, with one abstention), a two-state solution with special status granted to the 'City of Jerusalem' was precisely what UNSCOP envisaged as an equitable arrangement. Moreover, it had allotted to the Jewish state a larger area than that offered by Peel in 1937, or by Churchill's government in 1944. No less serious, from the Arab point of view, was the proposal to admit to the Jewish State 150,000 Jewish immigrants at a uniform monthly rate of 30,000 over a transitional period of two years. Trygve Lie, Secretary-General of the United Nations, a pro-partitionist, 'was ecstatic with the majority proposal . . . There had to be an independent Jewish state. He had unambiguously nailed his flag to the Zionist mast, and there was no turning back.'[19]

Neither the Foreign Office nor the Chiefs of Staff were happy at the idea of partition. They shied at any responsibility for putting into effect a partition plan, for helping to create a Jewish state. Ever since the concept had first appeared in Lord Peel's report this formidable combination had fought against the notion, arguing that it would ruin Britain's relations with the Arab and Muslim world. But the momentum towards partition was moving against them. Given the sophistication of Zionist lobbying and Great Power support, there was at least an even chance that a motion granting partition would be passed when the General Assembly came to debate the issue. Sir Frank

*Well-founded rumours had reached the Zionists that not all Arab leaders were as adamant in their opposition to Jewish statehood as Haj Amin made out. Some – the Emir Abdullah, Ali Mahar (Prime Minister of Egypt from August 1939 to September 1940), Azzam Pasha (Secretary-General of the Arab League), Ismail Sidqi Pasha (the Prime Minister of Egypt) for example – had expressed the view that 'it is difficult for them to negotiate on the basis of a Jewish State over the whole of Palestine. But they are ready to discuss partition'. They would do so, however, only if Britain led the way, declaring her support for partition. (See WL, XXII, nos 151, 193, pp. 128, 172–3.) Britain did not lead the way, however. And Haj Amin's reputation was such as to deter any but the bravest, or most foolhardy, of Arab leaders.

Roberts, Bevin's Principal Private Secretary, placed his master's policy, his ostensible aversion to partition, in a wider perspective. It was anchored on 'safeguarding the rim' from the spread of Communism, the 'rim' being defined as 'the British Empire, going through North Africa and the whole of the Middle East'. Because he, Bevin, 'wanted very much to get a new relationship with the Arab countries and with the Muslim world', the Zionist demand for a Jewish state threatened to unravel his strategy. Roberts thought that Bevin wasn't against a Jewish state per se. 'I think he accepted that this would probably be the solution, the Jews would have their state and the Arabs would have theirs. But he was looking for an agreed solution . . . he was thinking in terms of a settlement, I think, which would have been acceptable to both Arabs and Jews, and which would have given us certain rights.'

Responding to the UNSCOP report, the Foreign Office issued a statement on 19 September taking Bevin's line of thought a step further. Wishing to avoid any misunderstanding, the Office stated 'with all solemnity' that if it proved 'impossible to reach an agreed settlement', the government would base its policy 'on the assumption that they will have to surrender the mandate'. Administering the mandate 'has now become impossible, and in the absence of a settlement HMG must plan for an early withdrawal of British forces and the British administration from Palestine'. Sir Alexander Cadogan, Britain's representative to the United Nations, to be followed by Creech Jones, repeated this message to the General Assembly later that month. And as if to make absolutely certain that the world fully understood Britain's intention, Cunningham told a sceptical press corps that Britain was determined, 'in the event of no agreement between Jews and Arabs to withdraw from Palestine'. A unilateral withdrawal, he warned, would be at 'the expense of misery and considerable economic loss and chaos – possibly bloodshed'. However, he believed that somehow the two sides would 'get together'. But 'if agreement did not come, then Britain would go' and 'It is no use the press or anyone else looking for signs showing we are not going,' he restated.[20] Despite these unambiguous declarations of intent, many eyebrows were raised in disbelief.

All this only makes more explicit what was already very much on the cards. The UNSCOP report cleared the path towards partition. But the Palestinian boycott of the Committee, together with its absolute rejection of partition in any form, declining to compromise on what it considered to be a matter of principle – a stand which was perhaps laudable in its consistency, but, given the circumstances of the moment, was certainly bad politics – had rendered an agreed settlement inconceivable. In a dogged humour, the Arabs persisted in going for broke. Tewfik el-Khalidi, leader of the Reform Party and a member of the Arab Higher Committee, told Cunningham that it was the firm intention of the AHC not to cooperate with the United Nations Palestine Commission 'in any way'. Composed of five representatives from UNSCOP, dubbed the 'Five Lonely Pilgrims', the Commission was meant to collaborate with the British in administrative matters in winding up the mandate, and to continue its work during the transitional period, now reduced to two months.[21] Events soon overtook its purpose: by mid-May 1948 it had been disbanded.

The United Nations secretariat complex was located at Lake Success, Nassau County, on Long Island. The General Assembly was housed in New York – at Flushing Meadow, Queens – in a cheerless auditorium left over from the World Fair of 1939. It was here that the crucial debates on the future of Palestine would take place. Trafford Smith, a senior Colonial Office official attached to the British delegation at the United Nations, composed a short ditty celebrating the organisation's Palestine deliberations.

> War is lurking, Ugly and devouring, UK burking, Situation souring, Skies are murking, USSR lowing – What shall we do?
>
> Arabs stalling – Jews dig their toes in, [Peter] Bergson balling, Reinforcements goes in, UN crawling, Dare not put its nose in – I feel so blue!
>
> Truman dithering, Chaos supervening, [Rabbi Abba] Silver slithering, Hasn't any meaning, Hopes are withering, On each other leaning – Now, UNO![22]

Now that UNSCOP had given its majority verdict in favour of partition, the struggle for Palestine hinged on persuading the General Assembly to adopt its judgement – or not! Mainstream Zionists – Weizmann, Ben Gurion, Moshe Shertok, David Horowitz, the Jewish Agency and *Va'ad Leumi* leaderships – were firm in their advocacy of partition: the Revisionists, the *Irgun*, with their two sides of the Jordon philosophy, were minor players in this drama – despite 'Peter Bergson balling'. The Palestinian Arabs, led by the discredited Mufti, and the Arab world at large, were vehemently opposed to dividing up the country: they argued persistently in favour of an independent Arab Palestine, with a tolerated Jewish minority. Which side would garner the most votes when the General Assembly met to decide the issue? Which party would prove to be the most effective lobbyist? And so began one of the most intricate and dramatic lobbying exercises in modern diplomatic history.

The Zionists started this contest with a slight edge. But nothing was guaranteed. Certainly not the support of the Great Powers, notoriously fickle in their pledges, loyal only to their own perceived interests that could turn about overnight as circumstances changed. It would need a massive effort, from one side or the other, to gain the support of the Assembly: for the Zionists to secure the requisite two-thirds majority; for the Arabs to stymie a pro-partition resolution. Abba Eban, one of the Zionist lobbyists, took a rather detached, academic view of his task: 'There's never been a vote which is the result of abstract reflection . . . it's a parliament, in a parliament you lobby . . . There's no such thing as undue pressure, whatever pressure you can put, you put.' Eban thought the place to put it was in Latin America, where the United States was a key player after decades of American predominance.[23]

Sir John Fletcher-Cooke, a high official of the Palestine administration, now attached to the British delegation at the United Nations, gave his impression of the partitionists' tactics, as they exerted 'undue pressure'. He was particularly scathing of American 'bullying tactics'. When a vote was about to be taken, the Americans would brace an Arab delegate and say, ' "your colleague from", mentioning an Arab state, "would like to see you in the delegates lounge, or corridor". Hence less votes for the Arab cause.' Another 'well authenticated' case involved the head of the Philippine delegation, a Mr Romulo: he, apparently, was dragged off a ship in order to vote at the vital session of the General Assembly. (The Philippines voted in favour of partition.) Fletcher-Cooke – no doubt giving vent to the feeling of frustration felt by many of the British delegates – commented on the 'untidy' and 'irresponsible' handling of the session by United Nations officials. Comparing the two protagonists in the debate he thought the Jewish delegation 'absolutely first class', particularly when compared to the divided Arab states and Palestinians, whose case was presented by 'rather second-rate Arabs'.

More pressure in favour of partition was applied by two of the 'White Dominions', Canada and Australia – adopting an independent stand from the mother country. Lester Bowles Pearson, head of the Canadian delegation, took the Americans and John Martin (from the Foreign Office) and D. C. MacGillivray (a former liaison officer of the Palestine government to UNSCOP) to task on 16 November. 'The sole objective of the United States was to keep out of Palestine, that of the United Kingdom to get out,' he told the British officials. British policy was self-defeating. 'Delegates were getting impatient with her and she was being accused of deliberate sabotage of the United Nations effort.' Show some responsibility, he pleaded: 'be prepared to co-operate as a good member of the United Nations in implementation of any plan approved by the United Nations as a whole, although it might be one of which the United Kingdom herself disapproved.' Martin and MacGillivray advised their superiors not to ignore Pearson's 'storm warning'. They were heeded, but only up to a point. Pearson lobbied relentlessly in favour of partition. A popular figure, at ease with both Jews and Arabs, he mediated between the two superpowers, ensuring that both parties were in agreement regarding the textual details of the proposed resolution. David Horowitz had no doubt that Lester Pearson – a 'dynamic force and pathfinder', his influence at the United Nations 'tremendous' – made sure that 'Canada, more than any other country, played a decisive part at all stages of the U.N.O. discussions on Palestine'.[14]

Other commanding figures threw their weight behind partition. Herbert Vere Evatt, the Australian Foreign Minister, often thought of as 'secretive, devious, and duplicitous', played a crucial procedural role as chairman of the 'Ad Hoc Committee on Palestine' that prepared the way for the vote, skilfully presiding over its rulings, providing noteworthy leadership backing partition. He wrote in his memoirs: 'I regard the establishment of Israel as a great victory of the United Nations.' Sumner Welles was another. Forced into early retirement in 1943 as American Secretary of State after a homosexual scandal, he was now a prominent commentator and author on foreign affairs. His contacts were extensive and he used them to excellent effect, lobbying on behalf of the Zionists. Immediately after the vote Weizmann contacted him, thanking him for his 'moral support' and 'all you have done for my people . . . You were the first I tried to phone after I received the news.'[25]

The Zionists too were hyperactive. Weizmann was summoned to New York from his retreat at Rehovoth to bolster their propaganda offensive. Stationed in a suite at the Plaza Hotel, frequently sick and half blind, Weizmann indulged in the kind of private, individual diplomacy that best suited his style, augmenting the spadework carried out by the Jewish Agency delegation at Lake Success. Uncertain of France's position, and fearing this would influence the stand of Holland, Belgium and Luxembourg, he appealed to Leon Blum to intervene. (All four countries eventually voted in favour of partition.) He contacted Samuel Zemurray, an old friend and head of the United Fruit Corporation, to use his influence with the smaller republics of Central America, since 'the vote of Nicaragua weighs as much as that of the United States'. (Nicaragua voted in favour.) When it became apparent that the United States, succumbing to Arab pressure, wished to exclude the southern Negev desert from the proposed Jewish state, Weizmann, although sick with fever, travelled to Washington to convince Truman that the Negev, with its sea outlet to the Far East, was essential to the viability of the Jewish state. Truman – although given to anti-Jewish outbursts in the privacy of his diary* – when it came to the crunch remained faithful to his basic pro-Zionist outlook. He told Weizmann: 'Don't worry. Go home, and before you reach your hotel I will have put it right.' Truman was as good as his word. 'We sighed with relief,' chorused the Jewish Agency delegates once they heard the news, 'Dr. Weizmann's talk had been successful. The struggle for the frontiers ended in victory.'[26]

Help came from other quarters. Dorothy Thompson, a distinguished American journalist and broadcaster – once noted by *Time*

---

*Truman's diary for 21 July 1947 thought that the Jews 'are very selfish' and 'have no sense of proportion'. They care not how many others 'get murdered or mistreated as DPs as long as [they] get special treatment . . . neither Hitler nor Stalin has anything on them for cruelty or mistreatment to the underdog'. (Quoted in Louis, 'Conscience of the World . . .') Perhaps Truman was worn out by the relentless, and all too often tactless, pressure of the Jewish-Zionist lobby: it would not be the last time.

magazine as one of the two most influential women in America, the other being Eleanor Roosevelt – used her considerable powers to advance the Zionist case. 'The Jews will set up a Palestine state on May 16. Therefore partition *will occur* [her emphasis]. And anyone who knows Palestine Jewry – the ardour, the devotion, the fanaticism, the sacrifice that have gone into the creation of Jewish colonies, and the toughness of body and spirit engendered – knows that the state will be defended.' This, and other similar pieces, fashioned public opinion – which also gave voice in another way. New York Jewry rallied to the cause. Crowds of people, including many non-Jewish sympathisers, armed with banners and shouting pro-Zionist slogans swamped the grounds of Flushing Meadow. For the delegates, it was surely a most intimidating experience to have to cope with this rowdy vocal protest as they made their way to the General Assembly Hall. The ubiquitous Ben Hecht hit on an appropriate sporting analogy: the Jews, as the home baseball team, 'now had their turn to bat'.[27]

The vote on partition was originally scheduled to take place on 26 November. But as the debate progressed it became clear to the Zionists that a two-thirds majority was not assured. The Jewish representatives adopted desperate filibustering tactics. Acting on advice from the Assembly President, Oswaldo Aranha of Brazil, Nahum Goldmann buttonholed his friends, Enrique Rodriguez Fabregat (Uruguay) and Dr Jorge Garcia Granados (Guatemala), and requested that they take the floor again, and again: 'Read from the Bible, like in a Senate filibuster. Read the Psalms, the promises of the Prophet Isaiah.' Read anything, in fact, to postpone the session. The Arabs, suspecting something was up, shouted out, 'to vote! to vote!' Aranha once again came to the rescue: 'I have another list of speakers,' he informed the confused delegates. The filibuster tactic succeeded. 'Black Wednesday' passed. The crucial vote would take place three days later, on 29 November, a Sabbath.[28]

The United Nations was not the most congenial arena for Arab diplomacy: even though it benefited from a solid bloc of eleven Arab and Muslim countries (out of fifty-six member states), and only needed to win over eight more waverers to block a pro-partition decision. (From a Zionist perspective, the votes in doubt were China, Cuba, Ethiopia, Greece, Haiti, Liberia, the Philippines and Yugoslavia). Still, the odds were heavily stacked against them. The pro-partition line-up was a formidable one: Trygve Lie, Lester Pearson, Evatt, Aranha, Fabregat, Granados from inside the UN; while on the outside, Sumner Welles, Dorothy Thompson and New York Jewry were manipulating public opinion. American and Zionist heavy-handed pressure tactics seemed to be paying off. Gromyko had committed the Soviet Union. Above all, this was not Britain's shining hour. Its reputation tarnished by its Palestine record, Britain appeared to be steaming along rudderless, pursuing a 'Yes' and 'No' policy: 'Yes' to abandon its responsibility for the mandate; 'No' to enforce a UN decision. Nor were the Arab delegations effective enough in tackling the partitionists. Fletcher-Cooke had already noted that the Palestinian case was being put forward by 'second-raters'. Cunningham, on meeting Emile Ghoury, Secretary of the AHC, received the same impression, though he phrased it more diplomatically: 'The Palestinian Arabs are little organised to deal with the situation which would arise either from a UN decision to partition Palestine or from a failure to arrive at a decision.'

Even if the Arab delegations had been more savvy and adroit, more in touch with the prevailing spirit of the times, less given to full-blown rhetoric, it is doubtful whether the outcome would have been any different. They felt overwhelmed by the discriminatory sentiments, the open bias, flaunted shamelessly, or so it seemed to them, at Flushing Meadow. The Syrian delegate, Faris Khoury, noted flagrant American partisanship in favour of the Zionists: 'the United States has even threatened China with withholding a loan to it . . . as well as Chile, Paraguay, Costa Rica, and Brazil'. A frustrated Arab diplomat wrote: 'We in the United States could easily be in Tel Aviv – the only difference is the skies, the terrain, and the language . . . everything around us is Zionist . . . I cannot understand how a friendly government [the United States] could permit its citizens to attack friendly states [the Arab governments].'[29]

The winding-up speeches of the chief delegates produced few surprises. Gromyko refined his May statement, again acknowledging the Jews' 'deep historical ties' with Palestine, maintaining that the decision to partition Palestine 'is in keeping with the high principles and aims of the United Nations', of the tenet of 'the national self-determination of peoples'. He recognised the plight of the Jewish DPs, 'without a country, without homes', barely eking out an existence in 'conditions that are well known'. As for Arab complaints, he failed to adduce from them 'any convincing arguments apart from various general and unfounded statements and declarations'. The American representative, Herschel Johnson, registered his country's 'sincere belief . . . that the partition plan . . . with all its imperfections admitted, provides for the people of Palestine in that land the best practical means at the present time by which these high objectives may be obtained'. Sir Alexander Cadogan, speaking up for Britain, as if to leave no one in any doubt as to British policy – or lack of it – reiterated what had become his government's mantra: 'My Government does not consider that the Mandate required it to establish either a Jewish State or an Arab State in Palestine by force, or to coerce either people in the interests of the other; nor is it prepared now to accept any responsibility which would involve the use of British troops as the means of enforcing a decision against either people.'[30]

The British delegation must have viewed these proceedings with a mounting sense of disquiet. In particular this was true of Harold Beeley, a man of 'cold, incisive intellect', who served as Bevin's special adviser on Palestine. The Zionists thought he played 'a sinister role in our fortunes', and saw in him 'a moving spirit in Britain's anti-Zionist policy'. David Horowitz – one of the more perceptive Jewish Agency delegates who struck up a personal friendship with Beeley that, as he put it, survived the vicissitudes of political differences and behind-the-scenes polemic – described him thus:

> He was the type of person who, in spite of an icy temperament, develops an intensity of passion which holds him in a tight grip. He was not an anti-Semite. His grim unyielding antagonism to Zionism arose from his assessment and appreciation of British Imperial interests in the East, and perhaps also from a modicum of romantic, and irrational, sympathy for the Arabs. He remained an uncompromising and unrelenting foe.

Having guided Bevin in a contrary direction, Beeley now observed Britain's Palestine policy crumbling away before his eyes. Supremely assured of his analytical powers – he came, after all, from an academic background – he fell victim to his own self-confidence, revealing a puzzling inability to interpret correctly the rapidly changing political map. A Foreign Office traditionalist, he held that a Zionist-orientated policy would irretrievably damage Britain's relations in the Arab and Muslim world. Like his political masters, he believed that the Zionists had been 'deplorably successful' in selling the idea that only Palestine guaranteed Jewish DPs hope of a better life. Similarly, he assumed that survivors of the Holocaust – or at the very least, a considerable minority of them – could and should be reabsorbed into European society, apparently ignoring the feelings of the DPs themselves as expressed in the findings of the AAC report. Convinced that the Zionists would never achieve their majority vote, he aspired – against accumulating evidence after UNSCOP's report – to convince the Assembly of a one-state solution that would guarantee Jewish minority rights. With the Cold War hotting up, his supposition rested on the improbability of the United States and the Soviet Union joining forces on such a sensitive Middle East issue, where so much was at stake for both powers. But since Gromyko's May speech such cooperation, although not assured, was very much on the cards. 'Tantamount to a miracle', Weizmann called it; if so, it was a 'miracle' that seemed to escape Beeley's notice.

These were all warning signals, no more; but they went unheeded. Perhaps it was too late for the Beeleyites to change course. Unwilling to commit himself either way, Beeley dithered, advising the British delegation to abstain on the vote – as it did. It was not a stand that won them many friends, certainly not among the Zionists, nor, one suspects, among the Arabs. Churchill might well have repeated his barbed quip directed at Baldwin's administration years before: 'So they [the Government] go on in strange paradox, decided only to be undecided, resolved to be irresolute, adamant for drift, solid for fluidity, all-powerful to be impotent.'[31]

Beeley witnessed the finale to his Palestine policy. It was not the most uplifting of experiences, at least for him: 'The galleries were packed with an almost exclusively Zionist audience. They applauded declarations of support for Zionism. They hissed Arab speakers. They created the atmosphere of a football match, with the Arabs as the away team.' Oswaldo Aranha called for calm, but to no avail.[32] On 29 November 1947, as Beeley's 'football match' was being played, resolution 181, on partition, was adopted at the Assembly's 128th plenary session. The roll-call indicated just how divisive Beeley's policy had been, in particular for the Commonwealth, the sheet anchor of British imperial interests. The White Dominions – Canada, Australia, South Africa and New Zealand – voted in favour of partition, India and Pakistan against.*

The voting at Lake Success was broadcast throughout the world. In Palestine, Arabs and Jews tuned in, tension at breaking point, counting on a vote that would suit their purposes. The Arabs were to be bitterly disappointed. But in Jerusalem, 'ten pajama-clad' Jewish students

> crowded into a room with space enough for five and sat tensely around the battered radio for what seemed like hours while vain attempts were made to get clear reception. We got through just as the majority vote was made . . . Ecstatic, we hugged and kissed each other frantically and then stood rigidly to attention and sang *Hatikva* fervently. Out came the wine, biscuits and candy . . . All the students in the building scrambled up on to the roof, and under the warmth of the moonglow and wine, danced deliriously. Then we made a snake line to the nearest houses, banging on shutters and shouting the news. The streets were already full, ring upon ring of dancing groups circling in a frenzied *hora*.

'Roars of joy' spread throughout Jewish Jerusalem, accompanied by cries of 'The Jewish People Lives'.[33]

The hothouse atmosphere that prevailed in the days leading up to the vote gave rise to the most outlandish scenarios. Sir Henry Gurney, Chief Secretary of the Palestine Government, immediately scotched a far-fetched prospect. He would not recognise a *coup d'état*, a de facto government, 'a state within a state', he said, and saw 'no advantage in terminating the mandate before "D" Day'. It defies all rational analysis

*The roll-call went as follows: in favour, 33: Australia, Belgium, Bolivia, Brazil, Byelorussian SSR, Canada, Costa Rica, Czechoslovakia, Denmark, Dominican Republic, Ecuador, France, Guatemala, Haiti, Iceland, Liberia, Luxembourg, Netherlands, New Zealand, Nicaragua, Norway, Panama, Paraguay, Peru, Philippines, Poland, Sweden, Ukrainian SSR, Union of South Africa, USA, USSR, Uruguay and Venezuela.

Against, 13: Afghanistan, Cuba, Egypt, Greece, India, Iran, Iraq, Lebanon, Pakistan, Saudi Arabia, Syria, Turkey, Yemen.

Abstained, 10: Argentina, Chile, China, Columbia, El Salvador, Ethiopia, Honduras, Mexico, United Kingdom, Yugoslavia.

to suspect the Jewish Agency – the only candidate capable of effecting a coup – of even contemplating such a preposterous move, certainly not with victory at the United Nations within reach. Nor is there any evidence to uphold Gurney's extravagant suspicions. But it is a striking indication of how far mutual trust between the parties had broken down. A day after the partition vote Cunningham reported back to London in a more sober tone. Neither side regarded the United Nations decision as binding. The Arabs, relying on their 'superior strength', would strike 'once the British have ceased to shield the Yishuv'. Ben Gurion, in his own fashion, mirrored these sentiments. 'The claim of the Arabs to dominate Palestine had been soundly defeated,' he declared to the *Va'ad Leumi*, but 'to ignore Arab threats to force the issue by violence would be disastrous'. However, he assured his audience that in the event of violence 'the intellectual and moral superiority of the Jews would be decisive advantages'. Many Jews, continued Cunningham, regarded the partition frontiers 'as provisional and subject to enlargement as opportunity offers'. Tel Aviv, they claimed, would never be the Jewish capital, 'a privilege reserved for Jerusalem'. Unlike Gurney's idle hunches, Cunningham's report was distinguished by its perceptiveness.[34]

Susanna 'Espie' Emery, wrote to her mother that 'We are all feeling rather depressed, and very much disappointed, at the news of Partition being accepted by the U.N. The only thing to be said in favour of it is that the Arabs have quite failed to put forward a more just plan. I very much hoped that somebody would propose a workable plan of federation, but as nobody did so, I think Partition is better than no decision at all.' Recording the extreme anger of the Muslims, she feared that the Arabs 'will be provoked into a series of murderous attacks on Jews'. And what of the Christian population of Haifa? Espie considered that they would be 'safer in a Jewish state than in an Arab state. They do not think that at present, for of course they are full of resentment at the injustice of handing Haifa to the Jews; but if the Jews are sensible, there is no reason why Haifa should not continue to be a prosperous city with a very mixed population.' Espie was level-headed enough to recognise the crux of the problem: it all depended 'on the good sense and restraint' of the warring parties, she calculated, 'none of whom are accustomed to using good sense or restraint'.[35]

Partition was welcomed by Jewish communities throughout the

world. In Rome, Jews gathered beneath the Arch of Titus – who had razed to the ground the Second Temple in 70 CE – to offer prayers of thanksgiving: the state that had fallen two thousand years ago, they recited, had now been reborn. The *Yishuv* received the news with joyous demonstrations and communal dancing in the streets, on-lookers dragging astonished British policemen into the circles of dancers to join in the celebrations. Even the factions on the extreme right and left, the *Irgun* and *Hashomer Hatzair*, advocates of bi-nationalism, welcomed the decision as it allowed for large-scale immigration. Golda Meyerson addressed an excited crowd from the balcony of the Jewish Agency building in Jerusalem: 'We awaited this great day with awe. Now that it is here it is so great and wondrous that it surpasses human expression.' She was followed by Ben Gurion. 'Long live the Jewish state,' he cried and, touching the Zionist flag, shouted, 'We are a free People.' The moment was too charged for his audience. 'There were few dry eyes and few steady voices,' reported Zipporah Porath. In Tel Aviv, Haifa and Jerusalem 'drinks were on the House'. The more daring among the Jews clambered on to British armoured vehicles and jeeps, and guided them through the streets, flying the flag of a state that had yet to be established.[36]

The Arab world reacted in anger. Azzam Pasha had dispelled any illusions David Horowitz, Abba Eban and Jon Kimche (the noted pro-Zionist journalist, who had set up the meeting) might have held when they met at the Savoy Grill, London, in September 1947. Horowitz laid out a comprehensive plan 'for co-ordination of interests and a real peace between the two peoples'. 'The Arab world is not in a compromising mood,' replied Azzam Pasha, in a remarkably frank state of mind,

the fate of nations is not decided by rational logic. Nations never concede; they fight. You won't get anything by peaceful means or compromise. You can, perhaps, get something, but only by the force of arms. We shall try to defeat you. I'm not sure we'll succeed, but we'll try. We were able to drive out the Crusaders, but on the other hand we lost Spain and Persia. It may be that we shall lose Palestine. But it's too late to talk of peaceful solutions . . . The Arab world regards you as invaders and is ready to fight you. The conflict of interests is, for the most part, not amenable to any settlement except armed clash . . . You speak of the Middle East. We don't recognise that conception. We only think in terms of the Arab world. Nationalism, that's a greater force than any which drives us. We don't need economic development with your assistance. We have only one test, the test of strength . . . the problem now is only soluble by the force of arms.[37]

In the wake of the United Nations vote stormy demonstrations beset most Arab capitals. In Damascus, the United States legation was stormed. Haj Amin appealed to the Palestinian Arabs 'for energy and sacrifice at this moment of the parting of the ways'. The AHC, under Jamal al-Husayni's nominal leadership, proclaimed a three-day protest strike. In Jaffa, recounted Dr Lester, Director of Medical Services in Palestine, Arab patients refused to be treated by Jewish nurses: they were transferred to Jaffa Mental Hospital where 'they would feel safe for the time being'. In Jerusalem, the Polish and Swedish consulates – both countries had voted for partition – were attacked. In a spate of controlled spontaneity that spread throughout Palestine, anti-partition riots continued apace: highways were cut off, buses shot at, isolated settlements attacked. Spurred on by religious leaders calling for a jihad, hot-tempered demonstrators poured out of Jaffa Gate. Armed with axes and clubs they made their way downtown, attacking passers-by, looting, on occasion torching shops, ransacking a new commercial centre at the eastern end of Mamilla Street. The Jews retaliated. The *Irgun*, acting on its own authority, broke into the Arab-owned Rex Cinema on Princess Mary Street, ignited rolls of film and set the building ablaze. The British, either unwilling or unable to intervene, failed to restore law and order, as they had pledged to do under the mandate. Furious at perceived British indifference and/or prejudice, Amos Oz's father denounced them as the 'Anglo-Nazi foe', 'Amalek',* 'Perfidious Albion', to which his mother retorted: 'Amalek or not, who knows if we won't miss them soon.'[38]

A senior staff officer, General Sir Harold English Pyman, brought to his superiors a gloomy verdict on the efficiency of the Palestine government: 'There's every indication that the Civil Administration in

*Amalek, the grandson of Esau and ancestor of the Amalekites. Recurrent foes of the Israelites, they first attacked the Children of Israel while Moses was leading them out of Egypt into the Promised Land. Hereditary biblical enemies of Israel until defeated in turn by Joshua, Saul and David. Ever since, each generation of the Jewish people has confronted its own 'Amalek'.

Khalil al-Sakakini, Palestinian Arab educator and diarist, and his two daughters, Hala and Dumia.

Jamal al-Husayni, cousin of the Mufti, representing the Arab Higher Committee, arriving to give evidence before the Anglo-American Committee of Inquiry.

Haj Amin al-Husayni, the Mufti of Jerusalem, the dominant force in Palestinian politics throughout the mandatory period.

Abd al-Kadar al-Husayni, the legendary commander of Arab militia in the Judaean hills. His death severely weakened Arab resistence in the Jerusalem area.

(*Above left*) General Sir Alan Cunningham, the last High Commissioner of Palestine: eventually came round to support partition. (*Above right*) The 'imperturbable' Sir Henry Lovell Goldsworthy Gurney, the last Chief Secretary of the Palestine Administration.
(*Below*) Sir Harold Beeley (centre), Bevin's chief adviser on Palestine, at the United Nations.

Harry Truman. A persistent advocate of admitting immediately '100,000' Jewish immigrants into Palestine, a practice that considerably annoyed the British government.

Ernest Bevin (left), Foreign Secretary, and Clement Attlee, Prime Minister: 'Clem, about Palestine. According to my lads in the [Foreign] Office we've got it wrong.'

Chaim Weizmann (centre), President of World Zionist Organisation and Jewish Agency, putting the case for a Jewish state before the Anglo-American Committee of Inquiry. Moshe Shertok, Head of the Political Department of the Jewish Agency, on extreme left.

Wanted: Menachem Begin (left), self-styled Commander of the *Irgun*; and Natan Yellin-Mor (Friedman), Head of the Stern Gang.

Ben Gurion, at the Museum Hall, Tel Aviv, declaring the 'the establishment of the Jewish state in Palestine – to be called Israel.'

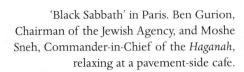

'Black Sabbath' in Paris. Ben Gurion, Chairman of the Jewish Agency, and Moshe Sneh, Commander-in-Chief of the *Haganah*, relaxing at a pavement-side cafe.

The 6th Airborne Division – *HaKalanioth* ('Poppies') – taking over the Jewish Agency building in Jerusalem on 'Black Sabbath'.

British soldiers searching for an arms cache at a Jewish settlement.

A 'Bevingrad' at the St. Julian quarter, Jerusalem.

The bodies of two sergeants, Cliff Martin and Mervyn Paice, hanging from a eucalyptus tree: they had been found guilty by an *Irgun* kangaroo court of belonging to a 'British terrorist organisation'. A 'Picture that will shock the world', cried the *Daily Express*.

A Jewish convoy reaches besieged Jerusalem, to the cheers of the onlookers.

The refugee ship *President Warfield* – renamed *Exodus* – making its way across the Mediterranean to Palestine.

The Anglo-American Committee of Inquiry arrives in Jerusalem. Back row, right to left: Richard Crossman, William Philips, James G. MacDonald, Bartley Crum, Frank Buxton, Frank Aydelotte, Lord Morrison of Tottenham, and Reginald E. Manningham-Buller. Front row, right to left: Sir Frederick Leggett, Wilfred Crick, Judge Joseph – 'Texas Joe' – Hutchinson, and Judge Sir John Singleton.

Palestine is losing its grip, and that certain Departments had virtually ceased to function.'[39] The lawless events of these days was but a fore-taste of what was to come. They proved to be the first phase of what the Israelis called their War of Independence and the Palestinian Arabs their *al-Nakba* (Catastrophe).

9

Civil War

'Jerusalem is like a fortress and every week there seems to be one building less,' wrote Mary Burgess to her mother in late November 1947, 'How one wishes things would settle down. It could be such a lovely country if the people in it were different.'[1] In the ensuing civil war the battle lines were clearly drawn: the Jews were fighting to safeguard the United Nations partition frontiers; the Arabs, to preserve the territorial entirety of their homeland. There is little point in attempting to forge a flawless moral case for one party at the expense of the other. Chaim Weizmann, appearing before the AAC, frankly admitted 'that the issue is not between right and wrong'. In putting the Zionist case for partition he pleaded that the Committee choose 'between the greater and lesser injustice', adding 'injustice is unavoidable'. One commentator has noted, in a different context, 'that all belligerents in all conflicts are morally compromised, but this is not to render all causes equally worthless'.[2]

As the fighting increased in intensity, the ability of the British authorities, civil and military, to control events, to maintain law and order in fulfilment of their mandatory obligations, crumbled away. According to one informed witness the Palestine government had lost 'its grip' and was simply not functioning as it should. As for the generals, they seem to have raised their hands in despair. Towards the end of the mandate, General Sir Gordon MacMillan, GOC Palestine, confessed that he felt unable to take responsibility for upholding law and order: a position, he claimed, that was endorsed by the Colonial Office (though no written evidence has yet been found confirming this). It was echoed by Major P. F. Towers-Clark, Cunningham's Military Attaché: 'The General's [Cunningham's] line is easy enough: we have simply not got enough troops to do anything about it, so we just have to let it go on.' On occasion, when local circumstances demanded it, troops did intervene, but these moments were the exception not the rule. During these last weeks of the mandate the overriding consideration of the authorities was to ensure that the evacuation of Palestine by British forces proceed as expeditiously and safely as possible. It meant securing the main lines of communication between the centres of British power and the key points of embarkation. In Jerusalem, British troops forcibly intervened to prevent the *Haganah* capturing the Sheik Jarrah neighbourhood that controlled the route to the Hebrew University on Mount Scopus, but through which also ran the main road to the north, essential to keep clear to guarantee a smooth British withdrawal. 'This area is vital to us,' judged Towers-Clark, 'for it commands our vital communications route out. The army reacted strongly (for the first time for a very long time) and sent troops in to clear the area of both armed Jews and Arabs and now occupy it.'[3]

Fifteen days into the civil war Cunningham assessed the deteriorating situation. The subtext of his report to London reads as a confession of administrative impotence, depicting an authority dragged along by events, certainly not in control of them. With neither side showing signs of restraint, he detailed an endless cycle of reprisals and counter-reprisals that resulted in 'many innocent lives being lost' – the death toll put at '84 Jews dead, 155 injured, 93 Arabs dead, 335 injured'. The AHC, still under the spell of the Mufti, remained a combative, rather than a conciliatory, force. In a fanciful flight of imagination Cunningham thought that 'a word from the Mufti' would calm the situation. But the only words Haj Amin uttered was an appeal for 'sacrifice at this moment of the parting of the ways'. Were the Arabs securing their aims? Cunningham didn't think so. 'Certainly the present frittering away of their resources in attacks which lead nowhere cannot suit their book, whatever they plan to do in the future.' Although better organised, the Jews were behaving no better. Cunningham described their activities as 'unmitigated folly', contending that the notorious dissident groups were working 'closely together' with the *Haganah*. The Jewish Agency disowned the dissidents, but justified *Haganah* actions 'as aggressive self-defence against definite targets, mainly at centres from which Arab attacks have taken place'. Cunningham remained unconvinced. 'I must state that the provocative action of the Jews and their admission that the *Haganah* is authorised to take what they call counter-action but what is in effect indiscriminate action against any Arabs, is hardly calculated to have a calming effect.'[4]

Some months on, the situation had not improved. Sectarian violence continued unabated, with the British caught in the middle, seemingly paralysed by a masterly inactivity, blamed by both sides for aiding the other. 'Well, I have been here for over a year now and that is just about long enough in a mad-house like this,' wrote Second Lieutenant Hodges to a friend. 'Especially just now when things are pretty critical, pretty is the right word, pretty bloody grim. Battles going on all round, shots pinging over the camp, snipers sniping and gunners gunning, it's all quite crazy. Luckily, however, we are not involved in these Arab-Jewish scraps, but it is all rather unnerving.'[5]

From early February to March 1948 – the partition resolution having led to an outbreak of savage inter-communal clashes and an apparent collapse of British authority – the United Nations was busy considering ways and means to avoid a catastrophe in Palestine upon the termination of the mandate. Talk at Lake Success had been matched by mounting violence in Palestine. In late December 1947, the *Irgun* had tossed a bomb into a crowd of Arabs gathered outside the Haifa oil refineries. No deaths were reported; but the two-thousand-odd Arab workers at the refineries, seeking revenge, had run amok: forty-one Jewish employees had been clubbed or slashed to death; seven others had been badly mangled, but survived. In retaliation, a *Haganah–Palmach* force had devastated the nearby Arab village of Balad el-Sheikh, inflicting scores of casualties.[6] And so it went on, one incident leading to another, retaliation following retaliation.

Events in and around Jerusalem gave the impression that the Arabs were gaining the upper hand. On 1 February the *Palestine Post* building was blown up. Twenty-one days later, three booby-trapped vehicles parked on Ben Yehuda Street, a main shopping centre, exploded, demolishing the surrounding buildings: rescue workers pulled more than fifty bodies from the rubble. On 1 March Arab saboteurs succeeded in placing a mined car in front of the Jewish Agency complex, the best-guarded spot in all Jewish Jerusalem, destroying a wing of the building, leaving thirteen killed and seventy wounded. These bombings also implicated the British: it emerged that army and police deserters were heavily involved. Thought to number some two hundred, these rogue elements were, in Towers-Clark's opinion, either 'youngsters with somewhat romantic minds, who have "Lawrence of Arabia" attitudes, or are ruffians who are in trouble with the army'. Clearly, the Ben Yehuda deserters were of the 'ruffian' type, if not of a more sinister character. An inquiry revealed that the 'British League-Palestine Branch' (an offshoot of Mosley's 'British League of Ex-Servicemen) claimed responsibility for the bombings. In a circular letter, that opened with a quote from the 'Protocols of the Elders of Zion', the 'British League' lambasted 'the vile Jew, backed by International Free Masonry, supported by international Communism and with the help of international Finance, [who] strode in the 20th century, [and] Under the cloak of Zionist ideals, but in reality for the purpose of creating a centre for international intrigue, claimed a Jewish National Home in Palestine'. Ending on a feverish note, it appealed to the 'Nations of the World, [to] arise and smite the Jews! Arabs, unite and liberate your country! Britons, awake and drive out the Jewish-dominated Labour Government! British soldiers and policemen, join the British League! Rule Britannia.'[7]

Jerusalem was under siege. In the Judaean hills a band of Arab irregulars under the vigorous and inspiring command of Abd al-Kadar al-Husayni, a veteran of the 1936–9 Arab rebellion and a cousin of the Mufti, had effectively cut off Jerusalem from the coastal plain. Unable to guarantee free access to the city, Cunningham explained his failure in dry topographical terms: 'It will be appreciated that to ensure absolute security on a stretch of road 37 kilometres long (from Latrun to Jerusalem), winding through rough and hilly country with frequent steep gradients and deep, narrow, tortuous defiles is a matter of extreme difficulty.' Zipporah Porath, an American Jewish student at the Hebrew University, put it more coloufully and personally: 'No parcel could be worth the danger of being ambushed in the hotbed of activity on the Jerusalem–Tel Aviv road. Every curve, clump of trees, cluster of rocks or mound of earth provided cover for Arab snipers. The road has become the most dangerous place in the country.' The Jewish authorities put on a brave face, informing the government that they 'have plenty of stores, and that the present stringency . . . is due to careful and close control and not to real shortage'. But according to Cunningham, the reality was very different: 'All indications however refute this allegation.' Food and water were rationed in the Jewish areas – though no doubt Arab neighbourhoods were affected as well. 'The only thing we aren't flooded with these days is food,' fussed Zipporah, 'Milk, meat, and fresh vegetables are getting hard to find. They have simply disappeared . . . Eggs are also in short supply. It isn't that there are fewer egg-laying chickens, it's just that they don't like laying eggs when they are disturbed by gunfire.' In addition, drugs and medicines had run out: operations were often carried out without anaesthetic. And with a breakdown of the electricity network, and paraffin in short supply, families often lived by candlelight or in darkness.[8]

Things were no better in Jerusalem's Arab districts. In Katamon, Khalil al-Sakakini welcomed in the New Year to the sound of 'explosions, artillery rockets and small firearms'. The *Haganah* kept a careful watch on the area, fearful that it would be turned into an armed camp. Three Arab leaders, Abou Dayieh, Emile Ghoury, and most significantly Abd al-Kadar, were spotted patrolling the streets in a jeep, presumably planning the disposition of Arab irregulars. A thousand metres or so to the north of Katamon lay the upmarket Jewish residential quarter of Rehavia, where many of the *Yishuv*'s leaders and high government officials lived. Sir Henry Gurney, one of them, wrote of 'a glorious battle between Katamon and Rehavia', with 'bullets and mortar bombs falling quite close to us'. This 'glorious battle', and its consequences, could easily serve as a template for many other neighbourhood clashes throughout Palestine.

Many comings-and-goings were noted at the Hotel Semiramis in Katamon, now identified as the Arab headquarters. On 5 January the *Haganah* blew it up. Hala al-Sakakini, Khalil's daughter, recorded the incident in her diary. 'We had terrible weather last night – rain, lightning, thunder and a violent howling wind. About a quarter past one we were awakened by an awful explosion that lighted the sky and shook the house. This explosion was followed by shots so near we had to leave our beds and creep to the corridor.' Early next morning Hala ventured outside: 'The eastern wing of Hotel Semiramis was completely destroyed. It was nothing but a heap of rubble. In spite of the pouring rain and bitter cold a large crowd had gathered at the scene. All faces were drawn and pale with sadness and fury. Women wept and men muttered curses.' Hala witnessed the aftermath:

All day long you could see people carrying their belongings and moving from their houses to safer ones in Katamon or to another quarter altogether. They reminded us of pictures we used to see of European refugees during the war. People were simply panic-stricken. The rumour spread that leaflets had been dropped by the Jews saying that they would make out of Katamon one heap of rubble. Whenever we saw people moving away we tried to encourage them to stay: 'You ought to be ashamed to leave. This is just what the Jews want you to do; you leave and they occupy your houses and then one day you will find that Katamon has become another Jewish quarter!'

Shooting and explosions continued. In the early morning of 14 March Hala saw 'trucks piled with furniture passing by. Many more families from Katamon are moving away, and they are not to blame. Who likes to be buried alive under debris?!' She complained bitterly at the lack of defence, of security measures against Jewish attacks. 'We cannot be expected to wait empty-handed for the Jews to come and blow us up.' Two days later Khalil wrote: 'Dear God, I don't know how we will hold out against the Jews' aggression. They are well-trained, organised, united, and armed with the latest weapons – all lacking on our side. When will we grasp that unity triumphs over disunity, that organisation prevails over anarchy, preparedness over neglect.' A local delegation approached the AHC for help. Arm and defend yourselves, they were told. The deputation protested: 'It is your duty to provide us with arms and guards,' enquiring pointedly, 'where's all the money sent by the Arab and Islamist states disappeared to?' Later, the AHC relented somewhat and assured the Katamon delegation that aid would be sent. (According to *Haganah* sources, about one hundred and seventy Syrians, Iraqis and Hebronites were dispatched to the area.) But a few days later Khalil recorded: 'Since midnight the Jews have been bombarding Katamon on a scale hitherto unknown.' Abd al-Kadar visited the besieged neighbourhood to offer advice; but the pounding continued unabated. 'Many of the residents of our quarter have left,' Khalil noted on 20 March, 'or for the Old City, or for Beth Jala, or for Amman or Egypt or other places. Only a very few of the property owners have remained.' Horrified by wildly inflated atrocity stories circulating, Hala's family thought 'seriously of leaving Jerusalem . . . The number of people in Katamon is decreasing every day and everybody wonders why we are not leaving too.' On 29 April they decided to leave for Egypt.

After a journey of thirteen hours by car, travelling through Hebron, the Sakakinis arrived in Cairo in the late evening. 'We were lucky to find two good double-rooms with a private bath in between at the Victoria Hotel.' Three days later they learned that the Jews had occupied all of Katamon. Hala was broken-hearted. 'How sad', she lamented, 'that Katamon, one of the newest, cleanest, and most beautiful quarters of Jerusalem, should turn into a battlefield.' 'The Arabs have only themselves to blame for this dismal result,' judged Sir Henry Gurney, 'a consequence of their use of this area as a snipers' post for months past.'[9]

According to Gurney's accounting 'over 2,000 had been killed and about 7,000 wounded' since the partition resolution (Towers-Clark put the number of killed at 2,200 and wounded at 4,500) – and there was no sign of a let-up.[10] Clearly, there was an urgent need to restore at least a modicum of law and order. One offbeat proposal came from Captain (retired) Thomas Henry Wintringham. To his contacts in Europe, North America, the Labour Party and the House of Commons he set out a scheme to raise 'a small international standing army' of about 15,000 volunteers, at a cost of 5–10 million dollars, 'to help in keeping the peace' in Palestine, a task the Security Council was evidently incapable of fulfilling. 'If no armed force is available,' Wintringham argued, 'it is natural to fear that Jewish and Arab armed forces are likely to be busier making war rather than the prevention of it.' However cogent and logical his case, and well-meaning his intention, Wintringham's novel project to neutralise the conflict in Palestine came to nothing.[11]

On 19 March, 'Black Friday', the American ambassador to the United Nations, Warren Austin, threw a bombshell. Since partition could not be discharged peacefully, he informed the Security Council that his country now supported a United Nations temporary trusteeship for Palestine. Envisaged as a kind of breathing space to allow the Jews and Arabs one last chance to reach an agreement, it would not, Austin made clear, prejudice 'the character of the eventual political settlement'.[12] Although clearly not familiar with the minutiae of Austin's scheme, Dorothy Blanche Morgan, an English teacher from Haifa, felt that this was a statesmanlike ruling. 'My dear Mother', she wrote,

We were much cheered yesterday morning at the news that America had dropped Partition & we hope it may ease the situation, though of course the Jews are furious, & most disappointed. You see the Hebrew newspapers are so full of lies that it is impossible for an ordinary Jewish citizen to get a clear view of the situation, & they have grown up under a mistaken idea. Even so, a great many of the decent Jews must be glad that a scheme which has already brought such misery is dropped.[13]

Needless to say, this was a serious misreading of the opinion of the overwhelming majority of 'decent Jews'.

Austin's démarche was the result of mixed signals and muddled thinking between the White House, the Pentagon and the State Department (perhaps they were too preoccupied with the onset of the Berlin crisis). Trusteeship had first appeared, and been discarded, in the AAC Report, while UNSCOP had just rejected it as a 'non-starter'. Truman was severely embarrassed. A day before Austin's announcement he had received Weizmann at the White House. Weizmann found the President 'sympathetic personally', indicating 'a firm resolve to press forward with partition'. 'How could this have happened?' Truman questioned one of his assistants. 'I assured Chaim Weizmann that we were for partition. He must think I am a plain liar.' Weizmann was assured, indirectly, that there would be no change in American policy.[14]

Sir Henry Gurney was in no doubt that Austin's proposal was counter-productive. 'It is playing for time, a Munich: it is putting the patient, who was almost on the operating table, back into bed where no other cure for his chronic disorders is at all likely to be found. UN trusteeship, if accepted, will be very difficult to end. In my experience temporary buildings are either bad or the most permanent of all – or both.' The Jews 'are shocked and stunned', he recorded, and surmised that 'when they recover their breath will pronounce their determination not to weaken in their political pursuit of a Jewish State'. Nor, Gurney considered, 'when they have thought about it a bit', will the Arabs 'be so happy after all. All the problems remain: immigration, illegal armies, no legislature, militant Zionism.' In accordance with Gurney's prediction, the Jewish Agency and Va'ad Leumi expressed 'regret and astonishment' at the recasting of American policy, and categorically rejected any suggestion to shelve the partition plan, even for a short period, affirming that a

Jewish state would be proclaimed upon the termination of the mandate; while the Arabs, also following Gurney's reasoning, were no less fierce in their opposition, noting that the proposed trusteeship provided for continued Jewish immigration – 100,000 in the first two years – and that Palestine's future constitution would rest or fall on Jewish compliance. Azzam Pasha made this perfectly clear when he saw Cunningham. Partition must not be revived, even under the guise of trusteeship, and certainly 'immigration must be discontinued completely'. Trusteeship, he summed up, would mean 'allowing a Jewish minority to obstruct indefinitely any democratic solution'.[15]

The British military, being on the spot, and fearing that the brunt of the burden would be borne by them, made a rapid assessment of what would be needed to impose trusteeship. The Chiefs of Staff estimated that it would take five divisions, backed by air power and naval contingents in proportion, to maintain a stable government in Palestine. This was clearly far beyond Britain's capability. Nor, with a European crisis looming over rights of access to Berlin, was there any sign that the Americans would contribute to such a force – while to ask the Russians for aid was unthinkable. So trusteeship ended as it had begun, as a non-starter. Partition remained, accepted by one side, rejected by the other. The fighting went on, increasing in intensity, with the British doomed to be stuck in the middle. 'Let us not deceive ourselves,' observed Towers-Clark, 'full-scale civil war is raging in this country and with the forces at our disposal we have no hope of stopping it.'

Just before dawn on 9 April 1948, a force of 130 *Irgun*-Stern Gang dissidents attacked Deir Yassin, a village of 700 inhabitants lying a few kilometres to the west of Jerusalem.[17] It was not a 'troublesome' village. Indeed, only recently it had signed an agreement with the *Haganah* that it would not give haven to Arab irregulars, following it up with a non-belligerency arrangement with its neighbouring Jewish settlement, Givat Shaul. It is not clear why the dissidents chose to strike at Deir Yassin: perhaps they wished to be associated, in a roundabout way, with 'Operation Nachshon', a *Haganah–Palmach* action to reopen the Jerusalem-Tel Aviv highway.* Reluctantly, David Shaltiel, the *Haganah*

*The code name derived from the biblical personage Nachshon Ben Aminadav, the first Jew to dare the waters of the Red Sea when the Jews fled Egypt. It was this audacious act that inspired 'Operation Nachshon', launched on 6 April.

commander, sensing he was powerless to prevent the 'splinter groups' from entering the village, gave his consent. But he warned the dissidents against blowing up the village: no buildings were to be destroyed, and if they managed to conquer Deir Yassin they would have to garrison it to prevent it falling to Arab irregulars. Lacking experience (apart from terrorist acts) in conventional warfare, the dissidents were ill-suited for the task they had set themselves. Advancing through the village and encountering opposition, they all too often overreacted, depopulating houses, reducing them to rubble with grenades and small-arms fire. The *Haganah* provided some logistical support, while a *Palmach* squad helped subdue the Mukhtar's house, the focal point of the fighting, after which it pulled out. A senior *Haganah* Special Operations officer, Lieutenant-Colonel Meir Pa'il, who accompanied the dissidents 'to see how they performed', witnessed the carnage. The *Palmach* commander, a friend of Pa'il, insisted that there was 'no pre-plan' to aid the dissidents. It occurred by chance. Having already overrun an area to the north of the village – part of the operation to open the road to Jerusalem – his squad heard firing to their rear. Realising that Jews were involved, they thought it their duty to rescue them. So the *Palmachniks* intervened, and immediately retreated to their previous position. The *Irgun*–Stern Gang action ended by late afternoon, Pa'il claiming that the 'massacre' was stopped by a group of Chassidic Jews (appearing from nowhere) who cursed the dissidents for 'un-Jewish acts'.[18]

There were numerous appalling reports – impressionistic, unver-ified, some deliberately embroidered – of that day at Deir Yassin. The wildest accounts circulated, cataloguing every gruesome detail: of the bellies of women, including pregnant women, being 'ripped open'; of all women aged between six and seventy being raped and paraded naked through the streets of west Jerusalem; of men, women and children being loaded on to buses, driven through the streets of Jerusalem, where they were jeered and stoned and spat upon, and then taken back to Deir Yassin and summarily shot.[19] The British, observing the events at Deir Yassin from afar, were exposed to the same first impressions and hearsay. All the indications point to 'around 250 casualties' accompanied by 'every circumstance of savagery', noted Cunningham. In one cave 'the heaped bodies of some 150 Arabs were found', while in a well 'a further 50 bodies' were seen. Arab allegations of Jewish atrocities, 'such as lining up and shooting with automatic weapons of unarmed men, women and children now seem to contain some truth . . . Women and children were stripped, lined up, photographed, then slaughtered by automatic fire and the survivors have told of even more incredible bestialities.'[20]

Sir Henry Gurney gave an account of a press conference the *Irgun-Stern* group staged on 10 April. 'The spokesmen claimed to have killed 200 Arabs in Deir Yassin . . . including 100 women and children. Certainly about 150 Arab women were brought into Jerusalem and dumped in the Street of the Prophets. This boasting of killing women and children is typical of the ruthlessness and degradation of these people.' A few days later Gurney's diary read: 'The bestialities of Deir Yassin are coming to light. They are too horrible for words and Belsen pales beside them. We have decided to publish them. As the Arabs know all about them already, publication cannot affect the "truce";* and it is right that the world should know what these people are, the dregs of utter degradation.' Gurney then attempted to balance the picture: 'The Arabs have been guilty of many horrible barbarities and are selling pictures of some of them. No doubt we shall have a competition in atrocity stories before long.'[21]

Moderate Jews were no less shocked. Zipporah Porath wrote to her mother: 'It is a conquest we are by no means proud of, although the extremist groups – *Etzel* [*Irgun*] and *Lechi* [Stern Gang] – are pretty pleased with themselves. It is outrageous and shameful and we are all horrified. That's the trouble with "extremists", they never know when to stop. Not everything can be excused by calling it war.' In the late afternoon of 9 April, Shaltiel approached Deir Yassin. Sickened at the scenes of gratuitous butchery, he told the dissidents' commander, 'We're not going to take responsibility for your murders' and withdrew his men to the edge of the village. Later, he issued a statement distancing himself – and the *Haganah* – from the bloodbath: 'For a full day, *Etzel* and *Lechi* soldiers stood and slaughtered men, women, and children, not in the course of the operation, but in a premeditated act which had as its intention slaughter

---

*A number of local truces had been proclaimed – and inevitably found wanting. Towards the end of April the United Nations appointed a Truce Commission to supervise these makeshift arrangements. Sir Henry Gurney viewed this initiative with conspicuous scorn: 'I fear that the U.N. make themselves more ridiculous and their impotence more obvious every day'. Gurney diaries, 24 April 1948, MEC.

and murder only. They also took spoils, and when they finished their work, they fled.' After learning of the events at Deir Yassin, Ben Gurion sent a message to King Abdullah of Transjordan conveying horror and regret at what had occurred. In the same vein, the Jewish Agency expressed its 'repugnance' at the massacre. These mandatory recitals of regret were dismissed as unworthy of notice by Cunningham: 'The Jewish Agency . . . has issued the usual notices of condemnation which however deceive nobody, especially as the dissidents themselves claim that *Haganah* let them pass through to the attack.'[22]

Deir Yassin became a byword for wanton savagery. Many of the horrendous stories of what happened, magnified to make a political point, have entered the folklore surrounding this tragic event – and indeed have never left it. Often spread by the Palestinians themselves, to pressurise Arab states to intervene, but also to blacken the name of the Jews, this tactic recoiled on its originators, sowing panic among the Palestinians: 'It demoralized the Palestinian population – and the Arab countries never came to our aid,' said Dr Amin Majaj. The head of Jerusalem's (Arab) National Committee, Dr Hussein Fakhri al-Khalidi, confirmed Majaj's point. At his press conference held after the incident he consciously distorted atrocity stories and exaggerated the number of killed in order to shock outside Arab leaders into intervening in the civil war. Arab governments' spokesmen took up the call, 'spreading rumours of rapes and killings on the part of the Jews, and thus encouraging people to flee'.[23]

What actually happened was bad enough, without any embellishments. No heavy armour was used, as was reported. Even Arab sources deny, or do not mention, cases of rape, or of the disembowelment of pregnant women.[24] Survivors were paraded through the streets of Jerusalem, were indeed jeered at and spat upon, but they were eventually dropped off in East Jerusalem. According to the latest Israeli and Palestinian research (conducted at Bir Zeit University in 1987) some hundred to a hundred and ten villagers were killed, including civilians, women and children. Bodies were dumped down wells, even torched, and houses were looted and prisoners robbed.[25] Israeli sources – released in the 1980s and 1990s – confirm that atrocities did take place: 'Combatants and non-combatants were gunned down in the course of house-to-house fighting; and subsequently after the battle, groups of prisoners and non-combatants were killed in separate sporadic acts of frenzy and revenge in different parts of the village. The remaining villagers were expelled.'[26] Meir Pa'il, present at the scene, remarked that 'no commanders directed the action, just groups of guerrillas running about full of lust for murder'. Although the events at Deir Yassin were truly horrendous, the most reliable reports do not suggest a large-scale organised massacre. Rather they suggest that what happened was the result of badly trained, inexperienced, probably hot-tempered dissidents, who were in all events hostile towards Arabs, losing their self-control in a battle in a built-up area for which they were ill prepared. None of this, however, excuses those responsible for turning Deir Yassin into a killing field, for which the *Irgun* and Stern Gang must be held fully culpable.*

Cunningham, as the senior British authority in the country, was, to say the least, considerably embarrassed by this episode. 'Arab reaction to this deliberate mass murder of innocent inhabitants . . . of an Arab village which, by Jewish admission, has taken little part in the disturbances is naturally extremely bitter,' he informed London, 'nor have the British escaped sharp criticism for their failure immediately to intervene or to punish the criminals.' Putting it bluntly, Cunningham explained that the British were unable to act decisively out of a fundamental inbuilt weakness: 'I should make it clear that the military authorities are not, repeat not, in a position to take action in this matter owing to their failing strength and increasing commitments.' One option remained open: the possibility of a punitive air strike. But even this notional demonstration

---

*Lacking military experience, Begin, although Commander of the *Irgun*, was not in 'full control' of the operation at Deir Yassin. But as was only to be expected, he strongly defended the action, discounting claims of any massacre, in what amounted to an *ex post facto* apologia at variance with most of the known facts and accounts, contemporary or subsequent. Claiming that Deir Yassin, a key point in the struggle for Jerusalem, was a fortress-like village garrisoned by Iraqi soldiers and Palestinian irregulars, he implied that it was a legitimate military target. Having fully coordinated the action with the *Haganah*, a force of about one hundred *Irgun* and Stern Gang fighters were sent in. After a 'humane warning' that went unheeded (probably unheard), fierce house-to-house fighting followed. A full-scale battle ensued: the attacking force suffering forty-one casualties, four of them fatal. Begin went on to castigate the Arabs for inventing and spreading false atrocity stories; but also chastised the Jewish (alluding also to British) authorities for besmirching the good name of the *Irgun* and Revisionists with similar concoctions. See Begin, *The Revolt*, pp. vi–viii, 162–5, and in the same vein, Shmuel Katz, MSS Brit. Emp., s.527, vol. 2, RH. For Begin not in 'full control', see Sofer, *Begin*, pp. 71–2.

of strength faded away and, instead, a face-saving announcement was circulated: 'An air strike against the Jewish dissidents in the village of Deir Yassin was arranged and was suspended when it became clear that the dissidents had left.' Towers-Clark, unhappy at the decision not to take action, thought: 'It is a pity that it had to be called off for both sides need a salutary lesson of what we can do.'[27]

The story of Deir Yassin, actual and supposed, remains indelibly written into the collective historical memory of mandatory Palestine (and of Israel/Palestine). Its immediate repercussions are more difficult to discern. Was it the trigger that led to the Palestinian refugee problem? Clearly not, as the flight of Palestinians had begun on the outbreak of the civil war, more than four months earlier. The atrocity rumours, spread mainly by word of mouth, affected for the most part the areas surrounding Jerusalem. In adjacent Arab villages, such as Malcha, Qaluniya and Beit Iks the inhabitants took flight. 'There is no doubt that the villagers are scared out of their wits,' noted Towers-Clark. Deir Yassin figures in the al-Sakakinis' diaries as sowing panic in the minds of the residents of Katamon. Otherwise, as has been pointed out, 'most Palestinians at the time had no access to radios or newspapers': knowledge of the warfare 'came solely from rumours and word of mouth'. In Haifa, in late April, when the fate of that city was in the balance, Farid Salab, a prominent Arab citizen, testified that all communications were down: Haifa was 'quite cut off – no telephones, etc.'. News of the massacre at Deir Yassin was not yet common knowledge in the city, he revealed.[28]

There was another repercussion. The name Deir Yassin became a kind of battle cry for Arabs bent on revenge. On 13 April cries of 'Deir Yassin' were heard as a Jewish convoy carrying medical staff to Hadassah Hospital on Mount Scopus was ambushed by hundreds of Arab irregulars as it passed through the Sheik Jarrah area. British troops were in the vicinity, but they stood by, intervening only at the last moment. Present at the scene was Lieutenant-Colonel Jack Malcolm Thorpe Fleming Churchill, nicknamed 'Fighting Jack Churchill', with twelve of his soldiers. (A true British eccentric, 'Fighting Jack' was reported to have fought throughout the world war armed with a bow, arrows and a claymore, insisting that 'any officer who goes into action without his sword is improperly dressed'.) Later, he testified that he had attempted to assist the Hadassah convoy, radioing for artillery support, a request that was turned down at brigade level. Although he could not guarantee the safety of those under attack, Churchill pleaded with them to seek refuge in his armoured vehicles; but the medical staff preferred to await the arrival of *Haganah* forces. Seventy-seven Jews were killed: only twenty-eight survived, most of them seriously wounded. 'The Jews were over-confident and endangered themselves,' Churchill later recalled. Following the slaughter, he coordinated the evacuation of Jewish doctors, students and patients from the Hadassah Hospital on Mount Scopus.[29] There were to be similar incidents.

April was a crucial month. At its beginning, before Deir Yassin, Cunningham reported on 'a disheartening week for the Yishuv . . . its leaders are deeply worried about the future'. Jerusalem was still under tight siege; efforts to relieve Jewish settlers at Gush Etzion, a group of four kibbutzim south of the city, had conspicuously failed. Arab irregular forces were even now operational: Abd al-Kadar along the Jerusalem corridor; Fawzi al-Kaukji, commanding his so-called 'Army of Liberation', a force of eight battalions comprised of Arab volunteers and sponsored by the Arab League, in central and northern Palestine; while other units were active in the Hebron and Ramleh-Lod areas. By the end of the month, after Deir Yassin – 'it helped a little bit,' Yigal Yadin, *Haganah*'s Chief of Operations, sardonically remarked – the military balance had swung heavily in favour of the *Yishuv*.

Of more consequence were the unorthodox methods of Jewish arms procurement. Ehud Avriel, a leading figure in *Rechesh*, the secret *Haganah* arms purchasing unit, recalled how it worked. In November 1947 he was based in Paris, at the headquarters of his organisation.

> We were like 'a state within a state' with extensive contacts in Europe. We were flooded with offers, some of them imaginary and some of them ludicrous, middlemen out for a fast buck. And then appeared a gentleman with a catalogue of arms from the Czech arms industry, which before the world war he had represented in his native Romania. He talked to me about purchasing Czech arms: his prices were realistic. He produced two air tickets and suggested we go to Prague the following morning, using forged documents to show I represented a foreign government interested in 'illegal' immigration.

In Prague, Avriel met Jan Masaryk, the Czech Foreign Minister. 'Masaryk was a close friend of Weizmann. On his own typewriter he typed a letter containing the necessary credentials on behalf of that other government I was supposed to represent and then gave it his remarkably impressive signature. Thus I was able to purchase Czech arms.' The arms were shipped to Palestine from ports in Yugoslavia, 'sympathetic to our cause. In order to slip the British sea blockade we used small commercial ships – 250–300 tons – and few sailors. In no way did these little boats arouse the suspicions of the British navy. Just in case, we covered the arms' boxes with onions, so that even if pricked by British bayonets the arms would not be discovered. They never were.'[30] *Rechesh* became a well-oiled machine that only improved over time, employing ever more sophisticated means of procuring arms.

It was in the United States, however, that Jewish arms smuggling was perfected to a fine art. The operation was orchestrated from Teddy Kollek's (later six times mayor of Jerusalem) suite at Hotel Fourteen on 14 East 60th Street, off Fifth Avenue: the famous Copacabana nightclub – reputedly run by the Mafia boss, Frank Costello – occupying the lower floor of the same building. 'My work touched on experiments in weapon production,' Kollek recorded, 'chemistry and physics, speculations on ship purchases; dealings with factories and junk yards; liaison with spies, mobsters, movie moguls, statesmen, bankers, professors, industrialists, and newspaper men; and no lack of illegalities, from petty to international.' The *Haganah* arms mission profited greatly from the vast amounts of army surplus supplies left over from the war. Everything was on offer, from boots, blankets and tents, to rifles, machine guns, ammunition, engine parts and aircraft, all waiting to be picked up by impatient customers. To facilitate the acquisition of these goods straw companies were set up, agents were alerted throughout the country and links formed with friendly countries, chiefly Panama and Nicaragua.

The problem was not simply to acquire these goods, but also to guarantee them safe passage to Palestine (and later to Israel), the *Haganah* emissaries knowing full well they were violating a United States arms embargo. To finance this vast operation Kollek relied on donations from wealthy Jewish backers as well as from the coffers of the Jewish Agency, monies that needed to be 'laundered' before they could be exploited for so-called 'legal' purposes. In large measure these problems were resolved by Kollek's discreet contacts with New York's Jewish-Italian mafia. Meyer Lansky, one of its leading lights, Jewish and pro-Zionist, approached Albert 'Mad Hatter' Anastasia (who ran 'Murder Inc.' together with Louis 'Lepke' Buchalter, another Jewish mobster) and his brother Tony: between them they controlled New York's waterfront. This formidable, and violent, alliance ensured that *Haganah* arms shipments to Palestine sailed, while arms shipments to Arab states conveniently fell overboard or were redirected to *Haganah* locations. Hotel Fourteen's business enterprises were not confined to New York: Chicago, Miami, Los Angeles, Las Vegas, even faraway Hawaii and the Philippines, were all targeted as profitable operational centres.

One of Kollek's chief agents, Al Schwimmer (later, founder of Israel Aircraft Industry), was responsible for laying the foundations of a Jewish air force. Under his direction the network bought, borrowed, or stole dozens of aircraft that included fighters, Constellations (military transport planes) and B17s, the 'Flying Fortresses'. From his days in Air Transport Control during the war, Schwimmer knew many pilots and mechanics, Jews and non-Jews. Scores of battle-trained ex-servicemen were recruited. Forming makeshift, but committed, crews, they flew these 'crates' from the States via Panama, Nicaragua and Dakar to Zetec, Czechoslovakia, then on to Palestine (or later Israel).

Transferring money – or bribes – to Kollek's shady contacts was always a problem, particularly as the FBI were keeping a close watch on Hotel Fourteen. 'I had an Irish ship captain with a ship full of munitions,' recalled Kollek, 'he had phony bills of lading and was to take the shipment outside the three-mile limit and transfer it on to another ship. But a large sum of money had to be handed over to him, and I didn't know how to get it to him. If I walked out of the door carrying the cash, the Feds would intercept me and wind up confiscating the munitions.' By chance, Teddy bumped into Frank Sinatra in the bar of the Copacabana – dubbed by those in the know, the 'Copahaganah'. It was common knowledge that Sinatra was sympathetic to the Zionist cause. Only the previous autumn he had sung at a rally at the Hollywood Bowl, attended by 20,000 Zionist supporters. Carefully, Kollek explained his dilemma. The solution was logical. 'I walked out of the front door of the building with a satchel and the Feds followed me. Out of the back door went Frank Sinatra, carrying a paper bag filled with cash. He went down to the pier, handed it over, and watched the ship sail.'[31] Perhaps for the only time in his career, Sinatra had played an unscripted role, that of 'bagman' for the *Haganah*.

Altogether, these multilayered initiatives at arms smuggling forged a critical mass to ensure the successful outcome of *Haganah*'s war effort.

Jewish gains were mirrored by Arab losses. On 9 April news reached Khalil al-Sakakini that Abd al-Kadar al-Husayni, the legendary Arab commander, had been killed in a battle to control the Kastel, a key point dominating the road to Jerusalem. An iconic figure to Palestinians, thousands followed his funeral procession, weeping and firing in the air; shops and markets were closed; all work was halted. Al-Kadar was buried on Temple Mount, an extraordinary honour. His death crippled Arab resistance in the Jerusalem area. By 20 April Operations *Nachshon* and *Harel* had provisionally cleared the road to the beleaguered city, allowing sufficient essential supplies to get through to sustain its Jewish population. Even Towers-Clark was impressed: 'The Jews have got another convoy, of 240 vehicles, through from Tel Aviv without incident. It is still too early to say whether the *Haganah* efforts on the road have been an outstanding success, but it begins to look like it and that I was wrong. They have done a good job if it is.'[32]

Further to the north, Fawzi al-Kaukji's 'Army of Liberation', 'its position desperate', immobilised in 'a state of suspended animation', was disintegrating, its mercenaries drifting off to their home bases in Syria or Iraq. Al-Kaukji, a sworn enemy of the al-Husaynis, often described as a 'menace to his own side', could boast of no military victories, only reverses, notably his humiliating failure to capture the settlement of Mishmar Haemek in mid-April. Sir Henry Gurney looked on in disgust as Fawzi's so-called 'Army' of foreign irregulars plundered its way across large tracts of Palestine: 'Palestine Liberation Army looting and robbing . . . this is what the Palestinian Arabs get from the assistance provided by the Arab States . . . this ill-organized and stupid intervention, in defiance of all our protests, has cost the Palestinian Arabs dearly, and one could say that it is all over bar the shouting and the re-opening of the road to Jerusalem.'[33] Elsewhere, other Arab bands faded away. Their fighting abilities were not entirely dissipated, but the lack of coordination, indeed often bitter enmity, between the chief Arab militias was a sure recipe for disaster.

Redeploying British troops to ensure their safe evacuation was a first priority for the authorities, a strategy that profited the *Haganah* as they took control of the main towns of Palestine – Jerusalem, the exception, was to remain a divided city until June 1967 – and much of the area allocated to the Jewish state under the partition plan. By end of April the *Haganah* were in command of Safad, Tiberius, Acre and Haifa; Jaffa was to follow by early May. Safad set the benchmark. According to a contemporary army report all efforts by the British to broker a cease-fire, which would have effectively left the town in the hands of the Arabs, had failed by 18 April. Frustrated, the British decided to evacuate their troops, their most immediate concern – a move that enabled the *Haganah* to take over Safad.[34]

Haifa – a major prize – fell to the Jews between 21 and 22 April. Major-General Hugh Stockwell, Commander of the Northern Sector and responsible for its security, recounted his attempts to mediate between the two sides. On the 21st he made crystal-clear to a committee of Jewish and Arab leaders that his main purpose was 'to secure routes and areas essential for the smooth and rapid evacuation of the British forces from Haifa': to meet this end he would brook 'no interference' with his 'dispositions'. During the night the Jews launched 'a major attack': by the early morning of 22 April they were 'in control of a large portion of the town'. By then many of the Arab notables had left the city, among them Ahmed al-Khalil, Chief Magistrate of Haifa, 'a man of considerable influence' who withdrew to Beirut by sea. By now, Stockwell recorded, the Arabs were 'in a state of considerable panic and I was faced with a large refugee problem'. Many of them were herded on to boats and shipped to Acre. Despite pleas to do so, Stockwell refused to allow Arab reinforcements 'to march on the town', fearing a 'renewed flare up of full scale fighting' and heavy loss of life, including British lives. 'I took this decision [a decision that later led to Arab accusations that Britain had handed over Haifa to the Jews] in the interests of humanity,' he explained. Stockwell summed up the course of events. 'The very rapid collapse of the Arab forces in Haifa leads me to suppose that there was a lack of unity and effort, either in Haifa, or from further afield.' As for the Jews, they are 'astonished at the speed and success of their operations and are still somewhat dazed by the resultant conditions . . . The Jews are gradually taking over Haifa and have set up Arab Liaison Offices in the Carmelia Court Hotel and in

general an air of stability is beginning to show itself.' The *Haganah*
people are 'quiet bodies', reported 'Jack', one of Susanna Emery's
friends, 'most punctilious and respectful . . . The Arabs have almost
completely evacuated [Haifa] and it is amazingly transformed.'[35]

Other observers put a different slant on things, even while acknowledging that the Jews in control 'have made the town quieter and safer
than it has been for months'. But it was at a human cost, for 'the
distress caused among the local Arabs has been great'. Susanna Emery
recognised the extent of personal, individual tragedy. 'Shortly after we
left Haifa, the Jews stormed into Haifa by three routes, driving the
Arab population down on to the beaches, where many of them were
sucked up by boats & taken to Beirut. During this savage attack on an
unarmed population, one of our big Arab girls who had recently left
school, & was studying 1st Aid to help her people, was shot dead as she
ran out onto the street to help a wounded neighbour.' On 29 April
Cunningham and Towers-Clark toured the town.

> It is even worse than I had expected. The whole Arab area is completely
> dead, with *Haganah* patrols in it, and the army confined solely to the
> bottom of the town . . . It is no wonder that the Arab population have
> almost all left, for how can one expect them to live in an area deserted
> by the army, where the *Haganah* lord it at will and against whom they
> have no protection? No doubting it, Haifa is a bad blot to our prestige.

A few days later Towers-Clark heard 'that a few Arabs are trickling
back into Haifa, where the Jews are taking a reasonable attitude and
doing their best to get them back in by diminishing armed *Haganah*
appearances. A reliable report says that the *Haganah* has disarmed
about half of the *Irgun* [they had been seen looting Arab property] in
Haifa.'[36]

Jaffa was another flashpoint. Considering it of little strategic value,
the *Haganah* did not regard its occupation as a high priority, figuring
to blockade it into surrender. The *Irgun* thought otherwise. 'Men of
the *Irgun*,' cried Begin. 'We are going out to conquer Jaffa.' The
conquest began with a mortar attack, but soon ran into trouble. The
Haganah, somewhat reluctantly, moved in to retrieve the situation.
And so did the British. Embarrassed at the 'bad blot' that had stained
their reputation at Haifa, they determined to make amends. 'By mid

morning,' a later account observed, 'the Arab position was very serious and it looked as if Haifa might be repeated. However we have reacted very strongly this time and troops were rushed to the scene to stem the tide.' Major Derek Cooper of the Life Guards commanded 'a scratch force of armoured cars, infantry and tanks' to repel Jewish fighters 'who were driving Arabs out of Jaffa'. By 28 April, the report continued, 'any possibility of further Jewish infiltration is out of the question and the area has become fairly quiet. The Jews have bitten off more than they can chew this time and at last the salutary tonic which has been so necessary has been delivered. We put in an air-strike onto one Jewish position, the first time that the RAF has been used.[37]

The British also made more vigorous efforts to obtain a lasting ceasefire. Acting as a go-between, William Vickery Fuller, District Commissioner for Lydda, brought the two sides together, the Jewish Agency and members of Jaffa's Municipal Council. His starting point was to declare Jaffa 'an undefended town'. By 5 May, both parties had agreed to a truce on this basis; but Ben Gurion added a proviso: 'The Agency cannot commit itself to anything in Palestine after the 15th May until the situation is clearer. The Agency would be pleased if the cease fire should continue after 15th May. If Jaffa wd not fire they wd not fire.' In any case, it was too late for such niceties. In effect, Jaffa had already fallen to the Jews. Fearful of savage Jewish reprisals – perhaps news of Deir Yassin had filtered through – the overwhelming majority of Jaffa's Arab citizens, together with their leaders, had bolted the city, their parlous situation aggravated by speculators jacking up the cost of transport, petrol and other essentials. All this was viewed by British observers with barely concealed contempt. 'I regret to say', penned Towers-Clark, 'that once again all the Arab leaders fled the town the moment it started. Almost without exception the wealthy influential Arabs have got out at the first sign of trouble. It has long been contended by many that the Effendi class is not fit to rule and events have proved this contention to be basically true, for almost all have either left the country altogether or gone into safe areas like Jericho . . . this conduct compares very ill with that of Jewish leaders.' Sir Henry Gurney was no less harsh: 'It is pathetic to see how the Arabs have been deserted by their leaders, and how the firebrands all seek refuge in Damascus, Amman and elsewhere when the real trouble starts.' And later: 'Really the Arabs are rabbits. Ninety per cent of the population have just run away and only some 5,000 remain.'[38]

At the end of April Cunningham forwarded to London a damning report on the operations of the *Haganah*, 'if indeed the mortaring of terrified women and children can be classed as such'. Jewish broadcasts, 'both in content and delivery, are remarkably like those of Nazi Germany'. Displaying 'a spirit of arrogance', *Haganah* forces 'are increasingly impudent and intrusive' as they take control of Haifa. Cunningham interpreted, correctly, overall Jewish policy, even if his phraseology was a bit extreme. 'Aggressive Defence', he commented, meant doing 'their utmost to consolidate territorial holdings and to cow neighbouring Arabs into a state of subjection in which they will be unwilling to offer further resistance themselves or to give help or encouragement to foreign Arab elements'. Caught in the middle, Cunningham was no less scathing of the Arab position: 'They are keenly critical of Britain and the Palestine Administration for their neglect, over the last twenty years, to control Jewish immigration, expansion and armament.' But, he pressed on, the Arabs could not only blame others for their wretched plight: they too were to blame:

> Fear breeds recrimination and they are perhaps wilfully blind to the fact that for months past they and their press have clamoured for the entry of the foreign Arab guerilla bands which, having successfully stirred up the Jews (and incidentally provided them with the excuse that they are now merely defending themselves against Arab aggression) are now proving quite unable to protect the local Arabs from the Jewish reaction. In their hearts the Arabs realise that their much vaunted Liberation Army is poorly equipped and badly led, brave though its members may be; they feel that their monetary subscriptions have been squandered and they themselves misled; they must pin the blame on someone, and who more deserving than the British. It was to preclude such a state of affairs that the Palestine Administration incessantly requested that armed Arab bands should at all costs be kept out of Palestine until the termination of the Mandate; but the bands entered and were defeated, and the inevitable wave of anti-British feeling is now being experienced.

Like his subordinates, he heaped scorn on the 'so-called' Arab leaders who 'are fleeing the country; and the Effendi class generally do not seem to be ashamed of watching the contest from the side-lines'.[39]

A week later Cunningham summed up the general situation. Haifa: 'Jews at Haifa are anxious that Arabs should now return and armed Jews have been removed by the army from Arab quarters.' Tiberius: 'Jews would welcome Arabs back but we can give no guarantee.' Safad: 'It would be advisable for Arabs to wait a bit.' Acre: 'Typhoid has broken out and until this is under control return might be inadvisable.' Jaffa:

> Only 5,000 Arabs remain. Municipal Services have completely broken down and remnants of Liberation Army are looting. Nearly all Councillors and members of National Committee have fled . . . perhaps it could be explained that this disaster at Jaffa is the fruit of premature military action against which Arab Governments have been repeatedly warned and that further premature action on their part will only add to the sufferings of the Arabs of Palestine who are now thoroughly tired of the Husayni regime and look only to King Abdullah to prevent worse befalling them.

Gurney followed suit, though more succinctly: 'Arab evacuation following Jewish attack following Arab attack. The Arabs have lost all confidence in their military leadership and look more and more to King Abdullah to rescue them from the inevitable consequences of intrigue and feckless chicanery.'[40]

In fact, Abdullah's Arab Legionnaires were already operating inside the areas allotted to the intended Palestinian state, the King having promised the Arab League that the *entire* Arab Legion' (author's emphasis) would intervene immediately after 15 May to ensure 'any military measures necessary to secure realisation of Arab aims'. Moshe Shertok protested vigorously to the President of the Security Council, Alfonso Lopez, that the 'Arab Legion be removed from Palestine forthwith', and be 'precluded from intervening in Palestine in any way'; but to no avail.[41] Units of the Arab Legion were instrumental in destroying the *Etzion* Bloc between 10 and 14 May. A crushing defeat for the *Yishuv*, it mourned over a hundred settlers slaughtered and hundreds more taken into captivity.* Abdullah's aims were not necessarily those of the Arab League. He aspired to raise up a Greater Syria – to include Lebanon and Palestine – as his personal fiefdom, an aim that put him at loggerheads not only with Syria, Lebanon, Saudi Arabia and Egypt but also the Jewish Agency. Meanwhile, Abdullah was shrewd enough to work to his own timetable and at his own pace, exploiting the capabilities of the British-led Arab Legion, the most effective Arab fighting force in the area, to his own advantage.

*The *Etzion* disaster could hardly be a consequence envisaged by the so-called collusion agreement between the Jewish Agency and Abdullah, a pact that supposedly partitioned Palestine between them, with the British nodding assent, to cheat the Palestinians out of their state. A conspiracy theory, it has been vigorously advanced by some, but which, upon closer examination, has been shown to be without real substance. By the end of the first Arab-Israeli war Abdullah was certainly in control of the West Bank, but this was not the endgame of a tripartite collusion or agreement, tacit or otherwise. In the absence of an authoritative Palestinian leadership – if one excludes the discredited Mufti – and given the Palestinian and Arab refusal to countenance partition, together with the total collapse of local Palestinian social and political structures, a power vacuum had emerged into which Abdullah slipped easily enough. Still, conspiracy theories have always retained a certain resonance among the gullible, the naive, the partisan – or headline-seekers!

The leading advocate of the collusion thesis is Avi Shlaim: see his *Collusion Across the Jordan: King Abdullah, the Zionist Movement, and the Partition of Palestine* (OUP, 1988); *The Politics of Partition: King Abdullah, the Zionists and Palestine, 1921–1951* (Clarendon Press, OUP, 1990); *Hussein. Lion of Jordan* (Allen Lane, 2007), p. 30; and 'The Debate About 1948', *International Journal of Middle Eastern Studies* (1995), p. 24. In *The Politics . . .*, Shlaim writes, 'Occasionally I may have pressed my arguments a little too far', but despite some verbal acrobatics he sticks, in essence, to his original thesis, see Preface, pp. vii–ix

The collusion thesis has been convincingly refuted in Avraham Sela, 'Transjordan, Israel and the 1948 War: Myth, Historiography and Reality', *Middle Eastern Studies* (October 1992), vol. 28, no. 4; Efraim Karsh, *Fabricating Israeli History. The 'New Historians'* (Frank Cass, revised ed., 2002), particularly section 3; and Joseph Heller, *The Birth of Israel, 1945–1949* (University Press of Florida, 2000), pp. 300–3.

10

Last Days

You see, what distinguished Sir Henry Gurney was his 'imperturbability', said Sir John Fletcher-Cooke, one of his top aides. On learning that a British police station had been blown up, and that 'everything was under control', Gurney went off 'for a quick round of golf . . . it would seem a pity to waste such a lovely afternoon. Come up for a drink about seven,' he bid Fletcher-Cooke, 'and tell me all about it.' In fact, Gurney's administration was barely functioning. Communications were erratic: no direct mail from London, only telegrams; while 'nearly all telephone lines were down'. There was no petrol or kerosine, and an acute shortage of diesel oil needed to pump water up 2,000 feet to supply Jerusalem; but in any case, 'water pipes blown up twice already'. Despite the chaos, some of the pleasures of civilised society were preserved. 'We came into our prison, the King David, last night . . . Hamburger, the Manager, went to great trouble to furnish rooms for us and to provide a dinner according to King David standards, which are as high as anywhere in the world. We sat down to a seven course dinner, beautifully cooked and served . . . I am bound to say it is not an unpleasant form of prison for the time being.' These were quiet days for Gurney. 'We played tennis this afternoon. If anyone had told me three months ago that we should be playing tennis within three days of the end of the Mandate, I should have laughed at him. But in fact we have run out of work.'[1]

The civil war was over bar the shouting: 'Arab morale broken . . . Arab collapse almost complete,' noted Towers-Clark. The Palestinian community, disorientated, in disarray, fragmented, at odds with itself, faced the *Yishuv*, united, set in its purpose, often ruthless in its methods. 'The Arab streets are curiously deserted,' reported *The Times*, commenting sharply on the 'exodus' of the 'more moneyed class'. Khalil al-Sakakini's words, never more pertinent, bear repeating: 'Dear God, I don't know how we will hold out against the Jews' aggression. They are well-trained, organised, united, and armed with the latest weapons – all lacking on our side. When will we grasp that unity triumphs over disunity, that organisation prevails over anarchy, preparedness over neglect.'[2]

Despite fierce criticism of his methods by some of his fellow Palestinians – corruption, cronyism, self-serving ways, even cold-blooded murder – the Mufti's stranglehold on the Palestinian national movement never slackened.[3] All attempts to form an All-Palestinian Government, with the Mufti pulling the strings, failed. The first, in February 1948, was vetoed by the Arab League; the second, in September, whose writ was confined to an enclave around Gaza, was simply a puppet regime manipulated by the Egyptians.[4] In effect, the Palestinians were denied an independent national identity: either by their own would-be leader, the Mufti, an anathema to all except his hollow coterie, whose policies led them into a cul-de-sac; or else by their Arab brothers, who were more concerned with pursuing their own, often conflicting, interests. Nor was their cause helped by the blood-curdling rhetoric trumpeted by Arab spokesmen. Now, on the eve of the first Arab-Israeli war, Azzam Pasha – 'the most honest and humane among Arab leaders', thought Ben Gurion – warned: 'We will erase you from the earth . . . This will be a war of extermination and a momentous massacre which will be spoken of like the Mongolian massacres and the Crusades.'[5] Such high-flown, vitriolic, threatening language, coming only three years after the Holocaust, could only strengthen the resolve of the *Yishuv* to hold firm; and would, no doubt, help conscript public opinion worldwide in favour of the Zionists and an independent Jewish state.

As for the Jews, 'The machinery for a Jewish state now seems to be complete,' concluded Gurney. Now in charge of a lame-duck administration, he marked time patiently as it limped on towards its final day. Something of the prevailing confusion can be discerned from Gurney's comical attempt to implement the November partition decision. 'The [Palestine] Police locked up their stores [worth over £1m] and brought the keys to the United Nations, who refused to receive them. I had to point out that the United Nations would be responsible for Palestine in a few hours' time [in accordance with the November resolution] and that we should leave the keys on their doorstep whether they accepted them or not; which we did.'[6]

14 May

At 6.45 a.m. on 14 May 1948 the Union Jack was lowered from the King David Hotel, where the Palestine government's administrative offices had been housed, to be replaced by the flag of the International Red Cross.[7] At 8 a.m, 'To the sound of a lament, played by a piper', General Sir Alan Cunningham, the High Commissioner, left Government House for the last time. Cunningham, a fair and honourable man, had bid farewell to the people of Palestine in a personal message broadcast the day before in words that resonate strongly even today.

> It is not my wish at this period of the British departure to turn back the pages and look at the past. It would be easy in doing so to say sometimes, 'Here we did right', and no doubt at other times, 'There we did wrong', for in this complex matter of the Government of Palestine the way ahead has not always been clear and the future often obscure. In this respect we are more than content to accept the judgment of history . . . I have never believed, and do not believe now, that the seed of agreement between Jew and Arab does not exist . . . Equally I am convinced that a solution of this problem is not to be reached through bullets or bombs, which in themselves have not brought a solution to any problem, but only misery in their train . . . I pray that peace may come immediately to Palestine. A peace emanating from the minds of the people themselves, the only true instrument through which it can be achieved . . . and it cannot be beyond the bounds of possibility that the future should hold for them mutual prosperity and understanding . . . in our hearts will remain the constant desire that co-operation, goodwill and amity may be re-established between us to our mutual benefit in the early future. Good Bye.

After inspecting a guard of honour of the Highland Light Infantry, Cunningham, safe in his armour-plated Daimler, and his entourage drove off to Kalundia airstrip on the outskirts of Jerusalem, successfully negotiating Jewish and Arab roadblocks, 'troops and guns covering

every danger point', from where he flew to Haifa. At Haifa airport, a
fifty-man detachment of the Palestine Police saluted him. After
'chatting quietly and shaking hands' with Shabtai Levi, the Jewish
Mayor, and his Arab Deputy, Haj Ta-Er Haraman, Cunningham made
his way to the dock area, lined with Comet tanks. His arrival at the
harbour 'caused little excitement among the Jews'. Wearing his
general's uniform, Cunningham made his way to the launch that
would convey him to the cruiser HMS *Euryalus*. 'Upon getting into the
launch he turned and looked soberly up across the docks. There stood
an honour guard of the King's Company of Grenadiers and Royal
Marine Commandos.' As the launch pulled away, he was piped aboard
the *Euryalus* to the sound of a seventeen-gun salvo. Protocol demanded
that he sail for Britain at midnight, the minute the mandate came to an
end. 'A few rockets and searchlights spotlighted the cruiser as it
steamed from harbour' for home, escorted by the aircraft carrier HMS
Ocean and three destroyers.

Despite Cunningham's prayer 'that peace may come immediately to
Palestine', violence continued unabated throughout the country.
Across its borders, Arab governments had declared their intention to
invade Palestine to overturn the partition decision. In a matter of hours
Tel Aviv would be bombed three times by Egyptian aircraft and the
first Arab-Israeli war would begin. These were chilling times for the
Yishuv, but times also of great promise. The British sea blockade had
finally been broken. On 14 May the 1,000-ton steamer *Andria*, flying the
Panamanian flag, sailed from Cyprus carrying 360 immigrants: the
British authorities made no attempt to interfere as the ship entered
Haifa bay.

At 4 p.m. on the same day, in Tel Aviv's Museum Hall, 16 Rothschild
Boulevard, Ben Gurion, flanked by the leaders of the *Yishuv*, with a
photograph of Herzl placed judiciously above his head, proclaimed
'the establishment of the Jewish State in Palestine – to be called Israel'.
It was not an easy decision to make. Just two days earlier, apprehensive
at what lay in the future, the *Yishuv*'s provisional Cabinet, by a vote of
6–4, decided narrowly in favour of declaring statehood. The gamble
paid off: eventually on the field of battle; more immediately in the
international arena. Two hours after Ben Gurion's proclamation, the
United States recognised the Provisional Government as the de facto
authority of the new state of Israel; three days later the Soviet Union

followed suit. Despite persistent parliamentary questioning, the British government agonised until February 1949 before recognising de facto the state of Israel. A few months later, in May, the United Nations received Israel, 'a peace-loving country', as an accredited member. In the course of a year the new state had attained full international legitimacy.

For the Jews – and not only the Jews – the establishment of Israel was a moment of historic significance: Herzl's improbable prophecy at Basel had come true, albeit a year late. Prayers were offered in synagogues throughout the world, where 'spontaneous and joyous demonstrations' took place. In New York, Weizmann, still bed-ridden, sent a message to a mass demonstration at Madison Square Garden.

> The recent confirmation by international judgment of our right to an equal place in the family of nations closes a two thousand year chapter of injustice, homelessness, and frustration in our history. We remember the six million martyrs of the last and bitterest trial of our exile, as we enter the new era in a spirit of rededication to the fundamental truth expounded by our prophets and sages. With God's help we shall continue to build the State of Israel on foundations of justice and equality for all its inhabitants and with good will and brotherhood towards the neighbouring Arab States, and indeed to all peoples of the world.

Meanwhile, in Tel Aviv, Ben Gurion prepared the fledgling state for war.[8]

For the Palestinians it signified the first stage of their *Nakba* (Catastrophe), its most visible manifestation the 325,000–350,000 refugees that had fled Palestine: that number would be doubled by the end of the first Arab-Israeli war.* There is no convincing evidence of a Zionist plot to ethnically cleanse, or transfer, the Palestinians from

*Understandably, precise figures are almost impossible to come by; but 650,000–700,000 seems to be the generally accepted figure. Bevin, however, in January 1949 put the number as low as 500,000, see *PD*, vol. 460, c.933, 26 January 1949.

their homeland, as has been argued by some.[9] *The by now notorious 'Plan Dalet', the supposed blueprint of this plot, reveals, after careful and responsible scrutiny, nothing of the kind. Drawn up in March 1948, 'The objective of this plan', it read, 'is to gain control of the areas of the Hebrew state (according to the partition frontiers) and defend its borders' – against an impending all-Arab attack.[10] From June 1946, the *Haganah* had been preparing in earnest for such an eventuality. That month an Arab conference, held in Bludan, Syria, called for the mobilisation of all Arab resources, money, arms and volunteers, the use of force – an army of 100,000 was mentioned – even anti-West sanctions, all to thwart a Zionist occupation of Palestine. The Jewish Agency, and Ben Gurion in particular, took these threats extremely seriously. 'Plan Dalet' was the latest manifestation of the measures intended to counter an inevitable Arab assault on the Jewish state.

The events of 1947–9 must be judged against the background of war, at first a civil war, aided by Arab irregulars, later a full-scale war launched by neighbouring Arab countries. It was a war waged to overturn the United Nations' decision to partition Palestine into Jewish and Palestinian states. What emerged was the total collapse of the Palestinian political leadership. Its upper and middle classes, those rich enough or well-connected enough to do so, fled the country. The net effect of this top-drawer exodus was to leave ordinary Palestinians leaderless and defenceless. Many left out of fear for the future, others were deliberately expelled, some took flight of their own accord. There can be no single one-dimensional explanation of the Palestinian refugee problem. Refugees are a tragic result of war, of every war in recorded history. And as in every war there were incidents of great brutality on both sides, cases of indiscriminate killings and expulsions. But two commentators, from different academic backgrounds, reach roughly the same conclusions. Dr Adel Husein Yahya, Director of the Palestinian Association for Cultural Exchange (PACE) at Ramallah,

*By the very nature of things there were some activists in the *Yishuv* who spoke of transfer. But it should be remembered that transfer was a perfectly legitimate concept during the interwar years, and for some time after. In its Palestinian context it was first raised by Lord Peel in his report of July 1937, and later at the Labour Party Conference of 1944. However, mainstream Zionism – and even Begin, judging from his pep talk to UNSCOP – was adamant in its aim to achieve a Jewish majority in Palestine through mass immigration, not transfer.

concludes: 'When refugees were asked why they left, the over-whelming majority of them, more than 92 percent, responded that they left out of fear . . . [or] to allow the Arab armies to fight . . . or out of plain ignorance on their part of the stakes involved . . . It thus seems that the flight of 1948 was a classic exodus, which occurs all too often in times of war.' Professor Benny Morris, of Ben Gurion University writes:

> The Palestinian refugee problem was born of war, not by design, Jewish or Arab. It was largely a by-product of Arab and Jewish fears and of the protracted, bitter fighting that characterised the first Arab-Israeli war; in smaller part, it was the deliberate creation of Jewish and Arab military commanders and politicians . . . What happened in Palestine/Israel over 1947–49 was so complex and varied, the situation radically changing from date to date and place to place, that a single-cause explanation of the exodus from most sites is untenable.[11]

It is illuminating to place the Palestinian refugee problem in a wider context. Two other refugee movements troubled the international community in the immediate post-war period: on the Indian Subcontinent, and in eastern and central Europe. Infinitely greater in scope, tens of millions were involved, and, no less painful in terms of personal tragedies, these upheavals were marked by planned massacres, mass rape and instances of ethnic cleansing. Bloody orgies of inter-communal violence stained the partitioning of the Subcontinent, frenzied bloodbaths that left a million dead and eleven million refugees driven from their homes. In Europe, almost three million Sudeten Germans were turfed out of Czechoslovakia and deported to Germany in a matter of months. The *New York Times* witnessed the forcible evacuation of thirteen million Germans from Poland, Czechoslovakia, Hungary and Yugoslavia: 'The scale of this resettlement, and the conditions in which it takes place are without precedent in history. No one seeing its horrors first hand can doubt that it is a crime against humanity for which history will exact a terrible retribution.[12]' No such retribution was exacted. These matters have largely faded away, no longer do they trouble the international community. What makes the Palestinian refugee problem unique is that it has been put on hold for sixty years, irrefutably for political reasons, humanitarian considerations having been shunted aside.

But the real tragedy of the *Nakba* is twofold. For the refugees, certainly. But of no less significance, and probably more so, it was an expression of the Palestinians' inability to foster authoritative national institutions: to borrow a well-worn phrase, to create 'a state within a state'. Instead, the Palestinians frittered away their potential strength in internecine fighting, an ongoing phenomenon since the early 1920s: Husaynis v. Nashashibis; clan v. clan; militia v. militia. Some reports spoke of more Palestinians being killed by rival Palestinian factions than by the British or the *Haganah*, although, yet again, precise figures are difficult to come by. Max Weber defined the state 'as an entity which claims a monopoly on the legitimate use of physical force'.[13] One can only speculate whether, had the Palestinians succeeded in creating 'a state within a state', they would have achieved all their aims. But one can assert with absolute certainty that the absence of such a creature guaranteed that they fail.

On 14 May the Foreign and Colonial Offices published a statement chronicling 'the history and policy of the Mandate'.[14] It highlighted how Palestine had developed under British patronage: improvements to the infrastructure of the country – roads, railways, postal and air communications, harbours – it noted considerable progress in Arab educational and health standards; and it commented on the remarkable growth of the Jewish National Home, its independent social welfare systems resting on a solid agricultural-industrial base. But despite these achievements, the statement was also a confession of failure. 'Eighty-four thousand troops, who received no cooperation from the Jewish community, had proved insufficient to maintain law and order . . . Since the war 388 British subjects had been killed in Palestine, while the military forces there had cost the British taxpayer £100,000,000.' Renewed Arab violence since the UN's partition decision, and the eruption of 'an open war' between the two peoples, 'showed that the loss of further lives was inevitable'. As Britain had repeatedly emphasised 'that, in the absence of agreement by both Arabs and Jews, they would not themselves enforce partition', the evacuation of Palestine – in the most humiliating of circumstances – was unavoidable.

Britain had undertaken responsibility for the Palestine mandate when its Empire, territorially at least, was at its apogee – though cracks were already appearing, particularly in India. It had done so believing firmly that the mandate was workable, despite warning signs to the contrary. All that was needed was a spirit of compromise, a measure of goodwill and cooperation between the interested parties, behaviour in accordance with the presumed British tradition of resolving thorny political problems. Unfortunately, the belligerent, extra-European nationalisms, gaining in militancy in the aftermath of the Second World War, were in no mood to adhere to this practice. So Britain stumbled along, at odds with its closest allies, subject to withering criticism at home and abroad, persisting in a policy it scarcely believed in. By 1948 it had neither the will nor resources to continue the mandate: it was a classic case of imperial overreach: psychologically, emotionally and materially. Eleven years earlier Lord Peel had pronounced the mandate 'unworkable', proposing that the government terminate 'the present mandate on the basis of partition'. Even in the chaotic situation that had evolved by May 1948, Peel's formula remained (and still remains) the best out of all possible options.

Sir Henry Gurney compared the last days of the British mandate to a Greek Tragedy.

'Chorus of British Delegates [to the United Nations] – We are going on May 15th. On May 15th we are going.'

Interruptions: 'Moshe Shertok [Sharett] – We are prepared to agree to anything provided that it includes partition, immigration and a Jewish state.

'Jamal al-Husayni – We are prepared to agree to anything that does not include partition, Jewish immigration and a Jewish state.

'Senator W. Austin – All I suggest is something that commits nobody to anything at all.

'President Truman (offstage) – I am still backing partition.

'Chorus – If you haven't heard us properly, let us say again that we are leaving on the 15th May. We have kept these people from each other's throats for the last 25 years, and if anyone else is prepared to do it let him say so now and do something about it. Only don't say we haven't warned you. If there is a vacuum, it is not our fault but yours, because you have assumed responsibility for Palestine from the 15th May. This is a thoroughly wicked child, though we brought it up as well as we could, and it was really very nice of you to take it over. It is rather urgent, because the child is getting more and more out of hand, and we are finding it almost impossible to look after it properly. Cutting it in half may well be the best thing that could happen to it, but we warned you that it wasn't likely to agree.

'This is the 15th May. We're off!'[15]

Glossary

Aliyah: Literally 'to ascend', 'to go up'.

AAC: Anglo-American Committee of Inquiry. Set up in November 1945, it reported in April 1946. Its main recommendation adopted Truman's call to admit immediately 100,000 Jewish immigrants.

AHC: Arab Higher Committee, the main political organ of the Palestinian Arabs. In November 1935 it called for the prohibition of Jewish immigration and the stoppage of land sales to Jews, and to establish an Arab government. It was dominated by the Mufti, Haj Amin al-Husayni. Disbanded in 1937 in the wake of the Peel report, it reinvented itself in the post-war years, though it was still run by the al-Husayni faction.

'Bevingrads': These were enclosed barbed-wire areas erected by the British in strategic areas in the main urban centres in the hope – not always realised – that they would afford British personnel greater protection from attacks by Jewish militias.

Eretz Israel: The Land of Israel.

Haganah (**Defence**): The principal military organisation of the Jewish community in Palestine. Linked to the Jewish Agency. Founded in 1920.

Irgun Zvai Leumi: (National Military Organisation) The military wing of the Revisionists. Established in 1931.

Kibbutz: Jewish communal settlement.

Mossad Le'aliyah Beth: The Jewish Agency body that facilitated 'illegal' immigration.

Nakba: Catastrophe.

Palmach: Acronym for *Plugoth HaMachatz*, or 'Assault Companies', the elite strike force of the *Haganah*.

'Slick': Slang for an arms cache.

Stern Gang: Or *Lechi*, acronym for *Lochmei Cheruth Israel* – 'Fighters for the Freedom of Israel'. An extreme offshoot of the *Irgun*, it was founded by Avraham 'Yair' Stern in September 1940.

UNSCOP: United Nations Special Committee on Palestine. Formed in May 1947, it reported the following September. It recommended the partition of Palestine into Jewish and Arab states.

URM: United Resistence Movement: an attempt to coordinate the actions of the *Haganah*, the *Irgun* and the Stern Gang. Created in October 1945, it was disbanded in July–August 1946.

Va'ad Leumi: National Council of the Jewish Community in mandatory Palestine.

Yishuv: The Jewish community in mandatory Palestine.

Notes

Endnotes Key:

MEC Middle East Centre at St Antony's College, Oxford

RH   Bodleian Library, Oxford, and its Library of Commonwealth and African Studies at Rhodes House

LHC Liddle Hart Centre for Military Archive at King's College, London

IWM Imperial War Museum, London

NA   National Archives, Kew, London

CZA Central Zionist Archives, Jerusalem

BC   Begin Centre, Jerusalem

WA   Weizmann Archives, Rehovoth

One – The Promised Land   **pp. 1–19**

• 1. See Marvin Lowenthal, ed., *The Diaries of Theodor Herzl* (Grosset and Dunlop, New York, 1962, Universal Library ed.), p. 224. • 2. See Chaim Weizmann, Trial and Error (East and West Library, London, 1950), p. 61 • 3. See Raphael Patai, *The Complete Diaries of Theodor Herzl* (New York, Herzl Press, 1960), vol. 1, p. 248, and Amos Elon, *Herzl* (New York, Holt, Rinehart & Winston, 1975), pp. 17–63, 87–8, 106–22, 126–9. • 4. See Arthur Koestler, *Promise and Fulfilment. Palestine 1917–1949* (London, Macmillan, 1949), p. 4. • 5. For Pinsker see David Vital, *The Origins of Zionism* (Oxford, Clarendon Press, 1975), pp. 122–32. Herzl wrote, a few days before the publication of *Der Judenstaat*: 'Dumbfounding agreement on the critical side, great similarity on the constructive. A pity I had not read it before my own pamphlet was printed. Still, it is a good thing I knew nothing of it – or perhaps I might have abandoned my own undertaking.' (Lowenthal, ed., *The Diaries of Theodor Herzl*, p.96). • 6. Quoted in *Encyclopaedia Judaica* (Jerusalem, 1972), vol. 4, c.1000. • 7. See Neville J. Mandel, *The Arabs and Palestine Before World War*

One (University of California Press, 1976), p. 229; Porath, p. 17; and ESCO, i, p. 54: McCarthy, p. 10, is again more modest but more precise, numbering the Jews at 38,754. • 8. Porath, i, p. 19, a reliable source, puts the figure at approximately 600,000; McCarthy, p. 10, less so, at 680,000. • 9. Porath, i, p. 20 and Walter Laqueur, *A History of Zionism* (New York, Schocken Books, 1976), pp. 224–5. • 10. Porath, i, pp. 23–5. • 11. Quotations in Elie Kedourie, *The Chatham House Version and other Middle-Eastern Studies* (London, Weidenfeld & Nicolson, 1970), pp. 332, 338–9, 341, taken from Khalil al-Sakakini diaries in Arabic, *Kadha ana ya dunya – such Am I, Oh World –* (Jerusalem, 1955), entries for 25 July 1908; 8 and 23 October 1908; 12, 14, 21 November 1908; and 26, 29 January 1919. • 12. Khalil al-Sakakini, *Such Am I, Oh World. Diaries of Khalil al-Sakakini* (Jerusalem, Keter Publishing House, 1990), p. 49, entry for 23 February 1914 (Hebrew ed.: translated from Arabic by Gideon Shilo). • 13. Mandel, p. xviii, and Porath, i, p. 26. 14. For a general discussion of religion and Orthodox Christians and Palestinian politics, see Elie Kedourie, 'Religion and Politics: The Diaries of Khalil Sakakini', *St Antony's Papers*, no. 4 (Chatto and Windus, 1958). • 15. See Mandel, p. xviii, and Porath, i, pp. 26–30. • 16. For these matters, see Mandel, in particular chapters 2 and 10, 'Early Arab Responses' and 'Towards Collision', and pp. 223–31; Porath, i, chapter 1 'The Rejection of Zionism and the Crystallization of Palestinian-Arab Ideology'; and Laqueur, p. 224. • 17. See Mayir Verete, 'Why was a British consulate established in Jerusalem', in *From Palmerston to Balfour. Collected Essays of Mayir Verete*, ed. Norman Rose (Frank Cass, London, 1992). • 18. See Philip Magnus, *Kitchener. Portrait of an Imperialist* (London, Penguin Books, 1968), pp. 27–8. • 19. Lowenthal, *The Diaries of Theodor Herzl*, p.382; and for 'Clapham Junction', Josiah Clement Wedgwood, *The Seventh Dominion* (London, 1928), p. 3. • 20. In Amos Elon, *Herzl* (New York, 1975), p. 71. • 21. For *Herzl* see, Alex Bein, *Theodor Herzl* (Philadelphia, 1942), pp. 455–6; Amos Elon, *Herzl* (1975), p. 388; and David Vital, *Zionism. The Formative Years* (Oxford, Clarendon Press, 1983), pp. 283–4. For an overall account, Norman Rose, *Weizmann. A Biography* (New York, Elisabeth Sifton Books, Viking, 1986), pp. 69–79. • 22. See Christopher Sykes, *Two Studies in Virtue* (London, 1953), section 2; Verete, 'The Idea of the Restoration of the Jews in English Protestant Thought', in Rose, ed., *From Palmerston to Balfour . . .*; also Norman Rose, *Chaim Weizmann. A Biography*, p. 79. And for a general discussion of gentile Zionism see Norman Rose, *The Gentile Zionists* (Frank Cass, London, 1973). • 23. Report in *The Times*, 10 November 1914. • 24. For the de Bunsen committee, see 'Minutes and Report of the Committee on Asiatic Turkey, 30 June 1915', in CAB.27/1. The drafting of the Sykes-Picot agreement may be followed in a series of diplomatic exchanges between Britain, France and Russia. The crux of the agreement is contained in Sir Edward Grey, the British

Foreign Secretary, to Paul Cambon, the French ambassador in London, 16 May 1916. For the correspondence see, *Documents of British Foreign Policy, 1919–1939*, First Series (HMSO, 1952), vol. IV, pp. 241–51. See also, Elie Kedourie, *In the Anglo-Arab Labyrinth* (Cambridge University Press, 1976), p.58; and Verete, 'The Balfour Declaration . . . footnote p.2, in Rose (ed.) *From Palmerston to Balfour . . .* • 25. For the exchange of letters, see *Cmd.5957, The Text of the Correspondence between Sir Henry McMahon and the Sherif Hussein of Mecca. July 1915–March 1916* (March 1939). For the most comprehensive and authoritative contribution to this debate, see Kedourie, . . . *Labyrinth*. • 26. See *The Letters and Papers of Chaim Weizmann. Series A, Letters* (OUP; Transaction Books; Rutgers University; Israel Universities Press, Jerusalem, 1968–80), vol. I, no .I, pp. 35–7 (hereafter, *WL*). • 27. See Viscount Samuel, *Memoirs* (The Cresset Press, London, 1945), pp. 139–42. Samuel's memorandum, 21 January 1915, in CAB.37/123/43, NA, and FO.800/100 NA; see also his paper, 11 March 1915, CAB.27/126 NA. Also Asquith, *Memories and Reflections* (Cassell, London, 1928), ii, pp.59–60, 65 and Stein, *Balfour Declaration*, pp. 109–12. • 28. In Trevor Wilson, ed., *The Political Diaries of C. P. Scott, 1911–1928* (Cornell University Press, Ithaca, 1970), p. 255. • 29. See Stephen Roskill, *Hankey. Man of Secrets* (London, Collins, 1972), vol. II, pp. 28–9. • 30. For a full and nuanced discussion of the rationale behind the Balfour Declaration, see Stein, *Balfour*; Verete, in Rose, ed., *From Palmerston . . .*, chapters I and 8; and Rose, *Weizmann*, chapter 8, 'The Charter'. • 31. Dr Henry King, president of Oberlin College, Ohio, and Charles Crane, a Chicago businessman, were the surviving commissioners from an intended international commission: the French and the British had pulled out at the last moment. Its main recommendation proposed a United States mandate for a Greater Syria, including Palestine and the Lebanon; but if that should prove to be impracticable, Great Britain – definitely not France – would be the preferred choice. The report is published in *Foreign Relations of the United States. The Paris Peace Conference, 1919* (Washington, 1947), xii, pp. 751ff (hereafter, *FRUS*). See also David Lloyd George, *The Truth About the Peace Treaties* (London, Victor Gollancz, 1938), ii, pp. 1078–80. • 32. See David Garnett, *The Letters of T. E. Lawrence* (London, Jonathan Cape, 1938), p. 196.

Two – 'Beginnings are always troublesome'   pp. 20–33

• 1. Storrs, *Orientations* (London, Ivor Nicholson & Watson, 1939), p. 352. • 2. Though others thought differently. See, for example, J. M. N. Jeffries, *Palestine, the Reality* (London, Longmans, 1939). • 3. See *WL*, p. 325, n2. This assessment was endorsed by War Office intelligence reports. Copies in Weizmann Archives, Weizmann Institute, Rehovoth, and the Lloyd George

Papers, House of Lords, F.86/8/4. • 4. See Clayton to Lord Curzon, 8 June 1919, *Documents of British Foreign Policy, 1919–1939*, First Series, vol. IV, (London, HMSO, 1952), no. 183, nr, p. 272. • 5. Storrs, p. 375. • 6. Text of agreement in *WL*, IX, pp. 86–7. • 7. Al-Budayri's recollections in GB165–0282, Box 2/4, deposited at the Middle East Centre, St Antony's College, Oxford (hereafter MEC); and Porath, i, p. 76. • 8. See Porath, i, pp. 110, 194. • 9. See *Cmd.1540, The Haycroft Report into the Disturbances of May 1921, with Correspondence* (October 1921). • 10. See *Cmd.1500*, 'Final Draft of Mandate', article 25; also *Cmd.1700*, 'The Churchill White Paper'. • 11. 'The Iron Wall' and 'Ethics of the Iron Wall' were originally published in Paris in Russian on 4 and 11 November 1923: an English translation of the former appeared in *Jewish Herald* (South Africa), 26 November 1937; of the latter, in *The Jewish Standard* (London), 5 September 1941. Of course, by 'Iron Wall' Jabotinsky did not mean an actual wall, but rather a protective military cordon. • 12. History of the *Haganah* (Hebrew), vol. 2, part 1, p. 188. • 13. See *Cmd.1500, The Final Draft of the Mandate* (August 1921), article, 25. • 14. See *Daily Express*, 28 October 1922; Maurice Cowling, *The Impact of Labour* (Cambridge University Press, 1971), p. 81; A. J. P. Taylor, *Beaverbrook* (London, Hamish Hamilton, 1972), pp. 200, 206; Chaim Weizmann, *Trial and Error*, pp. 351–2. • 15. See *Cmd.1700, Correspondence with the Palestine Arab Delegation and the Zionist Organisation. And a Statement of British Policy on Palestine* (June 1922). • 16. See Cabinet minutes, 27 June and 31 July 1923, CAB.23/46, and CAB.24/161, CP.351, NA. • 17. See *Cmd.1889, Papers Relating to Elections for the Legislative Council* (June 1923) and *Cmd.1989, Correspondence with the High Commissioner on the proposed formation of an Arab Agency* (October–November 1923). • 18. Recollections of Stewart Perowne (served in Palestine from 1925 to 1934: among other posts appointed as an Assistant District Commissioner) in GB165–0282, Box 1/6, MEC. • 19. See *WL*, vol. 1, series B, p. 296. • 20. Figures in *Cmd.3530, The Shaw Report on the Disturbances of August 1929* (March 1930), p. 8, and ESCO Foundation, *Palestine. A Study of Jewish, Arab, and British Policies*, vol. 1, pp. 405–6. • 21. Rose, *Weizmann*, pp. 30, 224. • 22. *Cmd.5479. The Report of the Palestine Royal Commission* (July 1937), p. 305. • 23. See Porath, i, pp. 304–9. • 24. Quoted in Bernard Wasserstein, *The British in Palestine: Mandatory Government and the Arab–Jewish Conflict, 1917–1929* (Oxford, Basil Blackwell, 1991, 2nd ed.), p. 142. • 25. See Theodore White, *In Search of History* (Harper & Row, New York, 1978), p. 61: diary entry for October 1938. For 'mental aberration', see Frederick William Geoffrey Blenkinsop . . ., who wrote a six-page memorandum, 2 November 1944, in which he made clear his lack of sympathy for Zionist aims and which contains the quoted phrase. In GB165–0030, MEC. • 26. Quoted in Wasserstein, p. 66, from an unpublished Commission of Inquiry report into the riots of April 1920, FO.371/5121/83 NA.

• 27. For 'very nice little dance', Colonel C. R. W. Norman (Head of Military Intelligence in Palestine, October 1946–July 1948) to his mother, 25 August 1947, 1706:87/57/4, IWM; and Richard Crossman, *Palestine Mission. A Personal Record* (London, Hamish Hamilton, 1947), pp. 132–3. • 28. Crossman's remark to an audience at Chatham House, 13 June 1946, in GB165–0068, File 1, MEC; Battershill's comments in MSS Brit. Emp., s.467, Box 10, file 2, RH; Mary Burgess to her mother, 3 November 1946, in MSS Brit. Emp., s.305, RH; and for Gurney diaries, entries for 27 March and 22 April 1948, GB165–0128, MEC. • 29. Interview with Ra'anan (Ronnie) Sivan, Jerusalem, June 2006. Sivan later served with distinction in the Israeli civil and foreign services.

Three – Rebellion   pp. 34–51

1. See *Cmd.3530, The Shaw Report on the Disturbances of August 1929* (March 1930), p. 65; and *Cmd.3229, A Memorandum by the Secretary of State for Colonies on the Wailing Wall* (November 1928); also *Cmd.3530*. • 2. See Miss Irvine to Miss Emery, 2 September 1929, GB165–0099, Box 1/1, Box 2/4, MEC. Also *Cmd.3530*, pp. 64, 65, 68. • 3. These events may be followed in: *Cmd.3229, A Memorandum by the Colonial Secretary on the Wailing Wall* (November 1928); *Cmd.3530, The Shaw Report on the Disturbances of August 1929* (March 1930); *Cmd.3582, A Statement of Policy with regard to Palestine* (May 1930); *Cmd.3686, The Hope Simpson Report on Immigration, Land Settlement and Development* (October 1930); and *Cmd.3692, A Statement of Policy* (Oct 1930) – the Passfield White Paper. For an overview see Rose, *The Gentile Zionists*, chapter 1. • 4. Chaim Weizmann, *Trial and Error*, p. 426. Also Moshe Pearlman, *Ben Gurion Looks Back* (Weidenfeld & Nicolson, 1965), pp. 70–1, 72–4. • 5. These remarks about Wauchope are taken from Ralph Postan's recollections in Box 1/13, MEC. For MacDonald to Ben Gurion, see Pearlman, p. 71 • 6. For Red Light district and restaurants, Flight Mechanic Graham Charles Tylee, 286:89/12/1, IWM; for swimming, Second Lieutenant R. Hodges to Stinger (?), 26 July 1947, 1321:87/14/1, IWM; and for polo and hunting, Colonel K. G. F. Chavasse, 7936:98/23/1, IWM. • 7. For immigration figures, see ESCO, i, pp. 404–6, ii, p. 674, and *Cmd.5479*, chapter X (the Peel report); for details regarding the 'Aryanisation' of Nazi Germany, and similar developments in central and eastern Europe, see Richard J. Evans, *The Third Reich in Power* (Penguin Books, 2005), chapter 6, 'Towards the Racial Utopia'. • 8. See *Cmd.5479* (the Peel report), p. 84 and ESCO, ii, p. 771. • 9. For al-Qassam, see Porath, *The Palestinian Arab National Movement*, ii, pp. 133–9; Arab demands in ESCO, ii, p. 785; and for Legislative Council, *Cmd.1889, Papers relating to Elections for the Legislative Council* (June 1923), and *Cmd.5119, Proposed New*

Constitution for Palestine (March 1936). • 10. For 'precedent', see Norman Rose, 'The Arab Rulers and Palestine, 1936: The British Reaction', *Journal of Modern History* (June 1972); and for 'forged a bond', see the Arab Office, *The Future of Palestine* (Geneva, 1947). • 11. See al-Sakakini diaries, 26 May, 10 and 17 October 1936, pp. 187–8, 191, 192. • 12. For al-Kaukji, see Porath, *The Palestinian Arab National Movement*, ii, pp. 188–92, 215. • 13. Blanche 'Baffy' Dugdale was the leading, and most influential, gentile Zionist of her generation, see her diaries, *'Baffy', the Diaries of Blanche Dugdale, 1936–1947* (Vallentine, Mitchell, London, 1973), p. 80, ed., Norman Rose. 'Ferocious eloquence' in John Connell, *Wavell, Scholar and Statesman* (London, 1964), p. 196. • 14. Wingate's papers in Liddell Hart Centre, King's College, London (hereafter LHC), LH 15/5/300. • 15. For the damaging effects Italian intervention had on British policy, see *British Documents on Foreign Policy* (London, 1950), Third series, vol. III, no. 326, 2 October 1938, and in particular for links between Haj Amin and Italy, see Lukasz Hirszowicz, *The Third Reich and the Arab East* (London, Routledge & Kegan Paul, 1966), p. 13. Also Rose, *The Gentile Zionists*, pp. 104–6. • 16. Hirszowicz, pp. 27–8. • 17. For Chiefs-of-Staff warnings, see, for example, 'A Review of Imperial Defence by Chiefs-of-Staff', 26 February 1937, CP (37), CAB.24/268; a meeting of Committee of Imperial Defence (CID), 5 July 1937, CP 183/37, CAB.24/270; Cabinet minutes for 14 July 1937, CAB.23/89; and 'A Report by Chiefs-of-Staff', 19 October 1937, CP 183 (37), CAB.14/271 – all in NA. For 'two divisions', see 'A Record of Anglo-French Conversations' held on 28 April 1938, *Documents on British Foreign Policy, 1919–1939*, Third Series, i, pp. 201, 208–9. These revelations were voiced as the two powers considered the ramifications of the *Anschluss*. • 18. For Royal Commission's findings, see *Cmd.5479* (the Peel Report), in particular, pp. i–viii, and chapter XIX, 'Conclusions and Recommendations'; for Wauchope, see Ralph Postan's recollections, Box 1/13, MEC, and for Battershill, MSS Brit. Emp. s.467, Box 15, File 5, RH; for British government concurring, *Cmd.5513*, 'Palestine Statement of Policy by HMG' (July 1937); opposition of Foreign Office in Anthony Eden's memorandum, 19 November 1937, CP282 (37), CAB.24/273, NA, and for Chiefs of Staff, see footnote 17. For parliamentary debates, see Lords, *PD*, vol. 106, c.599–674, 20 July 1937, and for Samuel, *Manchester Guardian*, 21 July 1937, and Commons, *PD*, vol. 326, c.2236–2367, 21 July 1937. For gentile Zionists' opposition, see Rose, *Gentile Zionists*, p. 149, n90; and Churchill quote in 'Notes of a Dinner Conversation', 8 June 1937, WA, Rehovoth, Israel. • 19. Porath, ii, pp. 231–35, 234, and report in *Ha'aretz*, 25 May 2007. • 20. References to Bludan, Andrews and administration's reaction in *The Times*, 10 and 27 September 1937, and 2 October 1937. For 'The Yids' see Lieutenant-General Lawrence Carr, a Brigade Commander, to his wife, 2 October 1937,

GB99, LHC. For quotations regarding Haj Amin, see General Sir Richard Nugent O'Connor Papers, 1938–9, GB99–3/4, LHC; also Tegart Papers, GB165–0282, Box 2/3, MEC. • 21. From Battershill's diary, 10 October 1938, MSS. Brit. Emp., s.467, Box 12, File 1, RH. • 22. For 'houses blown up', Carr to his wife, 17 October 1937, GB99, LHC; 'taking potshots' in Wakefield Street to his father, 8 July 1938, LHC; 'a bus loaded' in evidence of Roy Turner, a sergeant in the Palestine Police, MSS Brit. Emp., s.527/10, vol. 3, RH. For *Bureau Nationale Arabe*, see Arthur Creech-Jones papers, MSS Brit. Emp., s.332, Box 30/2, RH; and for violating Arab homes in Hala al-Sakakini, *Jerusalem and I* (Jordan, Economic Press Co., 1990), p. 59. • 23. 'Last cavalry charge' in Sir John's recollections, GB165–028, Box 1/17, MEC; Montgomery's ruling in General Sir Hugh Charles Stockwell's Papers, GB99–6/26, LHC. 'Precise figures' are taken from the Cunningham Papers, GB165–0072, Box 2/1, MEC, Royal Institute of International Affairs, *Great Britain and Palestine. Information Papers, No. 20, 1915–45* (London, 1946), 3rd ed., Cmd.5479, pp. 105–6, and *Encyclopaedia Judaica*, vol. 9, p. 350. For criticism of methods, see Evans to 'my darling Mev', 19 July 1936, MSS Brit. Emp., s.410, RH. • 24. Report in *Manchester Guardian*, 25 July 1937; David Niv, *The Irgun Zvai Leumi* (Tel Aviv, 1965–80), ii, pp. 78–80, in Hebrew. • 25. See GB99:5/1–13, LHC. • 26. *WL*, vol. 18, no. 364. • 27. Tegart Papers, GB165–0281, report of 22 April 1939, MEC. • 28. From papers of Sir John MacPherson, Chief Secretary, 1939–1943, MSS. Brit. Emp., s.487, RH. • 29. See Susanna (Espie) Pearce Emery, to her mother, 5 March 1939, GB165–0099, MEC. • 30. See Porath, ii, p. 292; and Rashid Khalidi, 'The Palestinians and 1948: the underlying causes of failure' in *The War for Palestine. Rewriting the History of 1948*, eds. Avi Shlaim and Eugene L. Rogan (Cambridge University Press, 2001), p. 28. • 31. See Shabtai Teveth, *Ben Gurion and the Palestinian Arabs. From Peace to War* (Oxford University Press, 1985), p. 130; David Ben-Gurion, *My Talks with Arab Leaders* (Jerusalem, Keter Books, 1972), p. 15; and Geoffrey Furlonge, *Palestine is My Country. The Story of Musa Alami* (London, John Murray, 1969), pp. 117, 126. See also a report in the *New York Times*, 18 March 1937. • 32. See Rose, *Weizmann*, p. 350. • 33. For MacDonald – GB165–0282, Box 1/10, MEC, and MacPherson Papers, MSS Brit. Emp., s.487, RH; and for Lloyd Phillips, letter of 20 May 1939, MSS Brit. Emp., s.499, 2/2, RH. • 34. See evidence of Sir Michael Hogan, Solicitor-General, Palestine, 1947, Box 1/8, MEC.

Four – War   pp. 52–70

1. See Halifax to Weizmann, 19 December 1939, WA; Cabinet discussions in CAB 65/2, 5, NA. Reports of casualties incurred during the demonstrations

in A312/16, 30, CZA, Jerusalem. • 2. For the Hitler–Haj Amin meeting, see *Documents on German Foreign Policy* (hereafter GD), Series D, vol. XIII, nos 515, 516, pp. 881–5. Hitler's recollections of Haj Amin in *Hitler's Table Talk, 1941–1944*, edited and with an Introduction by Hugh Trevor-Roper, (OUP, 1988), p. 547. For an overview of Haj Amin's contacts with and activities on behalf of the Axis powers, see in particular, Lukasz Hirszowicz, *The Third Reich and the Arab East*, pp. 34ff. Much has been written about Haj Amin. See also: Philip Mattar, *The Mufti of Jerusalem: Al-Hajj Amin Al-Husayni* (New York, Columbia University Press, 1988); R. Melka, 'Nazi Germany and the Palestine Question', *Middle Eastern Studies*, vol. 5, no. 3, October 1969; H. D. Schmidt, 'The Nazi Party in Palestine and the Levant, 1932–39', *International Affairs* (October 1952); David Yisraeli, 'The Third Reich and Palestine', *Middle Eastern Studies*, vol. 7, no. 3, October 1971; and Philip Mattar, 'The Mufti of Jerusalem and the Politics of Palestine', *Middle Eastern Studies*, vol. 42, no. 2, Spring 1988. • 3. See a report compiled by the Jewish Agency (apparently drafted by Lewis Namier) on the 'War Effort and War Potentialities of Palestine Jewry', A312/8, CZA. • 4. Quoted in Lossin, *Pillar of Fire*, p. 391. • 5. On these matters, see 'War Effort . . .', op. cit; statement by Sir James Grigg (Secretary of State for War), 6 August 1942, *PD*, Commons, vol. 382, c.1271–72; ESCO, ii, pp. 1027, 1028; Norman Rose, *Lewis Namier and Zionism* (Clarendon Press, 1980), pp. 101–13; Yehuda Bauer, *From Diplomacy to Resistance. A History of Jewish Palestine, 1939–1945* (Philadelphia, Jewish Publication Society of America, 1970), pp. 83–4; also Martin Gilbert, *Jewish History Atlas* (London, Weidenfeld & Nicolson, 1969), p. 91. • 6. See *PD*, Lords, vol. 121, c.102, 305, 25 November and 16 December 1941, statements by Lord Moyne and Lord Croft; Hirszowicz, p. 252; and ESCO, ii, p. 1007. • 7. From a note by MacPherson in MSS Brit. Emp., s.487, RH. • 8. See Brooke to Wilson, 20 July 1943; for 'reports circulating', Sir Percy James Grigg (Secretary of State for War) to Richard Casey (Minister of State, Middle East), 10 June 1943, both in Alanbrooke Papers, GB99, LHC. • 9. See MacPherson Papers, MSS Brit. Emp., s.487, RH. Ben Gurion in *'Baffy', The Diaries of Blanche Dugdale, 1936–1947*, 1 May 1940, p. 167. • 10. See *Palestine Post*, 17–20 November 1943, and WL, XXI, p. 100, n1, p. 103, n1. In December of the same year an arms search was carried out at kibbutz Hulda, not far from Rehovoth. Seven members were arrested, tried and handed down sentences ranging between two to six years. • 11. Report by George Lowe, a sergeant in the Intelligence Corps, in MSS Brit. Emp., s,527/10, vol. 2, RH.; also an account by Lieutenant-General Sir John Conyers, 2 July 1946, GB165–0075, MEC. • 12. Evidence of Daward al-Husseini and Rashid Shawwa, GB165–0282, Box 2/1, 3, MEC. • 13. As 'invaders' and 'pay the price', al-Sakakini diaries, quoted in Tom Segev, *One*

Palestine, Complete (New York, Henry Holt–Owl Books, 2001), pp. 461–5.
• 14. For the *Yishuv's* reaction, Rose (ed.), *Dugdale Diaries*, p. 198, and
Lossin, p. 342; for House of Commons, *Dugdale Diaries*, p. 198; and for
'Riegler telegram' and Allied declaration, Friedlander, *Nazi Germany and the
Jews, 1939–1945. The Years of Extermination* (New York, HarperCollins, 2007)
pp. 460–2. The precise number of Jews slaughtered during the war will
never be known. The most exact estimates of recent research puts the
number at nearly six million. • 15. See *GD*, Series C, vol. I, nos. 369, 399.
The agreement sanctioned the transmitting of funds to Palestine by
depositing marks with German exporters, ostensibly for the export of goods
to Palestine, and receiving from importers in Palestine the equivalent sum
in local currency. The agreements held – though their profitability steadily
decreased owing to pressure from the German government – until after
Kristallnacht in November 1938. • 16. See Saul Friedlander, pp. 87–9.
Revisionist circles and the Joint Distribution Committee were also parties
to this scheme. • 17. Quotations in Wasserstein, pp. 50–1, and Zweig, p. 84.
• 18. See Joseph Heller, *The Stern Gang. Ideology, Politics and Terror, 1940–1949*
(London, Frank Cass, 1995), p. 100, and chapter 4. Also a personal
communication from Professor Heller, 3 June 2007. • 19. See 'Begin and
Jabotinsky' in Sasson Sofer, *Begin. An Anatomy of Leadership* (Oxford, Basil
Blackwell, 1988), pp. 14–24. • 20. See Amos Oz, *A Tale of Love and Darkness*
(London, Vintage Books, 2005), pp. 60–1. Oz overheard these ruminations
at his uncle's home in Talpiot, Jerusalem. Professor Joseph Klausner, a
professor of modern Hebrew literature at the Hebrew University, was also
a leading Revisionist luminary, an ally of Jabotinsky, who would
periodically meet with his cronies to contemplate the contemporary
political landscape and reminisce about the past. In 1949, Klausner was put
forward as *Herut's* (Begin's party) candidate for the presidency of Israel, to
run against Chaim Weizmann. The result was a foregone conclusion:
Weizmann served as Israel's first President until his death in 1952. • 21.
Sofer, op. cit., pp. 62–7. • 22. See Yehuda Slutsky, *Toldoth HaHaganah –
History of the Haganah* (Tel Aviv, 1972), vol. 3, pp. 148, 1632, 1964. I am
grateful to Professor Joseph Heller for bringing these references to my
attention. The first, unsuccessful, attempt at bringing in 'illegal' immigrants
was made in 1934. By 1938, with the appearance of the *Mossad L'Aliyah Beth*,
the operation, now better organised, achieved a marked measure of
success. They did not act alone. The Revisionists were also heavily involved
in this traffic. From 1938 until the outbreak of war the *Mossad* brought in
about 6,000 immigrants, the Revisionists between 5,000 and 6,000, see
Bauer, *From Diplomacy . . .*, p. 61. • 23. For the debate, *PD*, Commons, vol.
347, c.1937–2056, and c.2129–90, 22 and 23 May 1939. Churchill spoke on the

second day; for 'establishing Palestine', see Norman Rose, 'Churchill and Zionism' in Robert Blake and Wm Roger Louis, eds, *Churchill. A Major New Assessment of his Life in Peace and War* (OUP, 1993), p. 163; for 'a great Jewish state', Churchill's minute in PREM 4/52/5, part 2, NA; and for Cabinet partition decision of 25 January 1944, CAB 65/45 NA. • 24. Text of Biltmore resolution in ESCO, ii, pp. 1084–5. • 25. Yellin-Mor's apologia in GB165–0282, Box 2/11, MEC. For further details regarding the Moyne killing, see Heller, pp. 137–8. For the failed kidnapping of MacMichael by the *Irgun*, see Sofer, p. 59; and for the abortive assassination attempt by the Stern Gang, Heller, p. 132. For other assessments of the repercussions of the Moyne execution, see Michael J. Cohen, 'The Moyne Assassination: A Political Analysis', *Middle Eastern Studies*, XV, (October 1979); and Y. Gelber, 'Zionists and British in Palestine in the Shadow of the Jewish Revolt, 1942–1944', *HaZionuth* (Hebrew), vol. 7. • 26. For John Martin, see Michael J. Cohen, *Churchill and the Jews* (London, Frank Cass, 1985), p. 259; Churchill's revulsion in *PD*, Commons, vol. 404, c.2242, 17 November 1944; for Leo Amery, *The Empire at Bay. The Leo Amery Diaries, 1929–1945*, eds John Barnes and David Nicholson (London, Hutchinson, 1988), p. 1018. Churchill's more conciliatory tone in his *Second World War*, vol. VI, p. 612. For Weizmann's reaction, *WL*, XXI, Weizmann to Churchill, 7 November and 7 December 1944, nos. 226 and 235, pp. 246, 251 and 228, n1; and for loss of son, Rose, *Weizmann*, p. 396. • 27. See Yigal Lossin, *Pillar of Fire: The Rebirth of Israel – A Visual History* (Shikmona Publishing Company, Jerusalem, 1983), p. 397. • 28. See Heller, *The Stern Gang*, p. 138, and Sofer, *Begin*, p. 73. Another source estimated that more than 250 terrorists were rounded up during the coming six months and deported from Palestine (Rose, *Namier*, p. 130, n146). • 29. Mansion House speech and Alexandria Protocol, quoted in J. C. Hurewitz, *The Struggle for Palestine*, (Schocken Books, New York, 1976), pp. 117, 192. • 30. See Furlonge, pp. 130–5, 137–41, and Walid Khalidi, 'On Albert Hourani, the Arab Office, and the Anglo-American Committee of 1946', *Journal of Palestine Studies*, vol. XXXV, no. 1, (Autumn, 2005), pp. 65–7, 71. • 31. See Mary Burgess to her family, 15 June 1946, MSS Brit. Emp., s.305, RH; and Susanna Pearce Emery to her mother, 16 June 1946, Box 3/2, MEC; also Sakakini, p. 222. • 32. See Joseph Heller, 'Roosevelt, Stalin and the Palestine Problem at Yalta' in *Wiener Library Bulletin* (London, 1977). For Weizmann's approaches to the Soviets, see *WL*, XX, no. 267, and XXI, no. 263, n3. • 33. For Ibn Saud's views, see Heller, 'Roosevelt, Stalin . . .', op. cit.; and *WL*, XXI, nos. 283, 293; and 'Notes of Roosevelt–Wise interview', 16 March 1945, WA. • 34. Weizmann–Churchill exchange in *WL*, XXII, no. 10 and n3. For Weizmann's reflection, see Bartley Crum, *Behind the Silken Curtain* (New York, Simon & Schuster, 1947), p. 169.

Five – The *100,000* pp. 71–103

1. See Tylee Papers, 286:89/12/1, IWM. • 2. See Hugh Dalton, *The Fateful Years. Memoirs, 1931–1945* (London, Frederick Muller, 1957), pp. 425–6. • 3. For Clifford's recollections, see MSS Brit. EMP., s.527, vol. 1, RH. • 4. Beeley's recollections in MSS Brit. Eem., s.527/10, vol. 1, RH. • 5. Initial Jewish Agency appeal for 100,000 in *WL*, XXII, no. 69, n9; for one and a half million Jews, Rose, *Weizmann*, p. 393; for Harrison Report and Truman-Attlee exchanges, see Harry S. Truman, *The Truman Memoirs. Years of Trial and Hope, 1946–1953* (London, Hodder & Stoughton, 1956), pp. 145–8, Kenneth Harris, *Attlee* (New York, W. W. Norton, 1982), pp. 390–2; Alan Bullock, *Ernest Bevin. Foreign Secretary* (London, Heinemann, 1983), pp. 175–6; Francis Williams, *A Prime Minister Remembers. The War and Post-War Memoirs of the Rt Hon. Earl Attlee* (London, Heinemann, 1961), pp. 183–91; and Hurewitz, pp. 229–30. For decision to continue with White Paper, see *Report of Palestine Committee*, 8 September 1945, CP(45)156, and CAB.128/3, NA. • 6. All quotations in this passage are taken from I. F. Stone, *Underground to Palestine* (New York, Boni & Gaer, 1946). • 7. See Rudolph Patzert, *Running the Palestine Blockade. The Last Voyage of the Paducah*, (Shrewsbury: Airlife Publishing Ltd, 1994). • 8. Conclusions of committee in Cunningham Papers, GB165–0072, Box 4/3 MEC. • 9. For Bevin briefing *Attlee*, Kenneth Harris, Attlee, p. 390. And for 13 November announcement and press conference, see *PD*, Commons, vol. 415, c.1927–34, and Alan Bullock, *Ernest Bevin. Foreign Secretary* (London, Heinemann, 1983), p. 181. • 10. Bullock, pp. 165, 182–3. Also, in same context, Wm Roger Louis, *The British Empire and the Middle East, 1945–1951: Arab Nationalism, the United States, and Postwar Imperialism* (Clarendon Press, OUP, 1984), pp. 383–96. • 11. In Bullock, p. 178; also Rose, *Weizmann*, p. 406. • 12. In Bartley Crum (a member of the AAC), *Behind the Silken Curtain* (New York, Simon & Schuster, 1947), p. 171. • 13. Sir Alan Cunningham's report, 1 December 1945, in GFB165–0072, Box 1, File 1, MEC. • 14. Bullock, *Bevin*, p. 178. • 15. Cunningham's communiqué of 1 December 1945 in GB165–0072, Box 1, File 1, MEC; Ben Gurion's speech of 21 November 1945 to Jewish Agency Executive in Cunningham Papers, GB165–0072, Box 4, File 3, MEC. • 16. See R. Dare Wilson (Major), *Cordon and Search. With the 6th Airborne Division in Palestine* (Aldershot, Gale & Polden Ltd, 1949), pp. 28–9; Lloyd Phillips to his father, 21 November 1946, MSS Brit. Emp., s.499, 4/1, RH; and Bevin's comment in Bullock, p. 178. • 17. See Amikam Nachmani, *Great Power Discord in Palestine. The Anglo-American Committee of Inquiry into the Problems of European Jewry and Palestine, 1945–46*, (Frank Cass, 1987) pp. 87–8. Nachmani's is the most comprehensive account of the workings of the Committee. Also

al-Sakakini, p. 221. • 18. From accounts by Colonel (later Major-General) Corran William Brooke Purdon, GB99–Purdon, LHC, and Brigadier (later Major-General) Charles Whish Dunbar, GB99–Dunbar, LHC. • 19. See Cunningham to Hall, 26 February 1946, GB165–0072, Box 1/1, MEC; Purdon Papers, GB99, LHC; and Joseph Heller, *The Birth of Israel. Ben Gurion and his Critics* (University Press of Florida, 2000), pp. 117–18, 123. • 20. Crossman, *Palestine Mission*, (Hamish Hamilton, 1947) pp. 25–6. • 21. See Wilson's note, MSS Brit. Emp., s.527/10, vol. 3, RH; also Crossman, *Palestine Mission* . . ., pp. 65–6, and diary entry, 30 December 1945, Crossman Papers, GB165–0068. MEC; also Bartley Crum, *Behind the Silken Curtain*, pp. 60–1. • 22. Their evidence in PRO 30/78/10, 11, 12, NA. For Piratin, Gluckstein, Brodetsky and Marks, see the unpublished Crossman diaries, GB165–0068, File 2, MEC. • 23. In Crossman, pp. 85, 89. • 24. Unpublished diary entry, 23 February (?) 1946, Crossman Papers, File 2, MEC. • 25. Crossman, p. 127, diary entry for 6 March 1946; and Crum, p. 161. • 26. Unless stated otherwise, all quotations in following passage in PRO 30/78/10, 11, 13 15, 18, 19, 21, 24, 25, 26 – Proceedings of the AAC, NA; Nachmani, pp. 171–9; Crossman's diary entries for 7, 12, 14 and 23 March 1946, MEC, and in Crossman, *Palestine Mission*, pp. 132–3, 139–40, 142, 166; Crum, pp. 174–80, 220–1, 225, 253, 258; Walid Khalidi, 'On Albert Hourani, the Arab Office, and the Anglo-American Committee of 1946', *Journal of Palestine Studies*, vol. XXXV, No. 1 (Autumn 2005); and 'Historical Document. The Case Against a Jewish State in Palestine: Albert Hourani's Statement to the Anglo-American Committee of Enquiry of 1946', *Journal of Palestine Studies*, vol. XXXV, No. 1 (Autumn 2005). • 27. Catling in MSS Medit., Series 20, RH; and Emery to her mother, March 1946, GB165–0099, MEC. • 28. In D'Arcy's report of 10 October 1945, Stockwell Papers, GB99, 6/1, LHC, also quoted in Naomi Shepherd, *Ploughing Sand* (Rutgers University Press, New Brunswick, NJ, 2000), p. 223. • 29. Diary entry, 23 March 1946, and Crossman, *Palestine* . . ., p. 168. • 30. See David Horowitz, *State in the Making* (New York, Knopf, 1953), p. 98, and Jon Kimche, Seven Fallen Pillars. The Middle East, 1945–1952 (London, Secker & Warburg), 1950, pp. 55–7. • 31. Diary entry for 12 March 1946, Crossman, pp. 139–40. • 31. Diary entry of 8 March 1946, and Crossman, *Palestine* . . ., p. 134. • 32. Crossman to Zita, 23 March 1946, and undated letter, but clearly written from Jerusalem in late March; also for strained atmosphere dogging the Commission, unpublished diary entry, 26 March 1946 – all in Crossman Papers, File 2, MEC. • 33. See Crossman, p. 157; Buxton, quoted in Nachmani, p. 178. • 34. Unpublished diary entry for 28 March 1946; see also Crossman, *Palestine* . . ., p. 173. • 35. See *Cmd.6806.* • 36. Horowitz, p. 90. • 37. Unpublished diary entry, 4 April 1946, Crossman Papers, MEC. • 38. Wadi Dides to Richard Crossman, 25 May 1946,

Crossman Papers, GB165–0068, File 1, MEC. For all-Arab conference, see Walid Khalidi, 'The Arab Perspective', p. 110, in Wm Roger Louis and Robert R. Stookey, eds., *The End of the Palestine Mandate* (University of Texas Press, Austin, 1986). • 39. Smart quoted in Wm Roger Louis, 'British Imperialism and the End of the Palestine Mandate', in *The End of the Palestine Mandate*, p. 9. Also Lloyd Phillips's letters to his father, 8, 12 May and 23 June 1946, MSS Brit. Emp., s.499, 4/2, RH. • 40. On Committees, Rose (ed.), *Dugdale Diaries*, p. 197. • 41. PD, Commons, vol. 422, c.197, 1 May 1946. • 42. These matters may be followed in closer detail in Bullock, *Bevin*, pp. 255–8, *Truman Memoirs*, ii, pp. 155–60, and Nachmani, pp. 215–18; also Susanna Pearce Emery to her mother, 5 May 1946, GB165–0099, Box 3/2, MEC. • 43. '*Gaffe*' and 'desultory' in Crossman, p. 199; 'grossly unfair' in Crossman to Attlee, 7 May 1946, GB165–0068, File 1, MEC. • 44. In Douglas Jay, *Change and Fortune* (London, Ebury Press, 1980), p. 133, quoted in Nachmani, p. 218. At the time, Jay served as a personal assistant to Attlee and witnessed the exchange, or lack of it. • 45. Crossman to Attlee–Attlee to Crossman, 7 and 9 May 1946, GB165–0068, File 1, MEC. • 46. Crossman to Hall, 17 June 1946, GB165–0068, File 1, MEC. • 47. See Abba Eban, 'Tragedy and Triumph' in *Chaim Weizmann. A Biography by Several Hands*, eds. Meyer W. Weisgal and Joel Carmichael (New York, Atheneum, 1963), p. 280. • 48. George Hall to Cunningham, 23 April 1946, Cunningham Papers, GB165–0072, Box 1/1; and Horowitz, pp. 97, 98.

Six – Black Sabbath   pp. 104–129

1. Heller, *The Stern Gang*, p. 160. • 2. See Major R. D. Wilson, *Cordon and Search. With the 6th Airborne Division in Palestine*, p. 57. • 3. George Hall to Cunningham, 23 April 1946, Cunningham Papers, GB165–0072, Box 1/1, MEC. • 4. Pyman Papers, GB99:7/1/2, LHC; and Cunningham Papers, GB165–0072, Box, 5/4, MEC. • 5. Barker's memorandum, 22 June 1946, Cunningham Papers, GB165–0072, Box 5, File 4, MEC. • 6. For an overall account of 'Agatha', see *The Palestine Post*, 30 June 1946. For Yagur, Barker memo, 22 June 1946, Cunningham Papers, GB165–0072, Box 5/4, MEC, and Lieutenant-Colonel Windeatt, diary entry, 4 July 1946, 90/20/1, LHC, the Cheshires, quoted in Naomi Shepherd, *Ploughing Sand*, p. 225; also *Pillar of Fire*, p. 435. • 7. See *Chaverim Mesaprim al Jimmie (Friends Reminisce About Jimmie)* (Jerusalem, Ariel Books, 1999), pp. 42–7, Hebrew. 'Jimmie', a Palmachnik, rose to iconic status in the unit's collective memory. • 8. See *The Palestine Post*, 30 June 1946; also R. Dare Wilson, *Cordon and Search. With the 6th Airborne Division in Palestine*, pp. 59–60. • 9. For further details of 'Operation Agatha' see Weizmann to Isaac Hertzog (Chief Rabbi of Palestine), 21 July 1946, *WL*, XXII,

no. 195, pp. 169–73, and *Pillar of Fire*, p. 435; 'a despicable race', quoted in Nicholas Bethell, *The Palestine Triangle* (London, André Deutsch, 1979), pp. 280–1; and an interview with Lord Charteris (then Provost of Eton College), 3 October 1984. • 10. Weizmann to Isaac Hertzog (Chief Rabbi of Palestine), 21 July 1946, op. cit. • 11. From *The Palestine Post*, 17 July 1946. • 12. See *Cmd.*6873, 'Palestine. Statement of Information Relating to Acts of Violence' (July 1946). • 13. The debate can be followed in *PD*, Commons, vol. 426, c.1860–1912, 1 July 1946. Extracts of Crossman's speech were printed in his *Palestine Mission*, Appendix V. • 14. Exchange of 17 and 31 January 1946, in Cunningham Papers: GB165–0072, Box 1/1, MEC. • 15. Horowitz, p. 114. • 16. Shaw to Crossman, 2 August 1946, Crossman Papers, File 1, MEC. • 17. From *Daily Express*, 23 July 1946. • 18. Lloyd Phillips to his father, 28 July 1946, MSS Brit. Emp., s.499, 4/2, RH. • 19. Mary Burgess to her family, 26 July 1946, MSS Brit. Emp., s.305, RH; and Susanna Emery to her mother, 28 July 1946, GB165–0099, Box 3, File 2, MEC. • 20. For Levi, see 'Interviews', GB165–0282, Box 2/11, MEC. • 21. Al *Sakakini*, entry for 22 July 1946, p. 222; Attlee in *PD*, Commons, vol. 425, c.1877–78, 23 July 1946; also *Davar*, 23 July 1946; and *Palestine Post*, 23 July 1946. • 22. Sofer, *Begin*, p. 72. For Begin's apologia, see his *The Revolt. The Story of the Irgun* (Steimatsky Group, Jerusalem, 2002), chapter XV; and for a detailed overview of the King David affair, see Bethell, 257–67. • 23. See Cunningham to Hall, 24 and 30 July 1946, GB165–0072, Box 1/1, MEC; and Cabinet Minutes, 25 July 1946, CAB.128/6, NA, also in Joseph Heller, 'From the "Black Sabbath" to Partition', *Zion* (Hebrew), vol. XLIII, pp. 3–4, 1978, p. 323. • 24. Text of Barker's letter in *The Times*, 29 July 1946; for 'rather strongly', Lieutenant-Colonel J. K. Windeatt, 90/20/1, LHC; and Cunningham to George Hall, 30 July 1946, GB165–0072, Box 1/2, MEC. • 25. Begin, *The Revolt*, p. 228. • 26. For 'Shark', see *Palestine Post*, 31 July and 13 August 1946, and Wilson, *Cordon . . .*, pp. 67–71. • 27. For above, see Wilson, *Cordon . . .*, pp. 6–7, 14, 99, 143. • 28. See *New York Times* and *New York Post*, 14 May 1947; also Bethell, p. 309. • 29. For the above passage on *A Flag . . .*, see Creech Jones Papers, MSS. Brit. Emp., s.332, Box, 32/1, RH; Louis, 'British Imperialism and the End of the British Mandate' in *The End of the Palestine Mandate*, p. 12; Bethell, *Palestine Triangle*, pp. 30–9; Bullock, *Bevin*, p. 277; and http://www.ajhs.org/publications/chapters/chapter.cfm?documentID=268, and http://www.wymaninstitute.org/articles/2004–04–flagisborn.php. • 30. For advertisements, the ZAC, and Crum and Niles, see Zvi Ganin, *Truman, American Jewry, and Israel, 1945–1948* (New York, Holmes & Meier, 1979), pp. 102–4, 105. • 31. For a summary of the speech, see Ganin, p. 104. • 32. From *The Times*, 7 October 1946, quoted in Cohen, p. 167. • 33. Attlee to Truman, 4 October 1946, PREM 8/627/5, NA, quoted in Louis, 'British Imperialism . . .', pp. 11–12; and Truman's answer, in Bethell, p. 282. • 34. For Dewey and other

Republicans, see Bethell, p. 283. • 35. Silver to Ben Gurion, 9 October 1946, quoted in Cohen, p. 170; also Ganin, p. 105. • 36. For Jewish Agency view, see WL, XXII, p. 200, no. 224, n3. • 37. For Truman's account of this affair, see *Truman Memoirs. Years of Trial and Hope, 1946–53*, p. 164.

Seven – Confrontation   pp. 130–150

1. Details of the operation in Roni Gitar, ed., *Chamishim HaShanim HaRishonoth: Yovel shel Kibbutz Nirim, 1946–1996 – The First Fifty Years: Kibbutz Nirim's Jubilee, 1946–1996* (Israel, Dahlia Publications, 1997), pp. 10–11; and the *Palestine Post*, 7 October 1946. • 2. These views were vividly put to the author by Richard Crossman and Lieutenant-Colonel Martin Charteris, see Interviews. Crossman statement in *PD*, Commons, vol. 426, c.1867–78, and *Palestine Mission*, Appendix V. • 3. Begin, *The Revolt*, pp. 42–3. • 4. For Ramat Gan and 'it was murder', Bethell, pp. 232–3, quoting War Office files; for railway workshop, Heller, *Stern Gang*, p. 160. • 5. See Cunningham to Creech Jones, 19 June 1946, Cunningham Papers, GB165–0072, Box 1, File 1, MEC; Lieutenant-Colonel Windeatt, diary entry, 4 July 1946, 90/20/1, LHC; and Field Marshal Bernard Law Montgomery, *Memoirs* (London, Collins, 1958), pp. 423–44; and WL, XXII, p. 155, n2. • 6. Overall figures in Cunningham Papers, GB165–00722, Box 1, File 1; and for 6th Airborne Division, Wilson, *Cordon*, p. 57. • 7. Figures in Henry Near, *The Kibbutz Movement. A History* (Vallentine Mitchell, 1997), vol. 2, Appendix 1, p. 362. • 8. The *Irgun* and *Lechi* actions recounted below may be followed in greater detail in J. Bowyer Bell, *Terror out of Zion. Irgun Zvai Leumi, LECHI (the Stern Gang), and the Palestine Underground, 1929–1949* (New York, St Martin's Press, 1977), chapters 2 and 3; Wilson, *Cordon*, Appendix N, pp. 251–73; Bethell, pp. 300, 303–4, 308, 337, 338–9, 340 ; and Cohen, pp. 233, 236, 238–9, 240, 242, 243–4, 247. • 9. Quoted in Naomi Shepherd, *Ploughing Sand*, p. 230, from minutes of a meeting, at Cunningham's request, with Rabbi Fishman and Leo Kohn, 1 January 1947, CZA, S25/10551. • 10. See Windham's recollections, Box 1/14, MEC; and for further details, Bethell, p. 300. • 11. I am grateful to Professor D. C. Watt for sharing with me his recollections of post-war Austria. • 12. Further details in Bell, pp. 180–1, 307–8, and Ezer Weizmann, *On Eagles' Wings* (New York, Macmillan, 1976), p. 48. • 13. John Julius Norwich, ed., *The Duff Cooper Diaries*, 28 August, 14 November and 6 December 1946, pp. 418, 423, 424. • 14. See Ya'akov Eliav, *Mevukash* (Tel Aviv, Ma'ariv Library, 1983), pp. 309–42, Hebrew; English edition: *Wanted* (New York, Shengold Publishers, 1984), pp. 235–61. The plan to contaminate London's water supply was edited out of the English edition of these bizarre memoirs. • 15. Keating to his chief at the BBC, 23 April 1947,

86/16/1, IWM. • 16. From the Tomlinson Papers, GB165–0360, MEC; also the reminiscences of Madge Lindsay, http://land of broken promises.co.uk/Palestine/OpPolly/OpPo12.htm. • 17. See Hugh Dalton, *High Tide and After*, pp. 187, 205. • 18. *Dugdale Diaries*, 11 March 1947, p. 249; Abba Eban recalled Bevin's pun in MSS Brit. Emp., s.527/10, vol. 1, RH: another version reads: 'there was no need for candles as they had the Israelites present', in Jon and David Kimche, *Both Sides of the Hill: Britain and the Palestine War* (London, Secker & Warburg, 1960), p. 22. • 19. For details and references of the 1942 proposals, see Norman Rose, *Churchill. An Unruly Life* (London, Simon & Schuster, 1994), pp. 329–30 and 395, n32. • 20. See *PD*, Commons, Fifth Series, vol. 420, c.1418–1424, 15 March 1946, and vol. 433, c.1395–98, 20 February 1947; also Bullock, p. 360. • 21. Records of the informal February conference with Arabs and Jews in CAB.133/85, NA, also *Cmd*.7044; Weizmann's comment in *WL*, XXII, p. 242 and n3. For Churchill, see *PD*, vol. 426, c.1253, 1 August 1946. • 22. Quoted in Hugh Dalton, *High Tide and After. Memoirs, 1945–1960*, p. 105; see also Attlee to *Bevin*, 1 December 1946, quoted in Bullock, *Bevin*, pp. 339–40, and in the same connection Bullock, pp. 243, 359, 362. • 23. These matters may be examined in more detail in Louis, *The British Empire in the Middle East*, pp. 93–102; David Reynolds, *Britannia Overruled* (London, Longman, 1991), p. 174. Also *The Truman Memoirs*, vol. 2, pp. 98–115, and Hugh Dalton, *High Tide . . .*, pp. 206–9. • 24. Figures for *Haganah*, etc. in *Cmd*.6873 (July 1946); also Creech Jones Papers, MSS Brit. Emp., s.332, Box 32/4, RH, and Cunningham Papers, note of 10 July 1947, GB165–0072, Box 4/4, MEC. Shaw's remark in GB165–0282, Box 1/3, MEC. Also interview with Charteris, 3 October 1984; and Horowitz, pp. 229–30. • 25. For details, see Major-General Richard Gale's (the Divisional Commander) report in GB165–0181, MEC. • 26. See Bell, pp. 190–1, and Bethell, pp. 303–4; and for Churchill, *PD*, vol. 484, c.1346, 12 March 1947. • 27. For Gruner's (perhaps apocryphal) story, see Stockwell Papers, 6/8, LHC, p. 3. • 28. Cunningham's measures to a security meeting, 11 April 1947, GB165–0072, Box 4/1, MEC; and for *Irgun* warning and orange hand grenades, Bell, pp. 199–200. • 29. Further details in Bell, pp. 204–19, and Bethell, p. 308. For Hecht's letter in full, see 'Black Sabbath', p. 123. 'A bad show' in Cunningham Papers, GB165: 0072, Box 4/1, MEC. • 30. Meeting between Ben Gurion and Cunningham. 25 April 1947, in Cunningham Papers, Box 4/1, MEC. Also interviews with Mordechai 'Morela' Bar-On (Colonel, Reserves), 20 March 2006; Raphael Vardi (Major-General, Reserves), 14 June 2006; Meir Pa'il (Colonel, Reserves), 19 June 2006; and Yehoshua 'Shaika' Gavish (Major-General, Reserves), 20 September 2007. And Cohen, pp. 237, 242–3. • 31. Captain Brown's diary, 6493: 97/19/1, IWM; see also the Watson Papers, 94/25/1, IWM, and Joanne

Buggins, 'The End of the British Mandate in Palestine: 'Reflections from the Papers of John Watson of the Forces Broadcasting Service', *Imperial War Museum Review* (1993), no. 8. The quotations are taken from letters to his mother between October 1945 and April 1948. (Watson was later court-martialled and imprisoned for losing his rifle: he maintained that it was stolen by Arabs.) Lieutenant Gourley's court martial in Shaw Papers, MSS Brit. Emp., s.456, RH. • 32. Names and ranks of 6th Airborne fatalities listed in *Cordon*, pp. 207–11. See Emery to her mother, 25 November 1945, and 24 February 1946 in Emery Papers, GB165–0099, Box 2/2, Box 3/2; and in same vein, Emery to her Bishop, 19 January 1946, GB165–0208, Box 1/4, all in MEC. And for 'will stick at nothing', Lloyd Phillips to his father, 3 August 1947, MSS Brit. Emp., s.499, 4/2, RH. • 33. Colonel Norman's memorandum, 23 June 1947, and lecture, 18 July 1947, in 1706: 87/57/4, IWM. • 34. Eleven countries were represented on UNSCOP: Australia, Canada, Czechoslovakia, Guatemala, India, Iran, the Netherlands, Peru, Sweden, Uruguay and Yugoslavia.

Eight – Partition   pp. 151–183

1. Ivan Lloyd Phillips to father, 15 June 1947, MSS Brit. Emp., s.499, 2/2, RH. • 2. Quotations from the English text of Gromyko's declaration issued by the Soviet embassy, London, in *Zionist Review*, 23 May 1947. See also Gabriel Gorodetsky, 'The Soviet Union's Role in the Creation of the State of Israel', *The Journal of Israeli History*, vol. 22, No. 1 (Spring 2003), pp. 4–20. • 3. Reactions to Gromyko's speech, *Zionist Review*, op. cit.; Shertok quoted in Louis, '"The Conscience of the World": The United Nations and Palestine in 1947' (unpublished paper delivered in Tel Aviv, April 2008); Abba Eban's recollections in MSS Brit. Emp., s.527/10, vol. 1, RH, and his essay, 'Tragedy and Triumph', in *Chaim Weizmann. A Biography by Several Hands*, pp. 296–9. See also David Horowitz, *State in the Making*, pp. 199–223. • 4. See Rose, *Weizmann*, p. 424; Horowitz, *State in the Making*, pp. 206–7, 219, and Jorge Garcia Granados, *The Birth of Israel* (New York, Knopf, 1949), pp. 140–5. • 5. See Horowitz, *State . . .*, p. 200; and for Eban's impressions, 27 July 1947, Crossman Papers, GB165–0068, File 3, MEC. • 6. Cunningham's plea of 27 June 1947 in GB165–0072, Box 4/1, MEC. And for transcript of *Irgun*–UNSCOP meeting, see GB165–0290, MEC. • 7. Creech Jones to Cunningham, 14 July 1947, GB165–0072, Box 2/1, MEC. • 8. For the above passage on the *Exodus* affair see, 'Minutes of Security Meeting, 7 March 1947, GB165–0072, Box 4/1; Creech Jones to Cunningham, 14 July 1947, GB165–0072, Box 2/1; Cunningham to Creech Jones, 18 July 1947, GB165–0072, Box 2/1, all in MEC. Captain S. B. de Courcy-Ireland's

memoirs, pp. 345, 394–400, IWM. For Stever and Kochavi, GB165–0282, Box
2/8, 9, MEC; for Noah Klieger, MSS Brit. Emp., s.527/10, vol. 3, RH. For
Abba Eban, MSS Brit. Emp., s.527/10, vol. 1, and 'Tragedy and Triumph',
pp. 296–8. See Duff Cooper Diaries, entries for 12, 19, 23, 24, 29 and 30 July,
and 8, 17, 21 August 1947, pp. 442–3, 444, 445, 446, 447. Also Bell, pp. 229–34;
Bethell, pp. 316–36, 340–3; Kimche, pp. 175–92; Horowitz, pp. 158–72, 178,
188–92; and Bullock, *Bevin*, pp. 440–50. • 9. For Begin and UNSCOP
meeting, see GB165–0290, MEC. And for further details related below on
the two sergeants affair, see Wilson, *Cordon*, pp. 131–4; David Charters, *The
British Army and the Jewish Insurgency in Palestine, 1945–47*, London, 1989, pp.
62–3, Bell, *Terror . . .*, pp. 222–8, 236–9, and Bethell, *The Palestine Triangle*, pp.
323–4, 336–40. • 10. Hodges to Stinger (?), 26 July 1947, 1321:87/14/1, LHC.
• 11. From A. M. Parry's account, 6249: 67/374, IWM; *Daily Express*, 1
August 1947; and Begin, *Revolt*, p. 290. Also Shmuel Katz's testimony. A
member of *Irgun* High Command, he argued that 'if the way to a Jewish
state was to be preceded by an avenue of gallows, it wouldn't only be Jewish
gallows', see MSS Brit. Emp., s.527/10, vol. 2, RH. • 12. See Creech Jones
announcement in the House, *PD*, vol. 441, c.2319, 12 August 1947. • 13.
Cunningham to Creech Jones, 31 July 1947, pointing out possible courses of
action, in GB165–0072, Box 2/1, MEC; from Watson's letters to his family,
August–September 1947, in Joanne Buggins, 'The End of the British
Mandate in Palestine: Reflections from the Papers of John Watson', *Imperial
War Museum Review*, no. 8 (1993); and for Cunningham's explaining his
soldiers' behaviour, Cunningham to Colonial Office, 15 November 1947,
quoted in Cohen, p. 245. • 14. See Cunningham to Creech Jones, 31 July
1947, op. cit.; *Palestine Post*, 1, 4 August 1947; and Lloyd Phillips to father, 3
August 1947, Brit. Emp., s.499, 4/2, RH. • 15. See *Daily Express*, *The Times*
and *Daily Telegraph*, 1 August 1947. • 16. See *PD*, vol. 441, c.636, 638, 31 July
1947. • 17. From Churchill's speech, 4 August 1947, quoted in Martin
Gilbert, *Winston Churchill. Never Despair, 1945–1965* (London, Heinemann,
1988), vol, VIII, p. 336. Churchill had urged the government to say 'that if the
United States will not come and share the burden of the Zionist cause, as
defined or agreed, we should now give notice that we will return our
Mandate to U.N.O. and that we will evacuate Palestine within a specified
period'. See *PD*, vol. 426, c.1255–57, 1 August 1946. • 18. For Commons
debate, see *PD*, vol. 441, c.2306–2388, 12 August 1947, in particular, c.2306,
2321, 2328, 2346, 2360, 2362–63. • 19. For UNSCOP's report, see United
Nations, Department of Public Information. Press and Publications Bureau
(New York, 31 August 1947), PAL/91. And for Trygve Lie, see James Barros,
Trygve Lie and the Cold War: The UN Secretary-General Pursues Peace, 1946–1953
(Dekalb, Illinois, 1989), p. 182, quoted in Louis, 'The Conscience of the

World . . .' • 20. Sir Frank Roberts's evidence in MSS Brit. Emp., s.527/10, vol. 2, RH; for the Foreign Office response to UNSCOP's report, Cunningham Papers, GB165–0072, Box 5/3, MEC; Cadogan's statement, 19 September 1947, GB165–0072, Box 5/3, MEC; Creech Jones and the UN, 26 September 1947 in MSS Brit. Emp., s.322, Box 32/1, RH; and Cunningham's message in GB165–0072, Box 4/4, MEC. • 21. El-Khalidi in Cunningham to Creech Jones, GB165–0072, 8 December 1947, Box 2/3, MEC; 'Pilgrims' in Horowitz, p. 324. • 22. See Trafford Smith, MSS Brit. Emp., s.530, Box 4/1, RH. • 23. For Eban, see MSS Brit. Emp., s.527/10, RH. • 24. MacGillivray's memorandum, 16 November 1947, in GB165–0193, MEC. Also for Pearson, Louis, 'Conscience of the World . . .', pp. 17–18; and Horowitz, pp. 279–80. • 25. For Evatt, see Louis, 'Conscience of the World . . .', pp. 19–20; and for Welles, WL, XXIII, Weizmann to Sumner Welles, 30 November 1947, no. 73, p. 52, and Louis, 'Conscience of the World . . .', p. 21. • 26. See WL, XXIII, nos 16–57; Chaim Weizmann, Trial and Error, pp. 561–3, 570; Vera Weizmann, The Impossible Takes Longer (London, Hamish Hamilton, 1967), pp. 219–20; Abba Eban, 'Tragedy and Triumph', pp. 301–2. And Rose, Weizmann, pp. 427–9. • 27. Dorothy Thompson in MSS Brit. Emp., s.530, Box 4/1, RH; and for Ben Hecht, Louis, The British Empire in the Middle East, pp. 486–7. • 28. See Lossin, p. 489, and Rose, Weizmann, p. 429. • 29. On Emile Ghoury, see Cunningham to Creech Jones, 22 November 1947, GB165–0072, Box 2/3, MEC; Arab diplomats quoted in Walid Khalidi, 'The Arab Perspective', in The End of the Palestine Mandate, eds. Wm Roger Louis and Robert W. Stookey (Austin, University of Texas Press, 1986), p. 120. • 30. Speeches in debate of 26 November 1947 in A/516, UN Archives; also   http://www.zionism-israel.com/zionism_ungromyko2.htm. • 31. For Horowitz on Beeley see Horowitz, State in the Making, p. 38; Weizmann's 'miracle' in WL, XXIII, no. 26, p. 23; Churchill's quip in PD, vol. 317, c.1107, 12 November 1936. • 32. Beeley's 'football match' quoted in Louis, 'Conscience of the World . . .', from his report to Foreign Office, January 1948, FO 371/68528, NA; Aranha in Lossin, p. 491. • 33. For 'pajama-clad', see Zipporah Porath to her family, 30 November 1947, in Letters from Jerusalem, 1947–1948 (Association of Americans and Canadians in Israel, Jerusalem, 1987), p. 44; and 'roars of joy' in Amos Oz, A Tale of Love and Darkness, pp. 342–3. • 34. See Gurney to Gibson (?), 10 October 1947, and a more 'sober' Cunningham to Creech Jones, 30 November 1947, GB165–0072, Box 6/1 and Box 2/3, MEC. • 35. Susanna 'Espie' Pearce Emery to her mother, 30 November 1947, GB165–0208, Box 1/3, MEC. • 36. See Lossin, Pillars . . ., p. 491; for 'Drinks . . .', Cunningham to Creech Jones, 12 December 1947, GB165–0072, Box 2/3 MEC. Also Zipporah Porath, p. 47, Amos Oz, Tale of . . ., p. 344. • 37. Horowitz, State in the Making, pp. 232–4.

• 38. Arab 'capitals' in Khalidi, p. 121; Haj Amin in Cunningham to Creech Jones, 30 November 1947, GB165:0072, Box 2/3, MEC; Lester in MSS Medit., Series 14, RH; and for events in Jerusalem, Porath, *Letters . . .*, p. 48, Amos Oz, pp. 346, 408, and Lossin, p. 495. • 39. General Pyman, Chief of Staff to General Miles Dempsey, C-i-C Land Forces, Middle East, reporting to Field Marshal Bernard Montgomery, Chief of the Imperial General Staff, in GB99:7/1/13, LHC.

Nine – Civil War   pp. 184–207

• 1. Mary Burgess to her mother, 23 November 1947, MSS Brit. Emp., s.305, RH. • 2. Weizmann in Crossman, *Palestine Mission*, p. 133, and 'all belligerents' in Max Hastings, reviewing *Human Smoke* by Nicholas Baker, *The Sunday Times*, 4 May 2008. • 3. For Palestine government losing 'its grip', see General Pyman's opinion, 'Partition', p. 182–83. 'Law and order' and 'keeping main lines of communication clear' in General MacMillan's evidence in MSS Brit. Emp., s.527, vol. 2, RH; and Towers-Clark, diary entry, 10 April 1948, in 14871:06/43/1, IWM. For Sheik Jarrah, see Towers-Clark, diary entry, 25 April 1948, IWM; and Avraham Sela, 'Transjordan, Israel and the 1948 War: Myth, Historiography and Reality', *Middle Eastern Studies*, vol. 28, no. 4 (October 1992), p. 629. • 4. Cunningham to Creech Jones, 15 December 1947, GB165:0072, Box 2/3, MEC. • 5. Letter of 24 March 1948, 1321:87/14/1, IWM. • 6. See Bell, p. 266, and Cohen, p. 308. • 7.. For British deserters, see Towers-Clark diary, 20 April 1948, in 14871: 06/43/1, IWM, and Porath, *Letters . . .*, entries for 3 and 22 February 1948, pp. 94, 105. British League pamphlet is printed in full in Koestler, Promise and Fulfilment, pp. 172–3; and Sir Henry Gurney diaries, 15 March 1948, GB:165–0128, MEC. • 8. Cunningham to Creech Jones, 9 April 1948, GB165:0072, Box 3/3, MEC; and Porath, *Letters . . .*, 12 December 1947, 6 and 30 January 1948, pp. 56, 75, 88. For 'plenty of stores', see Cunningham to Creech Jones, 9 April 1948, GB165:0072, Box 3/3, MEC; and for rationing, lack of medical supplies and electricity, Amos Oz, *A Tale . . .*, pp. 347, 351–2. • 9. For Katamon and the Sakakini family, see their diary entries in Hala al-Sakakini, *Jerusalem and I* (Jordan, Economic Press Co., 1990), for 5 January, 14 March, 14, 21, 29 and 30 April, and 2 May 1948, pp. 110–11, 115, 118–19, 120, 121–2; also Khalil al-Sakakini, *Such Am I, Oh World*, entries for 16 and 20 March 1948, pp. 230–2. For 'dismal result' see Gurney diaries, 1 and 3 May 1948, MEC. For a more detailed account of Semiramis affair, see Larry Collins and Dominique Lapierre, *O Jerusalem!* (New York, Simon & Schuster Paperbacks, 1972), pp. 128–33. Accounts differ regarding the number of fatalities: Collins and Lapierre put it at twenty-six, Hala al-Sakakini at eleven. • 10. Gurney diaries, 1 April 1948, MEC; and Towers-Clark diary, 23 April 1948, IWM. • 11. Wintringham to

Bill Stoneman, 24 January 1948, and to Wilfred ? (but an MP), 22 February 1948, IHW Archive 1, No. 1, LHC. • 12. Text of Austin's statement in *Foreign Relations of United States, 1948*, vol. 5, pp. 742–4. • 13. Morgan to her Mother, 21 March 1948, GB165:0208, Box 1/3, MEC. • 14. For above see *Truman Memoirs*, ii, pp. 171–2, 173–4; Weizmann, *Trial and Error*, p. 577; *WL*, XXIII, nos 137, n2, 146, n3; Weisgal and Carmichael, *A Biography . . .*, 309–10; Jonathan Daniels, *The Man of Independence* (1950), pp. 317–18; Eddie Jacobson, 'Two Presidents and a Haberdasher', *American Jewish Archives* (April 1968). And for 'non-starter', Sir John Fletcher-Cooke's comment in GB:165–0282, Box 1/7, MEC. • 15. See Gurney's diary, 20 March 1948, GB165–0128, File 1, MEC. For Jewish Agency reaction, *WL*, XXIII, no. 127, n1; also for Azzam Pasha, Cunningham to Creech Jones, 17 April 1948, GB165:0072, Box 3/3, MEC. • 16. For Chiefs of Staff, see Trafford Smith note, 15 April 1948, MSS Brit. Emp., s.530, Box 4/2, RH, and Towers-Clark, diary entry, 21 April 1948, 14871:06/43/1, IWM. And for 'full-scale civil war', Towers-Clark, diary entry, 22 April 1948, IWM. • 17. For a full, general account of the Deir Yassin massacre based on Israeli and Arab sources, see Benny Morris, 'The Historiography of Deir Yassin', *Journal of Israeli History* (March 2005), vol. 24, no. 1. • 18. Interview with Pa'il at Ramat Gan, 19 June 2006. • 19. See unnamed Arab witness in GB165:0282, Box 2/4, MEC; and Dr Amin Majaj, Series 527/10, vol. 2, RH. Also for 'summarily shot', Colonel (Reserve) Yitzchak Levy, Head of HIS (*Haganah* Intelligence Service) in 1948, reliving that day in 1971, see Morris, pp. 83–4. • 20. See Cunningham to Creech Jones, 13 April 1948, GB165:0072, Box 3/3, MEC, Cunningham to Colonial Office, 17 April 1948, CO 537/3869, NA, the latter quoted in Morris, p. 103, n35. I have linked quotations from both reports in the above passage. (The content of these communiqués to Creech Jones have not been corroborated by any other documentary evidence.) • 21. Gurney diaries, 10, 11, and 15 April 1948, GB165–0128, MEC. • 22. Porath, *Letters . . .*, 11 April 1948, p. 142; for Shaltiel, Bell, pp. 295–6; and 'mandatory recitals', Cunningham to Creech Jones, 13 April 1948, GB165–0072, Box 3/3, MEC. • 23. 'Sowing panic', evidence of Dr Amin Majaj, MSS Brit. Emp., s.527/10, vol. 2, RH. Dr. Hussein Fakhri al-Khalidi in Walid Khalidi, *Deir Yassin* (Beirut, Institute of Palestinian Studies, 1998), pp. 109, 128, quoted in Morris, p. 97; for 'spreading rumours' see Adel H. Yaha, 'The Birth of the Palestinian Refugee Problem in 1947–1949' in *Shared Histories. A Palestinian-Israeli Dialogue* (California, Left Coast Press, 2005), eds Paul Scham, Walid Salem and Benjamin Pogrund, p. 255. For other Arab accounts, see Collins and Lapierre, *O Jerusalem!*, pp. 274–6. • 24. See footnotes 72, 73 in Morris, p. 105; and Walid Khalidi, Deir Yassin, op. cit. • 25. See Morris, p. 96 and ns 38, 95. • 26. Morris, pp. 100–1. • 27. Cunningham to Creech Jones, 13 April 1948, GB165:0072, Box 3/3; see also General MacMillan's statement, MSS Brit. Emp., 5.527/10, vol. 3, RH. And Towers-Clark diary, 13 April 1948, 14871/06/1, IWM. • 28. Towers-Clark diary, 17 April 1948, IWM. For 'no access', see Yaha, 'The Birth of the Palestinian Refugee Problem', p. 221; and for Farid Salab, GB165:0282, Box 2/1, MEC. • 29. Testimony of Professor Chaim Cohen, a doctor at Hadassah Hospital, MSS Brit Emp., s.527/10, vol. 1, RH; also Shepherd, *Ploughing Sand*, pp. 234–5; and Robert Barr Smith, *Fighting Jack Churchill Survived: A Wartime Odyssey Beyond Compare, World War Two History, Profiles Column*, July 2005. • 30. For Avriel, see GB165–0282, Box 2/12, MEC. • 31. For the above passage, see Teddy Kollek, and his son, Amos, *For Jerusalem. A Life by Teddy Kollek* (Steimatsky's Agency, Tel Aviv, 1978), pp. 67–89, 237; Anthony David, *The Sky is the Limit. Al Schwimmer, The Founder of Israel Aircraft Industries* (Schocken Publishing House, Tel Aviv, 2008), pp. 60–95, Hebrew; Anthony Summers and Robbyn Swan, *Sinatra. The Life* (Corgi Books, 2006), p. 147; and Robert Lacy, *Little Man. Meyer Lansky and the Gangster Life* (Little Brown & Co., New York, 1991), pp. 202–3. • 32. Towers-Clark diary, 17 April 1948, IWM. • 33. See al-Sakakini diaries, 9 April 1948, 235; Lossin, *Pillars . . .*, p. 527. For Fawzi, see Towers-Clark diary, 19 April 1948, IWM; Gurney diaries, 5 May 1948, GB165–0128, MEC; and Alex Kirkbride, *From the Wings. Amman Memoirs, 1947–1951* (London, Frank Cass, 1976), pp. 7–8. • 34. Stockwell Papers, GB99:6/12, LHC; also Shepherd, *Ploughing Sand*, pp. 235–6. • 35. See Stockwell's report, 'Events During 21/22 April 1948', Stockwell Papers, GB99:6/15, LHC; also Jack(?) to Susanna 'Espie' Emery, 3 May 1948, Morgan Papers, GB165:0208, Box 1/4, MEC. And Farid Salab's and Ahmad al-Khalil's testimonies in GB165:0282, Box 2/1, Box 2/2, MEC. • 36. Unsigned report of events between 20 April–4 May 1948 in GB165:0208, Morgan Papers, Box 1/7, MEC; also Susanna 'Espie' Emery to family (date?), GB165:0099, Box 2/3, MEC. And Towers-Clark diary for situation in Haifa, 29 April and 5 May 1948, 14871:06/43/1, IWM. Sir Henry Gurney's impressions were much the same, see his diary, 29 April 1948, MEC. • 37. Begin's cry in *Revolt*, p. 354; 'salutary tonic' in Towers-Clark diary, 28 April 1948, IWM, also Gurney diaries, 29 April 1948, GB165:0128, MEC; for Cooper's 'scratch force' see his Obituary, *The Times*, 21 May 2007. In recognition of the success of his mission, Major Cooper was awarded the Military Cross. • 38. Fuller's report in GB165:0114, MEC. Towers-Clark diary, 25 April 1948, IWM; Gurney diaries, 28 April and 5 May 1948, MEC; and Basil Ennab in GB165:0282, Interview (undated) Box 2/1. For an overview of the Jaffa crisis, see Adam LeBor, *City of Oranges. Arabs and Jews in Jaffa* (London, Bloomsbury, 2006), chapter 9. • 39. Cunningham to Creech Jones, 30 April 1948, GB165:0072, Box 3/4, MEC. • 40. Cunningham to Creech Jones, 5 May 1948, GB165:0072, Box 3/5, MEC; and Gurney diary, GB165:0128,

22 April 1948, MEC. • 41. For 'entire Arab Legion', see Cunningham to
Creech Jones, 20 April 1948, Trafford Smith Papers, MSS Brit. Emp., s. 530,
Box 4; and for Shertok, Trafford Smith Papers, Box 4/2.

Ten – Last Days   pp. 208–217

• 1. For shortages, King David, and tennis, 20, 21, 29 April and 11 May 1948,
Gurney diaries, GB165:0128, MEC. • 2. 'Bar the shouting', Gurney diary, 5
May 1948, GB165:0128, MEC; Arab 'morale' and 'collapse', Towers-Clark
diary, 19 April and 10 May 1948, IWM. See also *The Times*, 5 May 1948, and
Khalil al-Sakakini diaries, *Such Am I . . .*, 16 March 1948, p. 230. • 3.
Testimonies in Creech Jones Papers, Brit. Emp., s.322, Box 30/8, RH, and
GB165:0282, Box 2/6, MEC: a petition by Palestinian Arab leaders now in
exile in Damascus; and by Anwar Khalib, who had served on Jamal al-
Husayni's AHC. • 4. See Avi Shlaim, 'Rise and Fall of the All-Palestine
Government in Gaza', *Journal of Palestine Studies*, vol. 20, no.1 (Autumn,
1990). • 5. Heller, *The Birth . . .*, p. 91, and Collins and Lapierre, *O Jerusalem!*,
p. 408. • 6. Gurney diaries, 22 April and 13 May 1948, GB165:0128, MEC.
• 7. Unless stated otherwise, the following passage can be followed in: *New
York Times*; *The Times*; *Palestine Post*; *Manchester Guardian*; *Daily Telegraph*;
Daily Herald and *Le Monde*, all from 14, 15 May 1948. Also Towers-Clark
diaries, 14 May 1948, IWM; the Gurney diaries, 13, 14 May 1948, MEC; and
Cunningham Papers, Box 6/1, MEC. • 8. See *New York Times*, 14 and 15 May
1948; and *WL*, XXIII, no. 158, p. 119. • 9. See Walid Khalidi, 'Plan Dalet: The
Zionist Master Plan for Conquest of Palestine', *Middle East Forum*
(November 1961); and more lately, but no more convincingly, Ilan Pappe,
The Ethnic Cleansing of Palestine (Onwards Publications, 2006). • 10. The
original text, in Hebrew, was first printed in Yehuda Slutsky, *Sefer Toldot
HaHaganah (History of the Haganah)* (Tel Aviv, Zionist Library, 1972), vol. 3,
Appendix 48, pp. 1955–60. Reasonable translations may be examined in
http://www.mideastweb.org/pland.htm. • 11. See Adel H. Yahya, 'The
Birth of the Palestinian Refugee Problem in 1947–48' . . ., pp. 220–1, and
Benny Morris, *The Birth of the Palestinian Refugee Problem, 1947–49*
(Cambridge University Press, 1987), pp. 286, 294. • 12. For India, see Piers
Brendon, *The Decline and Fall of the British Empire, 1781–1997*, pp. 404–5, 412–13;
and Ronald Hyam, *Britain's Declining Empire: The Road to Decolonisation,
1918–1968* (Cambridge, 2006), p. 115. For Europe, Tony Judt, *Postwar. A
History of Europe Since 1945* (London, Pimlico, 2007), pp. 25–6; for *New York
Times* quote, Michael R. Marrus, *The Unwanted. European Refugees in the
Twentieth Century* (OUP, 1985), pp. 329–30; Mark Mazower, *Dark Continent:
Europe's Twentieth Century* (Allen Lane, Penguin Press, 1998), p. 220; and

Antony Beevor, *Berlin. The Downfall, 1945* (Penguin Books, 2002). • 13. From Weber's *Politics as a Vocation*. I am grateful to Professor Shlomo Avineri for bringing this quotation to my attention. • 14. Full text in *New York Times*, 14 May 1948; abbreviated version in *The Times*, 14 May 1948. • 15. Gurney diaries, 16 April 1948, GB165:0128, MEC.

Bibliography

Unless stated otherwise, the place of publication is London

AAC Report. 'Cmd.6808 (HMSO)', 1946

Abboushi, W. F. *The Angry Arabs*, Philadelphia: Westminster Press, 1974

Abcarius, Michael, *Palestine: Through the Fog of Propaganda*, Hutchinson, 1946

Abdullah, King of Jordan, *My Memoirs Completed: 'Al-Takmilah'*, Longman, 1978

Abu-Lughod, Ibrahim, 'The War of 1948: Disputed Perspectives and Outcomes', *Journal of Palestine Studies* 18, no. 2 (Winter 1989), pp.119–27.

al-Alami, Musa, *The Future of Palestine – With a Preface by Musa Alami*, Beirut: Herman Books, 1970

—— 'The Lessons of Palestine,' *Middle East Journal* 3, no. 4 (October 1949), pp.373–405

Al-Hout, Bayan Neweihid, 'The Palestine Political Elite During the Mandate Period', *Journal of Palestine Studies* 9, no. 1 (1979), pp.85–111

Al-Sakakini, Hala, *Jerusalem and I*, Jordan: Economic Press Co., 1990

Al-Sakakini, Khalil, *Such Am I, Oh World. Diaries of Khalil al-Sakakini* (Hebrew, translated by Gideon Shilo), Jerusalem: Keter, 1990

Attlee, Clement Richard, *As It Happened*, Heinemann, 1954

Avizohar, Meir and Friedman, Isaiah (eds), *Studies in the Palestine Partition Plan, 1937–1947* (Hebrew), Be'er Sheva: Ben Gurion Research Centre, Ben Gurion University, 1984

Avriel, Ehud, *Open the Gates: A Personal Story of Illegal Immigration*, New York, 1975

Bauer, Yehuda, *Flight and Rescue: Brichah*, New York: Random House, 1970

——, *Jewish Reactions to the Holocaust*, Tel Aviv: Ministry of Defence, 1989

Beevor, Antony, *Berlin. The Downfall, 1945*, Allen Lane, Penguin Press, 1998, Penguin, 2002

Bell, J. Bowyer, *Terror Out of Zion: Irgun Zvai Leumi, LECHI, and the Palestine Underground, 1929-1949*, New York: St Martin's, 1977

Ben Gurion, David, *Ben Gurion Looks Back in Talks with Moshe Pearlman*, New York: Schocken Books, 1965

——, *Israel: A Personal History*, Tel Aviv: Sabra Books, 1972

——, *Letters to Paula*, Vallentine Mitchell, 1971

——, *Memoirs*, New York: World Publishing Co., 1970

——, *Memoirs*, 5 Vols. (Hebrew), Tel Aviv: Am Oved, 1971–82

——, *My Talks with Arab Leaders*, Jerusalem: Keter Books, 1972

——, *Recollections* (ed. Thomas R. Bransten), Tel Aviv: Bitan Books

Brendon, Piers, *The Decline and Fall of the British Empire, 1781–1997*, Jonathan Cape, 2007

Caplan, Neil, *Futile Diplomacy*, 2 Vols., Frank Cass, 1983

Carpi, Daniel and Yogev, *Zionism: Studies of the History of the Zionist Movement and the Jewish Community in Palestine*, Vol.3, Tel Aviv: Massada Press, 1975

Cathedra – Kollat, Cohen, Cohen, 'Discussion on the British Decision to Evacuate Palestine', *Cathedra* 15 (April 1980)

Charters, David, *The British Army and the Jewish Insurgency in Palestine, 1945–47*, Macmillan, 1989

Chazan, Meir, 'A Fighting Press: Reflections of Israel's War of Independence in Children's Newspapers. Also Review of Darr, Yael, 'Called Away from Our School Desks: The Yishiv in the Shadows of the Holocaust and in Anticipation of Statehood in Children's Literature of *Eretz Israel*, 1939–1948', *Journal of Israeli History* 24, no.1 (March 2005), pp.109-34

——, 'A Fighting Press: Reflections of Israel's War of Independence in Children's Newspapers,' *Journal of Israeli History* 24, no. 1 (March 2005), pp.109–34.

Cohen, Michael, *Palestine and the Great Powers, 1945–1948*, Princeton: Princeton University Press, 1982

——, *Palestine: Retreat from the Mandate. The Making of British Policy, 1936–45*, Paul Elek, 1978

Cottrell, Robert C., '*Izzy*', *A Biography of I. F. Stone*, New Brunswick, NJ: Rutgers, 1992

Crossman, Richard, *A Nation Reborn*, Hamish Hamilton, 1960

——, *Palestine Mission, A Personal Record*, Hamish Hamilton, 1947

Crum, Bartley C., *Behind the Silken Curtain*, New York: Simon & Schuster, 1947

Cunningham, Alan, 'The Last Days of the Mandate', *International Affairs* 24 (1948)

Dalton, Hugh, *The Fateful Years. Memoirs, 1931–1945*, Frederick Muller, 1957

——, *High Tide and After. Memoirs, 1945–1960*, Frederick Muller, 1962

David, Anthony, *The Sky is the Limit. Al Schwimmer, the Founder of Israel Aircraft Industries* (Hebrew), Jerusalem, Tel Aviv: Schocken Publishing House, 2008

Dayan, Moshe, *Story of My Life*, Sphere Books, 1976

Documents of British Foreign Policy, 1919–1939, First Series, V. IV, London: His Majesty's Stationery Office, 1952

Documents on German Foreign Policy, 1948–1944, Series D, V. V, HMSO

Eban, Abba, 'Tragedy and Triumph, 1939–1949' in *Chaim Weizmann. A Biography by Several Hands*, eds Meyer Weisgal and Joel Carmichael, New York: Atheneum, 1963

Editorial Board, *Kibbutz Yichiam. Fifty Years: 1946–1996*, Ma'arechet: Kibbutz Dahlia, 1997

Elath, Eliyahu, *The Struggle for Statehood, 1945–1948*. 3 vols (Hebrew), Tel Aviv: Am Oved, 1979

Eliav, Y., *Mevukash–Wanted*, Tel Aviv: Ma'ariv Library, 1983; New York: Shengold Publishers *Wanted* – (English ed.), 1984

Evans, Trefor ed. *The Killearn Diaries, 1934–46*, Sidgwick & Jackson, 1972

Evenson, Bruce J., 'Truman, Palestine, and the Cold War', *Middle Eastern Studies* 28, no.1 (1992), pp.120–56

Freidlander, Saul, *The Years of Extermination. Nazi Germany and the Jews, 1939–1945*, New York: HarperCollins, 2007

——, *When Memory Comes*, New York: Farrer, Straus & Giroux, 1979

Friesel, Evyatar, 'Through a Peculiar Lens: Zionism and Palestine in British Diaries, 1927–31', *Middle Eastern Studies* 29, no. 3 (1993), pp.419–44

Frilling, Tuvia and Troen, Ilan, 'Five Days in May From Ben Gurion's

Diary,' *Israel Studies* 3, no. 1 (Spring 1998)

Furlonge, Geoffrey, *Palestine is My Country. The Story of Musa Alami*, John Murray, 1969

Ganin, Zvi, *Truman, American Jewry, and Israel, 1945–1948*, New York: Holmes & Meier, 1979

Garcia Granados, Jorge, *The Birth of Israel: The Drama As I Saw It*, New York: A. Knopf, 1949

Gelber, Yoav, *Palestine 1948: War, Escape and the Emergence of the Palestine Refugee Problem*, Brighton, Sussex: Academic Press, 2001

Gitar, Roni, ed., *Chamishim HaShanim HaRishonoth: Yovel Kibbutz Nirim* (The First Fifty Years: Kibbutz Nirim's Jubilee), Israel: Dahlia Publications, 1997

Glubb, Sir John Bagot, *A Soldier with the Arabs*, Hodder and Stoughton, 1957

Golan, Tamar, 'Why Did Haifa's Arab Inhabitants Leave the City', *Cathedra* (Hebrew) 80 (1996), pp.175–207

Golani, Motti, 'The "Haifa Turning Point": The British Administration and the Civil War in Palestine, December 1947–May 1948,' *Middle Eastern Studies* 37, no. 2 (April 2001), pp.93–130

Gorni, Joseph, 'The British Labour Movement and Zionism, 1917–1948', In *The British Labour Movement and Zionism, 1917–1948*, Frank Cass, 1983

Gorodetsky, Gabriel, 'The Soviet Union's Role in the Creation of the State of Israel', *Journal of Israeli History* 22, no. 1 (Spring 2003)

Grant, Linda, 'The Real Exodus', *Guardian*, 30 June 2007

Graves, Philip R. ed., *Memoirs of King Abdullah*, Jonathan Cape, 1950

Gross, Jan T., *Fear. Anti-Semitism in Poland After Auschwitz – An Essay in Historical Interpretation*, Princeton: Princeton University Press, 2006

Grossman, David, *Sleeping on a Wire* (Translated from Hebrew by Haim Watzman), New York: Picador, 1993

Ha'aretz, 'As Though Auschwitz Wasn't Enough' (in Hebrew), 4 July 2006

Habachi, R., *The Partition of Palestine, 29 November 1947: An Analysis*, Beirut: Institute for Palestine Studies, 1967

Hadari, Ze'ev, *Second Exodus. The Full Story of Jewish Illegal Immigration to Palestine, 1945–1948*, Vallentine Mitchell, 1991

Hadawi, Sami, *Palestinian Rights and Losses in 1948*, Saqi Books, 1988

Haim, Sylvia ed., *Arab Nationalism: An Anthology*, Berkeley: University of California Press, 1962

Halpern, Ralph and Reinhartz, Yehuda eds., *Zionism and the Creation of a New Society*, Oxford: OUP, 1996

Hare, William, *The Struggle for the Holy Land: Arabs, Jews and the Emergence of Israel*, Lanham, MD: Madison Books, 1995

Haron, Miriam Joyce, 'The British Decision to Give the Palestine Question to the UN', *Middle Eastern Studies* 17, no. 2 (1981), pp.241–8

——, *Palestine and the Anglo-American Connection, 1945–1950*, New York: Peter Lang Publishing, 1986

Harris, Kenneth, *Attlee*, London: Weidenfeld & Nicolson, 1982

Hastings, Max, 'A Nation Built on Sand', *Guardian*, March 2006

Hattis, Sheila, *The Bi-National Idea in Palestine During Mandatory Times*, Haifa: Shikma, 1970

Hecht, Ben, Muni, Paul, Brando, Marlon, *A Flag is Born*, New York, 1946

Heller, Joseph, 'Alternative Narratives and Collective Memories: Israel's New Historians and the Use of Historical Context', *Middle Eastern Studies* 42, no. 4 (July 2006), pp.571-86

——, 'The Anglo-American Commission of Inquiry, 1945–46: The Zionist Reaction Reconsidered', in *Zionism and Arabism in Palestine and Israel*, eds., E. Kedourie and S. G. Haim, 1982

——, *The Birth of Israel, 1945–1949: Ben Gurion and His Critics*, Gainesville, Florida: University Press of Florida, 2000

——, 'From Black Saturday to Partition: The Summer of 1946 as a Turning Point', in Shavit ed., *Struggle, Revolt, Resistsance* (Hebrew), Jerusalem: Zalman Shazar Centre, 1987

——, '"Neither Masada – Nor Vichy": Diplomacy and Resistance in Zionist Politics, 1945–1947,' *International History Review* III, no. 4 (October 1981), pp.540–64

——, *The Stern Gang: Ideology, Politics and Terror, 1940–1949*, Frank Cass, 1995

——, *The Struggle for the Jewish State: Zionist Politics, 1936-1948* (Hebrew), Jerusalem: Zalman Shazar Centre, 1984

——, 'Zionist Policy and the Partition Plans in the 1940s', in Avizohar and Friedman (eds), *Studies in the Palestine Partition Plans* (Hebrew), Be'er Sheva: Ben Gurion University, 1984

Hertzberg, Arthur, 'American Zionism at an Impasse. A Movement in Search of a Pogrom', *Commentary*, October 1949, pp.340–5

Hertzog, Arthur, *The Zionist Idea*, New York: Atheneum, 1969

Hirszowicz, Lukasz, *The Third Reich and the Arab East*, Routledge & Kegan Paul, 1966

HMSO. *Palestine: Termination of the Mandate, 15 May 1948: Statement Prepared for Public Information by the Colonial Office and the Foreign Office*, 1948

Holliday, Eunice (ed. John C. Holliday), *Letters from Jerusalem During the Palestine Mandate*, New York and London: Radcliffe Press, 1997

Horowitz, Dan and Lissak, *The Origins of the Israeli Polity: Palestine Under the Mandate*, Chicago: Chicago University Press, 1978

Horowitz, David, *State in the Making*, New York: Knopf, 1953

Hourani, Albert, 'Musa Alami and the Palestine Problem, 1939–1949' in *Studia Palaestina: Studies in Honour of Constantine K. Zurayk*, ed. Hisham Nashabe, Beirut: Institute for Palestine Studies, 1988

——, 'Statement to the Anglo-American Committee of inquiry of 1946', *Journal of Palestine Studies* XXXV, no. 1 (Autumn 2005), pp.80–90

Hughes, Matthew, 'Lebanon's Armed Forces and the Arab-Israeli War, 1948–49', *Journal of Palestine Studies* XXXlV, no. 2 (Winter 2005), p.24–41

Hurewitz, J. C., *The Struggle for Palestine*, 2 vols, New York: Schocken Books, 1968

Hyam, Ronald, *Britain's Declining Empire: The Road to Decolonisation, 1918–1968*, Cambridge, CUP, 2006

Ilan, Amitzur, *America, Britain and Palestine: The Origin and Development of America's Intervention in Britain's Palestine Policy, 1938–1947*, Jerusalem: Yad Ben Zvi, 1979

Israel State Archives, *Palestine Broadcasting Service (Bulletin)*, Jerusalem: Israel State Archives, 1936–48

Jewish Agency, *The Jewish Case Before the Anglo-American Committee of Inquiry on Palestine*, Westport, Connecticut: Hyperion Press, 1947

Jones, Philip, *Britain and Palestine, 1914–1949. Archival Sources for the History of the Palestine Mandate*, Oxford: OUP, 1979

Judt, Tony, *Postwar. A History of Europe Since 1945*, Pimlico, 2007

Kadish, Alon. 'Evacuation of British Army from Safad, 1947–1948', in *A Community at War in the Jews of Safed*, ed. Shmariyn Paz: in *A Commumity at War: the Jews of Safed*, ed. Shmariyu Pazi, Jerusalem, 2006

—— 'The British Army in Menashe', in *Etzel's Struggle against the*

British, ed. Yo'iakov Markovsky, Jerusalem, 2008

Kana'ana, Sherit, and Zeitawi, *Deir Yassin. Destroyed Village Series*, Birzeit: Birzeit University Publications, 1991

Karsh, Epfraim, *Fabricating Israeli History: The 'New Historians'*, 1997, rev. ed. Frank Cass, 2002

——, 'Nakbat Haifa: Collapse and Dispersion of a Major Palestinian Community', *Middle Eastern Studies* 37, no. 4 (October 2001), pp.25–70

——, 'Re-Writing Israel's History', *Middle East Quarterly* 3, no. 2 (1996), pp.19-29

Kedourie, Elie, *Arabic Political Memoirs and Other Studies*, Frank Cass, 1974

——, *Chatham House version and other Middle-Eastern Studies*, Weidenfeld and Nicholson, 1970

——, 'Great Britain and Palestine: The Turning Point,' in *Islam in the Modern World* (ed. Elie Kedourie), Mansell, 1980

——, 'Religion and Politics; The Diaries of Khalil Sakakini.' *St Antony's Papers*, No. 4 (1958)

Khalidi, Rashid, 'The Palestinians and 1948: The Underlying Causes of Failure', in *The War for Palestine: Rewriting the History of 1948*, eds., Shain, A, and Rogen, E, Cambridge: Cambridge University Press, 2001, pp.12–36

Khalidi, Tarif, 'Palestine Historiography: 1900–1948', *Journal of Palestine Studies* 10, no. 3 (1981), pp.59–76

Khalidi, Walid, *All That Remains: The Palestinian Villages Occupied and Depopulated by Israel in 1948*, Washington, DC: Institute for Palestine Studies, 1992

——, *Before Their Diaspora: A Photographic History of the Palestinians, 1876–1948*, Washington, DC: Institute for Palestine Studies, 1991

——, *Deir Yassin, Al Jam'at 9/4/1948*, Beirut: Institute of Palestine Studies, 1998

——, 'On Albert Hourani, the Arab Office, and the Anglo-American Committee of 1946', *Journal of Palestine Studies* XXXV, no. 1 (Autumn 2005), pp.60–79

——, *Palestine Reborn*, I.B. Taurus, 1992

——, 'Why Did the Palestinians Leave, Revisited', *Journal of Palestine Studies* XXXlV, no. 2 (Winter 2005), pp.42-54

Khalidi, Walid ed., *From Haven to Conquest: Readings in Zionism and the*

Palestine Problem Until 1949, Washington, DC: Institute for Palestine Studies, 1971

Kimche, Jon, *Seven Fallen Pillars. The Middle East, 1945–1952*, Secker & Warburg, 1950: revised and enlarged, 1953

Kimche, Jon and David, *The Secret Roads – The 'Illegal' Immigration of a People, 1938–1948*, Secker & Warburg, 1955

Kirkbride, Sir Alec, *From the Wings: Amman Memoirs, 1947–51*, Frank Cass, 1976

Koestler, Arthur, *Arrow in the Blue*, Collins, 1952

——, *Promise and Fulfilment: Palestine, 1917–1949*, Macmillan, 1949

——, *Thieves in the Night. Chronicle of an Experiment*, Macmillan, 1946

Kollek, Teddy and Amos, *For Jerusalem: A Life by Teddy Kollek with His Son, Amos Kollek*, Weidenfeld & Nicolson, 1978

Kollek, Teddy, 'Kollek "Never Denied Spying for the British"' (in Hebrew), *Ha'aretz*, 30 March 2007

Krunecker, David, 'At 12.37 Jerusalem Shook to a Tremendous Explosion' (in Hebrew), *Ha'aretz*, 18 July 2006

Lacy, Robert, *Little Man. Meyer Lansky and the Gangster Life*, New York: Little, Brown & Co., 1991

LeBor, Adam, *City of Oranges. Arabs and Jews in Jaffa*, Bloomsbury, 2006.

Levett, Gordon, *Flying Under Two Flags*, Frank Cass, 1994

Lewis, Bernard, 'The New Anti-Semitism: First Religion, Then Race, Then What?' *American Scholar* (2004), pp.25–36

Lindhein, Irma, 'Palestine Diary', *On Guard* 1, nos 1, 2 (July–August 1946)

Lissak, Moshe, Shapira, Anita and Cohen, Gabriel, *The History of the Jewish Community in Eretz-Israel Since 1882: The Period of the British Mandate*, Part 2, Jerusalem: Bialik Institute, 1995

Louis, Wm Roger, *The British Empire in the Middle East, 1945–1951. Arab Nationalism, the United States, and Postwar Imperialism*, Oxford: Clarendon Press OUP, 1984; paperback ed., 1985

——, 'Sir Alan Cunningham and the End of British Rule in Palestine', *Journal of Imperial and Commonwealth History* 16, no. 3 (1988), pp.128–47

——, '"The Conscience of the World": The United Nations and Palestine in 1947', *unpublished paper*, 14 April 2008

Louis, Wm Roger, and Stookey Robert R., *The End of the Palestine Mandate*, Austin: University of Texas Press, 1985

McCarthy, Justin, *The Population of Palestine*, New York: Columbia University Press, 1990

Mana, Adel H., *Memories of Father's House* (Hebrew private publication)

Mandel, Neville, *The Arabs and Zionism Before World War 1*, Berkeley: University of California Press, 1976

Marrus, Michael R., *Unwanted. European Refugees in the Twentieth Century*, New York and Oxford: Oxford University Press, 1985

Masalha, Nur, *Expulsion of the Palestinians: The Concept of 'Transfer' in Zionist Political Thought, 1882–1948*, Washington, DC: Institute for Palestine Studies, 1992

Mattar, Philip, *The Mufti of Jerusalem: Al-Hajj Amin Al-Huseini*, New York: Columbia University Press, 1988

——, 'The Mufti of Jerusalem and the Politics of Palestine', *Middle East Studies* 42, no. 2 (Spring 1988)

Mayer, Thomas, 'Arab Unity of Action and the Palestine Question, 1945–48', *Middle Eastern Studies* 22 (1986)

Mazower, Mark, *Dark Continent: Europe's Twentieth Century*, Allen Lane, Penguin Press, 1998

Meinertzhagen, Richard, *Middle East Diary, 1917–1956*, Cresset Press, 1959

Meir, Golda, *My Life*, Weidenfeld and Nicolson, 1975

Melman, Yossi, 'Survivors, Forgotten but Now Remembered' (in Hebrew), *Ha'aretz*, 16 August 2007

Migdal, Joel S. 'Direct Contact with the West: The British Mandate,' in *Palestinian Society and Politics*, Princeton: Princeton University Press, 1980

Migdal, Joel S. ed., *Palestinian Society and Politics*, Princeton: Princeton University Press, 1980

Miller, Rory, 'Sir Edward Spears' Jewish Problem: A Leading Anti-Zionist and His Relationship with Anglo-Jewry, 1945–48', *Journal of Israeli History* 19, no. 1 (Spring 1998)

Monroe, Elizabeth, *Britain's Moment in the Middle East, 1914–1956*, Chatto & Windus, 1963

——, 'Mr Bevin's Arab Policy', *Middle East Affairs* 11, St Antony's Papers (ed. Albert Hourani, 1961)

Montgomery, Field Marshal Sir Bernard, *The Memoirs of Field Marshal Montgomery*, Collins, 1958

Morris, Benny, *The Birth of the Palestinian Refugee Problem, 1947–1949*, Cambridge: Cambridge University Press, 1987

——, *Correcting a Mistake: Jews and Arabs in Palestine/Israel*, Jerusalem: Am Oved, 2000

——, 'The Historiography of Deir Yassin', *Journal of Israeli History* 24, no. 1 (March 2005), pp.79–107

——, 'Revisiting the Palestinian Exodus of 1948', in *The War for Palestine* . . , pp.37-59, Cambridge: Cambridge University Press, 2001

——, *Righteous Victims*, New York: Knopf, 1999

Moughrabi, Fouad and El-Nazer, Pat, 'What Do Palestinian Americans Think? Results of a Public Opinion Survey', *Journal of Palestine Studies* 18, no. 4 (1989), pp.91–101

Muslih, Muhammad M., *The Origins of Palestinian Nationalism*, New York: Columbia University Press, 1990

Nachmani, Amikam, *Great Power Discord in Palestine: The Anglo-American Committee of Inquiry in the Problems of European Jewry and Palestine, 1945–46*, Frank Cass, 1987

Nashif, Taysir, 'Palestine Arab and Jewish Leadership in the Mandate Period', *Journal of Palestine Studies* 6 (1977), pp.113–17

Near, Henry, *The Kibbutz Movement. A History*, Vallentine Mitchell, 1997

Nevo, Joseph, 'The Arabs of Palestine, 1947–1948: Military and Political Activity', *Middle Eastern Studies* 23 (January 1987)

Niv, David, *The Irgun Zvai Leumi: Battle for Freedom, 1944–1946*, 6 vols (Hebrew), Tel Aviv: Hadar, 1973

Norwich, John Julius, *The Duff Cooper Diaries*, Weidenfeld & Nicolson, 2005, Phoenix Paperback, 2006

Ofer, Dalia, *Escaping the Holocaust: Illegal Immigration to the Land of Israel, 1939–1944*, New York, OUP, 1990

Ovendale, Ritchie, 'The Palestine Policy of the British Labour Government, 1947: The Decision to Withdraw', *International Affairs* 56 (1980)

Oz, Amos, *A Tale of Love and Darkness*, Vintage Books, 2005

Ozacky-Lazar, Sarah and Khaba, Mustafa, 'The *Haganah* in Arab and Palestinian Historiography and the Media', *Israel Studies* 7, no. 3 (Fall 2002), pp.43-60

Palumbo, Michael, *The Palestine Catastrophe: The 1948 Expulsion of a People from Their Homeland*, Faber and Faber, 1987

Pappe, Ilan, *Britain and the Arab-Israeli Conflict, 1948–51*, Macmillan/ St Antony's College, Oxford, 1988

——, *The Ethnic Cleansing of Palestine*, London and New York: Oneworld Publications, 2006

———, *The Making of the Arab-Israeli Conflict, 1947–1951*, I. B. Taurus, 1992

Parents, *Chaverim Misaprim Al Jimmie (friends promise about Jimmie)*, Jerusalem: Ariel Books, 1999

Patzert, Captain Rudolph W., *Running the Palestine Blockade. The Last Voyage of the Paducah*, Shrewsbury: Airlife Publishing Ltd, 1994

Pensler, Derek J., 'Herzl and the Palestinian Arabs: Myth and Counter-Myth', *Journal of Israeli History* 24, no. 1 (March 2005), pp.65–77

Porath, Yehoshua. *The Emergence of the Palestinian-Arab Nationalist Movement, 1918–1929; 1929–1939*, 2 Vols., Frank Cass, 1974

———, *In Search of Arab Unity, 1930–1945*, Frank Cass, 1986

Porath, Zipporah, *Letters from Jerusalem, 1947–1948*, Jerusalem: Association of Americans and Canadians in Israel, 1987

Reinharz, Yehuda, Shapira, Anita, *Essential Papers on Zionism*, New York: NYU Press, 1996

Rose, Norman, 'The Arab Rulers and Palestine, 1936: The British Reaction', *Journal of Modern History* 44 (June 1972)

———, *Chaim Weizmann. A Biography*, New York: Viking Press, 1986

———, 'Churchill and Zionism', in *Churchill: A Major New Assessment of His Life in Peace and War*, eds. Robert Blake and Wm. R. Louis , Oxford: OUP (1993)

———, 'The Debate on Partition, 1937–38: The Anglo-Zionist Aspect. 1. The Proposal', *Middle Eastern Studies*, October 1970

———, 'The Debate on Partition, 1937–38: The Anglo-Zionist Aspect. 2. The Withdrawal', *Middle Eastern Studies*, January 1971

———, *Lewis Namier and Zionism*, Oxford: Oxford University Press, Clarendon Press, 1980

———, 'Weizmann, Ben Gurion and the 1946 Crisis in the Zionist Movement', *Studies in Zionism*, Spring 1990

Rose, Norman, ed. *'Baffy': The Diaries of Blanche Dugdale, 1936–1947*, Vallentine, Mitchell, 1973

Rosenthal, Yemima ed., *Documents on Foreign Policy of Israel. Armistice Negotiations with the Arab States, December 1948–July 1949*, vol. 3. Jerusalem: Israel State Archives, 1983

Royal Institute of International Affairs, *Great Britain and Palestine, 1915–1945*, 1946

Rubenstien, Danny, 'A Murder Waiting to Happen', *Ha'aretz*, 30 September 2006

Rubin, Barry, *The Arab States and the Palestine Conflict*, New York: Syracuse University Press, 1981

Said, Edward W., 'Afterword: The Consequences of 1948', in *The War for Palestine . .* , Cambridge: Cambridge University Press, 2001, pp.206–19

——, *Out of Place*, Granta Books, 1999

Samuel, Edwin, *A Lifetime in Jerusalem*, Vallentine Mitchell, 1970

Sayigh, Rosemary, *Palestinians: From Peasants to Revolutionaries*, 2nd Press, 1979

Scham, Paul, Salem, Walid, and Benjamin Pogrund, eds., *Shared Histories*, Walnut Creek, California: Left Coast Press Inc., 2005

Segev, Tom, *1949. The First Israelis*, New York: Free Press, 1986

——, 'Creative Oblivion', *Ha'aretz*, 3 August 2007

——, *One Palestine Complete*, New York: Heny Holt–Owl Books, 2001

——, *The Seventh Million: The Israelis and the Holocaust*, New York: Hill & Wang, 1993

Sela, Avraham, 'Arab Historiography of the 1948 War. The Quest for Legitimacy', in *New Perspectives on Israeli History*, ed. Laurence Silberstein, pp.124–54. New York: New York University Press, 1991

——, 'Transjordan, Israel and the 1948 War: Myth, Historiography and Reality', *Middle Eastern Studies* 28, no. 4 (October 1992), pp.623–88

Shacham, Natan, *Tamid Anuchnu* (in Hebrew), Merchavia: Hashomer Hatzair, 1952

Shapira, Anita, *Land and Power: The Zionist Resort to Force, 1881-1948*, New York: OUP, 1992

——, 'Politics and Collective Memory: The Debate Over the "New Historians" in Israel', *History and Memory* 7 (1995), pp.9–40

Shepherd, Naomi, *Ploughing Sand: British Rule in Palestine, 1917–1948*, New Brunswick, Rutgers University Press, 2000

Sherman, A. J., *Mandate Days: British Lives in Palestine, 1918–1948*, Thames and Hudson, 1997

Shlaim, Avi, *Collusion Across the Jordan: King Abdullah, the Zionist Movement and the Partition of Palestine*, Oxford: OUP, Clarendon Press, 1988

——, *The Iron Wall*, Penguin Press, 2000

——, 'Israel and the Arab Coalition in 1948', in *The War for Palestine . .* , Cambridge: Cambridge University Press, 2001, pp.79–103

Shlaim, Avi and Rogen, Eugene L. eds., *The War for Palestine. Rewriting the History of 1948*, Cambridge: Cambridge University Press, 2001

Simons, Chaim, *International Proposals to Transfer Arabs from Palestine, 1895–1947: A Historical Survey*, Hoboken, NJ: Ktav Publishing House, 1988–93

Slonim, S., 'The 1948 American Embargo on Arms to Palestine,' *Political Science Quarterly* 94, no.3 (Fall 1979)

Slutsky, Yehuda *et al.*, *History of the Haganah: From Resistance to War*, 8 vols (Hebrew), Tel Aviv: Ma'arachot, 1954–72

Smith, Pamela Ann, *Palestine and the Palestinians, 1876–1983*, Croom Helm 1984

Smith, Robert Barr, 'Fighting Jack Churchill Survived: A War Odyssey Beyond Compare', *World War Two History, Profiles Column*, July 2005

Sofer, Sasson, *Begin: An Anatomy of Leadership*, Oxford: Basil Blackwell, 1988

——, *Zionism and the Foundations of Zionist Diplomacy*, Cambridge: Cambridge University Press, 1998

Srouji, Elias, 'The Fall of a Galilean Village During the 1948 Palestine War: An Eyewitness Account', *Journal of Palestine Studies* XXXlll, no. 2 (Winter 2004), pp.71–80

——, 'The Last Days of "Free Galilee": Memories of 1948', *Journal of Palestine Studies* XXXlll, no. 1 (Fall 2003), pp.55–67

Stone, I. F, *This Is Israel* (Foreword by Bartley C. Crum; Photographs by Robert Capa, Jerry Cooke and Tim Gidal) New York: Boni & Gaer, 1948

——, *Underground to Palestine*, New York: Boni & Gaer, 1946

Summers, Anthony and Swan Robbyn, *Sinatra. The Life*, Corgi, 2006

Tal, David, 'The Forgotten War: Jewish-Palestinian Strife in Mandatory Palestine, December 1947–May 1948', *Israel Affairs* 6, nos .3–4 (Spring–Summer 2000)

——, 'The Historiography of the 1948 War in Palestine: The Missing Dimension', *Journal of Israeli History* 24, no. 1 (March 2005), pp.183–202

Tamiri, Salim, and Zureik, *The UNRWA Archives on Palestinian Refugees*, Jerusalem: Institute of Jerusalem Studies, 1997

Tannous, Izzat, *The Activities of the Haganah, Irgun and Stern Bands as*

Recorded in British Command Paper, No. 6873, New York: Palestine
Arab Refugee Office, 1988

——, *Expulsion of Palestinian Arabs: Dark Page in Jewish History*, New
York: Palestine Liberation Organisation, 1968

——, *The Palestinians: A Detailed Documented Eyewitness History of
Palestine Under the Mandate*, New York: IGT Co., 1988

Teveth, Shabtai, *Ben Gurion and the Palestinian Arabs: From Peace to
War*, Oxford: OUP, 1985

——, *Ben Gurion: The Burning Ground, 1886–1948*, Robert Hale, 1987

——, 'The Palestinian Arab Refugee Problem and Its Origins', *Middle
Eastern Studies* 26, no. 2 (April 1990), pp.214–49

Toubbeh, Jamil, *Day of the Long Night: A Palestinian Refugee Remembers
the Nakba*, McFarland & Co, Inc., 1998

Truman, Harry S., *Memoirs: Years of Trial and Hope, 1946–1953 . . .* , vol
2, Hodder & Stoughton, 1956

Wasserstein, Bernard, *Britain and the Jews of Europe, 1939–1945*, Oxford:
Clarendon Press, 1979

——, *The British in Palestine: The Mandatory Government and the Arab-
Jewish Conflict, 1917–1929*, Oxford: Basil Blackwell, 1991

——, *British Officials and the Arab-Jewish Conflict in Palestine, 1917-1929*,
Oxford: OUP, 1974

——, *Herbert Samuel, a Political Life*, Oxford: Clarendon Press, 1992

Weiss, Jeffrey and Craig, *I Am My Brother's Keeper. American Volunteers
in Israel's War for Independence, 1947–1949*, Atglen, PA: Schiffer
Publishing Ltd, 1998

Weitz, Yechiam, 'Jewish Refugees and Zionist Policy During the
Holocaust', *Middle Eastern Studies* 30, no. 2 (1994), pp.351–68

Wheatcroft, Geoffrey, *The Controversy of Zion*, Sinclair-Stevenson,
1996

White, Theodore, *In Search of History*, New York: Harper & Row,
1978

Wilson, Mary C., *King Abdullah, Britain and the Making of Jordan*,
Cambridge: Cambridge University Press, 1987

Wilson, Major R. D., *Cordon and Search. With 6th Airborne Division in
Palestine*, Aldershot: Gale & Polden, Ltd, 1949

Yapp, M. E. 'In Israel's Archives', *Times Literary Supplement*, 27 April
2007

Yasin, Abd al-Qadir, 'The Palestinian Press Rhetoric Under the British

Mandate' (Arabic), *Samid al-Iqtisadi* 17, no. 102 (1995), pp.41–62

Yizhar, S., *Khirbet Khizeh,* Jerusalem: Ibis, Eng. ed., 2008

Zertal, Idit, *From Catastrophe to Power: Holocaust Survivors and the Emergence of Israel,* Berkeley: University of California Press, 1998

Zweig, Ronald W., *Britain and Palestine During the Second World War,* Royal Historical Society, The Boydell Press, 1986

Picture Credits

Khalil al-Sakakini and his two daughters, Hala and Dumia (reproduced by kind permission of Dr Tom Segev)

Jamal al-Husayni (reproduced by kind permission of the Central Zionist Archives)

Haj Amin al-Husayni (Central Zionist Archives)

Abd al-Kadar al-Husayni, the legendary commander of Arab militia in the Judaean hills (reproduced by kind permission of *Pillar of Fire*)

General Sir Alan Cunningham, the last High Commissioner of Palestine (Central Zionist Archives)

The 'imperturbable' Sir Henry Lovell Goldsworthy Gurney, the last Chief Secretary of the Palestine Administration (Central Zionist Archives)

Sir Harold Beeley, Bevin's chief adviser on Palestine, at the United Nations (Corbis)

Harry Truman (Corbis)

Ernest Bevin, Foreign Secretary, and Clement Attlee, Prime Minister (Corbis)

Chaim Weizmann, President of World Zionist Organisation and Jewish Agency; and Moshe Shertok, Head of the Political Department of the Jewish Agency (Central Zionist Archives)

Menachem Begin, self-styled Commander of the *Irgun*; and Natan Yellin-Mor, Head of the Stern Gang (Central Zionist Archives)

Ben Gurion, at the Museum Hall, Tel Aviv, declaring 'the establishment of the Jewish state in Palestine – to be called Israel' (Central Zionist Archives)

'Black Sabbath' in Paris. Ben Gurion, Chairman of the Jewish Agency, and Moshe Sneh, Commander-in-Chief of the *Haganah*, relaxing at a pavement-side café (reproduced by kind permission of *Pillar of Fire*)

The 6th Airborne Division – *HaKalanioth* ('Poppies') – taking over the Jewish Agency building in Jerusalem on 'Black Sabbath' (Central Zionist Archives)

British soldiers searching for an arms cache at a Jewish settlement (Central Zionist Archives)

A 'Bevingrad' at the St Julian quarter, Jerusalem (Central Zionist Archives)

The bodies of two sergeants, Cliff Martin and Mervyn Paice, hanging from a eucalyptus tree (Central Zionist Archives)

A Jewish convey reaches besieged Jerusalem, to the cheers of the onlookers (Central Zionist Archives)

The refugee ship *President Warfield* – renamed *Exodus* – making its way across the Mediterranean to Palestine (Central Zionist Archives)

The Anglo-American Committee of Inquiry arrives in Jerusalem (Central Zionist Archives)

Acknowledgements

Realising a project of this kind depends upon the goodwill and encouragement of many people and during the course of my work I have incurred many debts. I remain particularly grateful to the archivists and staff of the numerous archives, libraries, and institutions that generously extended their facilities to me, their courtesy and proficiency greatly eased my task: to the Middle East Centre Archive at St Antony's College, Oxford; the Bodleian Library, Oxford, and its Library of Commonwealth and African Studies at Rhodes House, Oxford; the Liddell Hart Centre for Military Archives at King's College, London; the Imperial War Museum, London; the British Library, London and its Newspaper Collection at Colindale; the Institute for Historical Research, London; the Library for Humanities and Social Sciences and the National Library at the Hebrew University, Jerusalem; the Weizmann Archives, Rehovoth; the Central Zionist Archives, Jerusalem and the Begin Centre, Jerusalem.

Crown copyright material at the National Archives (formerly the Public Record Office) at Kew, London, is reproduced by kind permission of the Controller of Her Majesty's Stationery Office. I would also like to thank the authors and publishers – listed in the bibliography – for quotations I have used from works of which they hold the copyright; and to register in advance my apologies for those cases that I have inadvertently overlooked.

I am especially grateful to my numerous colleagues, friends and acquaintances for allowing me to tax their patience, all too often picking their brains in what perhaps appeared to them as little more than casual conversations: the late Sir Isaiah Berlin; Colonel (Reserves) Mordecai Bar-On; the late Lord Bullock; the late Lord Charteris; the late Richard Crossman; the 'Epicurians' (they know who they are);

Major-General (Reserves) Yehoshua (Shaika) Gavish; Professor Joseph Heller; the late Professor Albert Hourani; Professor Eli Joffe; Professor Alon Kadish; Professor Wm Roger Louis; Mr Martin Lubowski; Dr Adel Mana; Professor Amikam Nachmani; Professor Perela Nesher-Warburg; Colonel (Reserves) Meir Pa'il; Diana Reich; Dr Tom Segev; Professor Avraham Sela; Mr Ra'anan Sivan; Professor Sasson Sofer; Dr Steve Uran; Major-General (Reserves) Raphael Vardi; Professor Gaby Warburg; Professor D. C. Watt and the participants in *Shared Histories. A Palestinian-Israeli Dialogue* (see bibliography).

I owe a special debt of gratitude to Dr Inbal Rose who, with a merciless eye, scrutinised my manuscript, rescuing me from far too many errors of grammar and style.

Andrew Lownie has been the most forbearing, optimistic and supportive of agents, cheerfully promoting and sustaining this project from the outset: I owe him much. Many thanks are due to the staff at The Bodley Head (Random House), in particular to my editor Will Sulkin, for his expertise, patience and tact, and no less his sense of humour; also to Drummond Moir for his resourceful input to the production of this book, and also to Kay Peddle and Ilsa Yardley.

Authorship is a solitary business. As always, my greatest debt is to my family: to my wife, Tslilla, and daughter and son-in-law, Inbal and Amit, for their patience and understanding. All too often, while they were dealing with pressing domestic matters, my mind was elsewhere, preoccupied with distant and obscure historical controversies. Without their mutual support and encouragement this book would not have been written.

Index